OH3725N

# PHILOSOPHY
# OF *Introductory Studies*
# EDUCATION

### PHILIP G. SMITH
Indiana University, Bloomington

*Harper & Row*

NEW YORK, EVANSTON, AND LONDON

# Contents

# Editor's Introduction

THIS BOOK, especially timely because its publication comes shortly before the author's accession to the presidency of the Philosophy of Education Society, will be read with interest because its orientation is rather unusual among texts dealing with educational philosophy.

There are other texts that are ostensibly designed to help a student *build* a philosophy of education, or possibly a philosophic understanding of education, but none of these seem to go about it quite as Dr. Smith's book does. The author's purpose is expressed on pp. 68–70, wherein he distinguishes philosophy *of* education from philosophies *and, in,* and *for* education. Placing this book within the category of books by Broudy, Kneller (ed.), Phenix, Scheffler (ed.), and Smith and Ennis (eds.), he proposes that this is a book on philosophy *of* education. In so being, it is "a study of the nature of the enterprise" of education, "a more or less independent disciplined area of study, comparable [to a degree at least] to philosophy of science," hence, "a changed conception of philosophy itself." Except for the texts by Broudy and Phenix, the above represent symposia; and those by Broudy and Phenix are ostensibly realist in philosophic orientation. Smith, though presumably sympathetic to pragmatic orientation, is, in this book, highly detached as to personal alignment, and in this way has written a book that is quite unique. Critics may make the charge that Dr. Smith has been noncommittal in approach, but they should take the foregoing into account before judging this a flaw.

Possibly, Dr. Smith is carrying forward and making more explicit the basic orientation of his mentor, the late Dr. H. Gordon Hullfish, with whom he collaborated in writing a previous book. If so, we feel that he has been successful. We consider this a significant book.

Ernest E. Bayles

# *Preface*

THIS BOOK is intended for use in a first course in philosophy of education at the level of advanced undergraduate or beginning graduate study. No attempt has been made to put the course inside the covers of the book. I hope, rather, that the book contains enough information and ideas to enable students to profit from lectures, discussions, and assignments under the direction of a good instructor. The writing is brief enough so that the entire book can be assigned within a semester, yet the range of topics is comprehensive enough to permit the instructor plenty of elbow room. Such structured flexibility seems to be called for by the widely varied situations encountered these days by those who teach philosophy of education.

Any writing that attempts to be both brief and comprehensive is almost sure to have noticeable inadequacies. Fortunately, however, in selecting a textbook, instructors generally look for usefulness rather than perfection. In any event, while I must accept full responsibility for all of the shortcomings, it is a pleasure to acknowledge some of the assistance I have received.

Most of all, I am indebted to a great many students at several universities who, more patient than I would have been, listened and responded to much of the material in this book in the form of lectures. If there are lucid spots in the writing, it is because these students, from time to time, forced me into using understandable language.

I am also grateful to J. Donald Butler who read an early draft of the manuscript and made helpful comments, and to Ernest E.

Bayles who, very unselfishly, stayed with the manuscript and continued to make useful suggestions long after men of lesser stature would have been alienated by my obdurate refusal to change certain passages.

Elizabeth Maccia read Chapter 5 and made helpful comments and Lewis Bayles did the same for Chapter 8. Acknowledgements for the use of copyrighted materials appear at appropriate points throughout the book.

P.G.S.

*Bloomington, Indiana*
*1964*

# Philosophy of Education

# CHAPTER 1

# What Is Philosophy?

LITERALLY, the word *philosophy* means *love of wisdom*. Some of the early philosophers were fond of pointing out that they did not claim to be wise men—merely lovers of wisdom. They were seekers after wisdom and, as teachers, they believed their role was one of helping others in the search for wisdom. There were other teachers known as *sophists*, a word which means literally *one who is wise*. Many sophists viewed teaching not so much as a process of assisting the student in a search for wisdom but rather as a matter of telling or giving the student, for a fee, certain information, skills, and conclusions, that made up the content of the education of a wise man. Such different points of view concerning what constitutes good teaching are still found today on most of our campuses.

Although it is the sophist view of teaching that is predominant in our schools, it is the term *philosopher* that is held in high esteem rather than such terms as *sophistry* and *sophisticate*. In all fairness to the early sophists, one should note that probably the main reason why our language reflects less respect for the sophist tradition than for the philosophic is because it turned out that the speculations of the early philosophers concerning the nature of man and the universe gained much wider popularity than speculations on the same topics by the early sophists. Actually, many of the sophists were reasonably modest men. They were teachers of such useful subjects as rhetoric, public speaking, and the like. For the most part they tended to be rather skeptical about man's ability to solve, with much certainty or finality, such basic problems as "What is the nature of reality?" "What is the nature of knowledge?" and "What is the nature of value?" On the other hand, the answers given to these questions by philosophers such as Plato and Aristotle have exerted a dominating influence on human thought for more than two thousand years. Today the very language we use reflects, both in content and in structure, the thinking of these early Greek philosophers.

## PHILOSOPHY AS AN ACTIVITY

In discussing the life and times of Socrates, Plutarch wrote:

Socrates neither set out benches for his students, nor sat on a platform, nor set hours for his lectures. He was philosophizing all the time —while he was joking, while he was drinking, while he was soldiering, whenever he met you on the street, and at the end when he was in prison and drinking the poison. He was the first to show that all your life, all the time, in everything you do, whatever you are doing, is the time for philosophy.

It is evident that for Socrates philosophy was an activity. A philosopher was a man who *philosophized*. Great philosophers have always understood this and, though most of them have devoted endless study to the work of other philosophers, each has struggled to state anew what seemed to him to be the most fundamental problems of man, and then, in his own terms, to develop a comprehensive and systematic body of speculative answers. A few have philosophized with such dazzling success that the effect of their work has frequently been more dominating than stimulating, so far as the philosophizing activity of teachers and students is concerned. Thus it is that many professors of philosophy become philosophically sophisticated and, in sophist fashion, dispense to students such information about philosophy as is thought requisite for an educated man. Thus, the title *philosopher* frequently becomes associated with the man who knows philosophy even though he engages in little or no philosophizing.

In recent times there has been an interesting return to an emphasis on philosophy as an activity. Wittgenstein, one of the influential persons in this movement, once said: "Philosophy is

not a theory but an activity. A philosophical work consists essentially of elucidations. The result of philosophy is not a number of
'philosophical propositions,' but to make propositions clear."[1]
According to this view philosophy is something that one does
rather than a body of subject matter to be studied. This movement has become especially popular in England, so that today it
is not uncommon to hear British philosophers speak of *doing
philosophy*. Many contemporary students of philosophy believe,
however, that the followers of this movement are doing philosophy in a much too limited way, for their activity is restricted
largely to an analysis of language as used in ordinary discourse
and in the more technical discussions of science and philosophy.
Such linguistic analysis tends to become quite technical and to
focus on the minute complexities of problems of limited scope.
The work tends, therefore, to take on an esoteric quality that is
likely to discourage the uninitiated. In reaction to these developments, one of the greatest of British philosophers has said, "Philosophy proper deals with matters of interest to the general
educated public and loses much of its value if only a few professionals can understand what is said."[2]

The most common way in which teachers of philosophy have
strayed from the philosophizing tradition is by confusing the history of philosophy with the philosophic activity. Certainly a
knowledge and understanding of what philosophers have
thought and felt about important problems is worthwhile.
Indeed, discovering what problems various philosophers have
considered important is, in itself, very frequently a stimulating
and rewarding activity. It is not uncommon for students to discover that some of the world's greatest minds have struggled
with the same problems that have disturbed them, problems that
in the student's mind have remained so vague and amorphous
that one hesitates to discues them; yet they have a feeling of persistent importance attached to them so that they crop up again

[1] Ludwig Wittgenstein, *Tractatus Logico-Philosophicus*, Harcourt, Brace
& World, New York, 1922, p. 27.
[2] Bertrand Russell, *Human Knowledge*, Simon and Schuster, New York,
1948, p. v.

and again in moments of solitary contemplation. To discover in the writings of some world renowned philosopher one's own private questions and speculations transformed into a series of well-formulated problems is often the very spur needed to start one on the road to more careful and persistent consideration of basic beliefs. And, of course, to follow the thinking of a first-rate mind, as it strives for clarity and precision of thought, may well be an excellent preparation for the struggle of pushing one's own life into more reflective levels.

Careful study of the philosophic activity of others remains, however, a study of history. No matter how thoroughly one understands someone else's philosophy, it is never a good substitute for understanding oneself—for transforming that conglomeration of beliefs and attitudes, that most of us depend upon, into at least the outline of a more comprehensive and harmonious outlook. This is one reason why Socrates repeatedly advised, *Know thyself.* C. I. Lewis, professor of philosophy at Harvard University, once said, "It is—I take it—a distinguishing characteristic of philosophy that it is everybody's business. The man who is his own lawyer or physician will be poorly served; but everyone both can and must be his own philosopher."[3] Thus, it is sometimes said that everyone has a philosophy whether he knows it or not.

It usually turns out that each of us, as he begins to think more carefully about his basic beliefs, discovers that he has been serving himself rather poorly as a philosopher. We often find that either we don't know what we really do believe or else we are at a loss for any very convincing evidence or argument in support of our convictions. Moreover, we commonly find that, as we ponder the things we think we believe, they tend to conflict, one with another, rather than stand together in mutual support. How is it that we have managed to live so many years in such confusion? Why haven't our friends and associates noticed our difficulty and prodded us into doing something about it? And then we discover that our confusion has hardly been noticeable because so many of us are in the same boat.

[3] C. I. Lewis, *Mind and the World Order,* Scribner, New York, 1929, p. 2.

Thus it is that we realize that to hold opinions about philosophic questions is not the same as to have a philosophy. To assert these opinions is one thing whereas to philosophize is something more.

In point of fact what does this universally possessed philosophy come to? It comes to something having less kinship with anything to be called a philosophy than with the job lot of odds and ends in Tom Sawyer's pocket. Insofar as the vast majority of us are equipped with anything resembling an outlook upon life and the world, it consists of a substratum of superstition about the supernatural, a smattering of social theory, a nest of group prejudices, a few wise saws, a rumor or two from science, a number of slipshod observations of life. To call this hodgepodge a philosophy is to take unwarranted liberty with language.[4]

## LEARNING TO PHILOSOPHIZE

Socrates evidently believed that prior to earthly existence the spirit or soul of man existed in a realm of pure forms, a realm of ideal and perfect objects. As a result of the birth trauma, the memory of this empyreal existence was erased from the conscious mind. Through contemplation, especially when prodded and assisted by a sagacious teacher, many individuals could, however, recall some aspects of their prior existence and come to the realization that the objects of this world were but imperfect transitory copies of the pure, eternal forms. The most important knowledge was, of course, knowledge of the ideal or perfect forms and, as this knowledge was gained by recollection, the role of the teacher was that of "drawing out of the student" and bringing to the level of conscious recognition that which he already knew. In order to accomplish this, Socrates developed a method of teaching by questioning. He invited students *to teach him,* to give him the best answers they could to the questions he posed; and then, of course, he helped them to examine critically their own answers, to modify them, and to make them more and more adequate until finally by their own efforts they arrived at the truth. Socrates was sometimes called a "gadfly" and an "intel-

[4] Max C. Otto, *Things and Ideals.* Holt, New York, 1924, p. 34.

lectual midwife." His activity finally became such a threat to entrenched ideas and interests that he was arrested and condemned to death for "corrupting his students."

Today we seldom encounter anyone who believes that knowledge is attained by recollecting a prior existence. But the Socratic method of teaching is generally recognized as an educationally sound procedure. Many philosophers, from Aristotle to John Dewey, have recognized that we learn to do by doing, and psychologists generally agree that we tend to appreciate most those things which we gain, at least in part, by our own efforts. We learn to philosophize by philosophizing.

Unfortunately, most of us do not find a Socrates to confront us with the kind of questions that impel us into a reflective or critical examination of our basic beliefs. As we have already noted, our friends and associates are likely to be leading the same sort of unreflective life as we, based on a similar conglomeration of attitudes, prejudices, and bits of knowledge sufficient to enable us to get on with our daily lives. Nor is it likely that by a simple act of will we can decide some morning to reconstruct ourselves so that thereafter we become our own Socrates, raising our own fundamental questions, challenging our own answers, striving always for the greatest possible depth and adequacy in thinking. Yet, if each of us both can and must be his own philosopher, each must learn to be his own Socrates.

This is one reason why many persons undertake a study of philosophy. They suspect that their own ideas are inadequate and they find in the study of philosophy the stimulation and challenge they need in order to attempt a more reflective mode of life. They read philosophy not only to find what questions great minds have considered most important and what answers most adequate but also to discover the *method of philosophy*. When one studies philosophy in this way, he is likely to discover that "to philosophize is not merely to read and to know philosophy; it is to think and to feel philosophically."[5]

[5] Harold H. Titus, *Living Issues in Philosophy*, 2nd ed., American Books, New York, 1953, p. 6.

## PHILOSOPHIC-MINDEDNESS

Learning to think and to feel philosophically may be compared to learning to be a good salesman. Good salesmanship is not merely something added to a person who is basically a poor salesman. Many large corporations have learned that it is not enough for a person simply to know the proper techniques of selling. They have discovered that a good salesman is a kind of person different from a poor salesman. Involved here are differences in temperament, attitudes, and personality. Studies have been made of the temperament and personality characteristics of successful salesmen. When individuals possessing such characteristics are selected for practical instruction in the techniques of selling the corporation's products, a much higher degree of success may then be anticipated.

We do not have much systematic study of how to effect a change in basic temperament and personality. Still, great teachers have always recognized that some basic reconstruction of individuals is necessarily involved in all true education. Today we are coming to a realization that one of the weaknesses of most of our institutions of higher learning is that four years of college life somehow fails to touch basic personality structure. Concerning fundamental values, a graduating senior is very largely the same *person* he was as an entering freshman.

Anyone who is serious about learning to philosophize should face the fact that, if successful, he will become a somewhat different person. The thought may be frightening. But why should it be? Physiologists tell us that we continually are becoming new persons. Many cells of our body are created, wear out, and are sloughed away. Such physiological changes are usually so gradual, however, that even after several years separation our old friends normally recognize us on sight. We should not be afraid to cast away some of our old, outworn, inadequate attitudes and beliefs. It is not likely that the change will be so radical or accomplished in so short a time that our identity will be lost. If old friends object to our gradually acquiring a more mature and enriched personality, then perhaps we should reevaluate their friendship.

## THE DIMENSIONS OF PHILOSOPHIC THINKING

When the characteristics of philosophic-minded persons are studied, they appear to cluster along three interrelated dimensions—comprehensiveness, penetration, and flexibility. Although these qualities characterize the total behavior of such persons, from the standpoint of the philosophizing activity we are interested in the way they are exhibited in the thinking of a person; in his problem-solving behavior, in his reflective life. Once these characteristics are understood it appears reasonable to hope that each of us, by constantly striving to develop these qualities in his own thinking, may gradually become a new person who may philosophize for himself with increasing adequacy and satisfaction.

### Comprehensiveness

Perhaps the most obvious characteristic of a philosophic-minded person is his striving for comprehensiveness of outlook. Philosophy has sometimes been described as the attempt to see life steadily and see it as a whole, and Whitehead has said, "The philosophic attitude is a resolute attempt to enlarge the understanding of the scope of application of every notion which enters into our current thought."[6] During and after World War II this same quality of comprehensiveness was emphasized by the armed forces as soldiers were encouraged to "see the big picture." There is a common-sense saying that we fail to see the forest because we are looking at the trees.

In order to think comprehensively we must resist the press of the immediate and the particular. We frequently find ourselves so snowed under with small though pressing problems that we never find the time to step back, so to speak, and view these

---

[6] Alfred North Whitehead, *Modes of Thought*, Macmillan, New York, 1938, p. 234.

troublesome matters in larger perspective. What are we trying to accomplish in the long run? How does our activity gear in with the work of others who may hold the same long-range goals? To raise and doggedly consider these kinds of questions is to launch oneself into philosophizing activity. Pursued far enough, such questions inevitably carry one into philosophically deep waters, but it is the persistent push rather than swimming at some prescribed philosophic depth that is the mark of philosophic-mindedness. If you strive for comprehensiveness of thought in those problems that seem important to you, the quality of your philosophizing is likely to become far superior to that of a pedantic and artificial rehash of "the traditional problems of philosophy."

One of the blocks to comprehensiveness of thought is the popular misconception concerning the relation of the theoretical and the practical. Some individuals display a temperamental intolerance for theoretical considerations. Such persons believe, no doubt, that most theory is a matter of impractical dreaming based on impossible ideals, while the work of the world is carried on by the tough-minded acceptance of "things as they are."

It is difficult to see how one can maintain such an attitude in the face of recent scientific developments. The world has been given a most dramatic illustration of how the theoretical, abstract, esoteric speculations of, say, an Einstein, are converted into the hard realities of an atomic bomb, a nuclear-powered submarine, or controlled, medical-radiation therapy. In less dramatic terms it should be equally apparent that to see things as they are is to see them in light of their antecedents and possible consequences. Everything that exists has both history and potential. What could be more practical than a sound theory concerning the hidden potentials of things? Ideals—even impossible ideals—can perform the very practical role of directing our attention to frequently overlooked possibilities in things as they are, enabling us to move in the direction of at least partial realization of our long-range goals. The attitude of "half a loaf is better than none" is all that is needed to get the most lofty ideals ready to go to work. And a comprehensive view of the persistent problems confronting one provides the most practical setting for the daily functioning of ideals.

As comprehensiveness develops, what may formerly have seemed an aimless flow of more or less isolated events becomes a sequence amenable to purpose and direction. Life takes on historical thickness and future possiblities become just as important spurs to action as are present actualities. The tendency to think of theory *versus* practice disappears, for a comprehensive thinker realizes that the only hope of making practice more purposeful and effective is to work in light of a more adequate theory. Anyone can take the first steps in the direction of greater comprehensiveness and we should remember that we learn by doing. But as Aristotle cautioned, "there must also be a full term of years for this exercise, for one swallow or one fine day does not make a spring, nor does one day nor any small space of time make a blessed or happy man."

## Penetration

If the immediate and the particular tend to press in on us, forcing us into a less comprehensive view, we may also be tyrannized by the obvious. The philosophic-minded seldom are long content with obvious answers or even with the obvious way of posing questions. One of the inadequacies of common sense is that it tends to proceed on the most common assumptions. There is so much taken for granted that it becomes difficult to get beyond the usual slogans, the clichés, the stereotypes. We must dig to the roots of questions or problems in order to discover fundamental dffiiculties.

An obstacle to penetration is the fact that, if we are not to flounder hopelessly in our daily affairs, we must live much of life as if we fully understood what is going on. It is only a hesitant neurotic who is obsessed with doubts and overwhelmed with feelings of inadequacy. What is needed is not vague doubts about things in general but specific questions designed to reveal what is fundamental in a situation. In the absence of *reasonable doubt* we must presume that we and others are innocent of fundamental confusion. But it is sometimes quite reasonable to question what others take for granted and to insist upon a review of fundamentals. There is no infallible rule to offer concerning what and when to question. Indeed, one of the marks of genius seems to be an uncanny sense of timing concerning when to plunge ahead in spite of doubts and when to refuse to budge until common assumptions have been reexamined. Inasmuch as most of us are given rather more to hasty action than to excessive deliberation and inasmuch as it is only infrequently that a short delay will have disastrous or irreversible consequences, it would seem wise to suggest that greater depth of thinking, even though time-consuming, would generally have salutary results.

Sometimes we fail because the particulars of a situation are unrelatable in terms of superficial aspects. A more penetrating look may bring to light fundamental relations that enable us to see them as a whole. And, of course, once the fundamentals of a situation have been grasped, the way is clear for those sound generalizations that enable us to deal effectively with a wide range of similar situations.

It is by a combination of penetration and comprehensiveness that we develop what is so dear to a philosopher, namely, basic principles. A principle is a generalization, a succinct expression of what has proved to be fundamental in a vast amount of well-digested experience. It is thus a vehicle for bringing to bear upon subsequent experience the best that has been distilled, not only from our own past experience, but from the experience of the race. It is only as we develop a comprehensive and harmonious set of principles that we may feel, with some justification, that we really are beginning to understand what is going on in this world and what we really want to do.

### Flexibility

A third set of characteristics distinguishing the philosophic-minded has to do with flexibility of thinking. Some persons are inhibited, in their approach to problems, by unfortunate "psychological set" or rigidity. Under unusual emotional stress it is not uncommon for almost anyone to behave in ways that are both quite rigid and quite inappropriate to a problem at hand. We have all heard stories of how some unfortunate fellow, trapped in a burning building, loses his head and tries with bare hands to batter down a wall or wildly jumps from a hopelessly high window.

In psychological laboratories, many experiments have been performed in which a subject is confronted with a series of probblems each of which yields to a single method of attack. Following this series of successful solutions, the subject is presented with a problem having superficial similarities but which requires a change in approach before success can be attained. It is surprising how frequently the subject will again and again try the old method with repeated failures leading only to increasing frustration, rather than attempt penetrating reappraisal of the situation.

Habitual ways of behaving—of thinking and feeling, and of dealing with problems—become habitual because they seemingly have proved to be generally successful. Habits, routines, orderly procedures are essential to successful living. Yet, if there is any truth to the old saying that nothing is permanent except change, it is clear that what we need is flexible rather than fixed habits. To be in command of a repertoire of procedures or behavior, each of which may be employed with smooth, habitual efficiency, is to have at hand a wide selection of tools for successful living. On the other hand, to be a slave of fixed habits, of dogmatic opinions, and of sterotyped behavior is to invite frustration and failure every time one slips, or is pushed, from accustomed grooves.

Flexibility involves creativity and there are many blocks to creative, imaginative thinking. No doubt there is a wide range of difference with respect to hereditary and early environmental factors, but there is reason to believe that many of us suffer from numerous emotional blocks, largely unrecognized, which prevent us from attaining more than a fraction of our actual potential. One such common block is the fear that our ideas may not stand with criticism. The truth is that most of them probably are quite faulty and inadequate—some of our ideas are probably ridiculous. It appears, however, that the number of good ideas one has is roughly proportional to the total number of ideas. Concern about our batting average is largely inappropriate in the matter of creative thought. The important thing is to swing at the ball. This is why, in the now famous brain storming technique, participants are encouraged to "keep swinging" with no critical or depreciatory comments permitted. Later, the entire crop of ideas is culled and only the more promising are selected for further thought and development. The point is, there is a time to be highly creative and a time to be highly critical and it appears that, for many, it is not wise to attempt both at the same time.

There are many specific errors in thinking that contribute to inflexibility. One of the most common is known as *black or white thinking*. Even he who prides himself on broad-mindedness—on always being willing to look at both sides of the question—may be a habitual victim of black or white thinking. Actually, most important questions or issues have *many sides*. A person who claims to be considering both sides may, in reality, be thinking in terms of his side or his point of view in contrast to the other side, which consists of a vague group of all other possible points of view. The philosophic-minded cultivate the habit of viewing issues from a relatively large number of alternatives or points of view. Consequently, they are more inclined to investigate issues rather than to debate them.

Another common error is to commit what has traditionally been called the *genetic fallacy*. This form of inflexibility is a matter of allowing opinions about the source of an idea to influence unduly one's judgment about its worth. For example, it is not uncommon for, say, a school administrator to tag various persons in the community according to some outstanding fact about their interests or connections. Mr. X is a labor-union man, Mr. Y is a socialist, Mr. Z is an arch conservative. After a while the administrator may feel that he "has their number and knows how to deal with them." When some suggestion or criticism about the schools

arises, the administrator may ask first, "Who made this suggestion?" and upon learning that it originated with, say, Mr. Y, dismiss the matter with the remark, "Well, that's nothing but
another socialistic suggestion." The genetic fallacy is thus
sometimes called the _nothing-but fallacy._

It is clear that under this method of dealing with ideas, the
worth of an idea, as idea, may never be investigated at all. The
other side of the coin is that ideas from honored sources are
likely to be accepted in uncritical fashion. Herein lies a paradox
of good teaching. The respected, successful teacher must continually fight against being _so_ honored that students accept
without question everything he says.

Nothing that has been said about flexibility should be construed to mean that a philosophic-minded person is wishy-washy
or indecisive. Students sometimes confuse any forceful, precise
statement with dogmatism and believe that a truly liberal or
broad-minded person must of necessity be a fence straddler or
an intellectual dilettante. Intelligent men of action who are continually called upon to make decisions soon learn that two
demons wait to pounce upon them at every turn. The first says,
"Don't make a mistake, wait until you're certain"; the second
counsels, "Make up your mind quickly and stick to it. Be consistent." The philosophic-minded brush aside these demons and
move forward on the bases of tentative appraisals and hypotheses, welcoming opportunities for reappraisal and reconstruction
of judgment and action. The hand of a surgeon does not shake
merely because he is less than certain in his diagnosis. Nor does
he hesitate to change his mind in the face of new evidence. The
question of flexible versus fixed habits is just as relevant to the
way we think—to the way we behave intellectually—as to overt
behavior. And the rules for making and breaking habits apply to
thinking, the same as to other forms of behavior.

## PHILOSOPHY AS CONTENT

We have previously noted that almost any question, pursued
far enough, will bring one to the level of philosophic speculation.

It is almost inevitable, therefore, that a philosophic-minded person will find himself eventually confronting fundamental problems, which have been traditionally called *philosophic problems* in contrast to scientific problems, religious problems, social problems, etc. If one goes about his daily affairs with more and more comprehensiveness, penetration, and flexibility of thought, how can he avoid facing basic questions such as: "What is the nature of reality?" "What is the nature of truth and knowledge?" "What is the nature of value?"

These three questions provide us with the three basic divisions of philosophy. The name given to the branch that deals with the nature of reality is *ontology*. The branch concerned with the nature of knowledge and truth is called *epistemology*, whereas studies of the nature of value are known as *axiology*. We must not be surprised, however, that, in a subject having a written history of more than two thousand years, many writers have developed various schemes of classification. For example, many persons use the word *metaphysics* to refer to the branch we have called ontology. Some writers say that metaphysics is concerned with the nature of reality, whereas ontology is merely one subdivison of metaphysics, namely, that concerned with the nature of *being* or of all conceivable existent entities. Under this system of classification, the other subdivision of metaphysics is known as cosmology, that is, the study of the nature of the fundamental causes and processes of the universe conceived as a cosmos or orderly system. On the other hand, still other writers restrict the word *metaphysical* to matters concerning *supernatural* forces or events. Thus, they may speak of a metaphysical ontology in contrast to a nonmetaphysical ontology. The intent is, of course, thus to differentiate speculation about the nature of reality that rests on supernatural forces and events from speculation based exclusively on natural forces. Finally, when ontological questions are combined with *theology*, that is, with speculation about the nature of God and his works and intentions, a capital R is frequently used in such a question as, "What is the nature of Reality?"

There is general agreement among writers that epistemology

is that branch of philosophy concerned with the sources, the nature, and the limitations of human knowledge. This should not be confused with *logic*, which is sometimes viewed as a subdivision of epistemology, but is more frequently viewed as an additional special branch or tool of philosophy. Logic is the systematic treatment of the nature of clear and exact thinking. It involves the study of what constitutes valid reasoning in all of its many possible forms.

The most common subdivisions of axiology are *ethics* and *aesthetics*. Ethics is concerned with problems of right conduct, with the nature of good and evil, of moral principles, and the like. Aesthetics deals with problems that center in our affective life or feelings, especially feelings about beauty and about the principles that govern creation and appreciation of the beautiful.

## SCHOOLS OF PHILOSOPHY

When a person develops a systematic set of answers to the basic questions of philosophy, he creates *a philosophy*. When such creations are analyzed and compared, we find that they may be grouped or classified on the basis of similarity in the manner of dealing with certain issues. Actually, there are no universally acceptable standards of classification by which philosophic thought may be incontrovertibly placed in groups or schools. Nevertheless, the following ways of classifying enjoy considerable acceptance.

With respect to the nature of reality, a major classification is that of supernaturalism in contrast to naturalism. The history of Western philosophy begins with naturalistic thought. Reality was conceived as continuous, in the sense that whatever actually exists is neither more nor less real than any other actual entity. There is only one level of reality. It was not long, however, until speculation arose concerning the possibility of hypernatural or supernatural forces or beings. Was there not some First Cause, some Creator of the natural universe? Would not such a Force or Being be a superior form of reality? Would not such a Reality be supernatural, that is, not bound by natural laws?

Once this basic bifurcation of reality was conceived, it was an easy step to extend this dualistic thinking into the creation of numerous discontinuities or dualisms such as good and evil, the spiritual and the material, mind and matter, soul and body, worldly and other-worldly. Any philosophy that systematically posits or assumes any hypernatural forces or beings is known as *supernaturalism*. All other philosophies are *naturalistic*. There are many forms of naturalism ranging from materialism to positivism to pragmatic humanism. A good rule of thumb for dividing philosophy into supernaturalistic and naturalistic is to note whether the basic assumptions of the system would lead one to anticipate miracles. Such a rule is not entirely adequate but at least it should prevent one from falling into certain gross errors, such as assuming that all forms of naturalism must be materialistic and atheistic.

A second ontological distinction may be drawn in terms of what the basic stuff of reality is considered to be. In the last analysis, is reality made up of material atoms—small bits of concrete, matterlike stuff? Or is reality ultimately composed of immaterial forms, forces or ideas—mindlike stuff? According to the way it answers this question, a philosophy is classified as *materialism* or *idealism*. A major division within idealism occurs over the question of whether reality (especially as expressed by universals or general ideas) has objective or subjective status. Objective idealism is sometimes called *realism* in contrast to certain forms of subjectivism. We have noted that Plato, an objective idealist, believed that there exists a realm of pure form, a realm of perfect, unchanging ideas. For example, the essence or idea of chair, that is, its *chairness*, enjoyed objective existence. It is more real than the imperfect copies (i.e., the actual chairs) with which we deal in our daily lives. Thus it is that such a view. is sometimes called *Platonic realism* in contrast to the belief that there are no universal essences in reality, the term chairness being merely a name for a man-made abstraction.

Additional distinctions are made when epistemological questions are considered. Those philosophies which hold that the objects of cognition exist independent of, and are not basically altered by, the process of being known, are again called *realism* in contrast to such views as *subjective idealism,* which holds that knowledge is limited to mental states or ideas, or to *pragmatism,* which denies the subjective-objective discontinuity as a basic division of reality and insists that both knower and known are abstractions from experience. Concerning the ways in which knowledge is gained, *empiricism* holds to sense experience as the source. When a philosophy insists that sense experience "is all that exists or can be known" it is called *phenomenalism.*

In contrast to empiricism, the view that reasoning is the primary source of knowledge is known as *rationalism,* and the insistence that some form of "direct grasp or intuition" is an important additional source of knowledge frequently is known as *mysticism.* With respect to methods for gaining knowledge or warranted beliefs, pragmatism may be thought of as a synthesis of empiricism and rationalism with the accent on *experimentation* rather than on either sense experience or pure reason.

In matters of axiology there is a common two-way division based on the question of whether it is possible to have *knowledge of value* or merely *emotions about value.* If one has knowledge of value, then such knowledge can be expressed in statements and such statements (i.e., assertions or judgments about value) can be investigated and determined to be, at least in principle, either true or false. On the other hand, if no knowledge of value is possible, then our assertions of value are neither true nor false, they are merely exclamations, or at best, exhortations or directives. Those who hold that value-statements may convey knowledge are known as *cognitivists,* others are called *noncognitivists.* The first group may be subdivided into *naturalists,* who believe that value-assertions may be investigated by natural or experimental forms of inquiry, and *nonnaturalists,* who believe that some form of intuition or hypternatural form of knowing is involved in knowledge of value, or that, at least, knowledge of value is knowledge of a nonnatural property.

Noncognitivists may be subdivided into *emotivists,* who hold strictly to a separation of valuing and knowing, and the *informalists,* who in a somewhat less astringent way view man's emotional language as subject to orderly analysis.

## THE USE AND MISUSE OF LABELS

It should be apparent that this brief discussion of the classifications or schools of philosophy is, at best, only grossly accurate. The intention has been to present some terminology that may prove helpful in the more detailed examinations to be undertaken in later chapters. Frequent use of a good dictionary plus thoughtful consideration of the context in which troublesome terms appear should enable a student gradually to develop a reasonable degree of language proficiency for reading, thinking, and writing in the area of philosophy of education.

Grouping and naming seems to be a basic characteristic of human thought. Until distinctions of some sort are drawn, experience remains a vague blur. We have already noted that the question of whether the distinctions man draws correspond to some objectively real divisions of the universe or are basically functional distinctions developed for the control of inquiry, is one of the perennial problems of philosophy. It is a problem, incidently, that has a definite bearing on education. But for the present, it is important to note that it is by grouping and naming that we begin to gain control over a subject matter. Indeed, this is one of the ways that material becomes a subject matter, that is, becomes logically organized human knowledge.

A word of caution is necessary, however, for it is easy to allow the names of various classifications or divisions of material to become labels that are used as substitutes for thought rather than as tools for thinking. For example, once a student is in possession of such labels as idealism, realism, and pragmatism, there is a tendency to consider them neat compartments into which ideas, philosophers, philosophies (and even teachers and educational procedures) may be tossed. Such use of philosophic labels invariably does violence to the thought and behavior of individuals.

When it is asked whether you are an idealist, a realist, or a pragmatist, the question appears structurally similar to the question, "Which do you prefer—Chevrolet, Ford, or Plymouth?" Actually, however, as the following chart may suggest, the question is more like, "Which do you prefer—a General Motors car, power steering, or an internal-combustion engine?"

It turns out that the philosophic classifications appearing on the chart are not designations for alternate sets of systematic answers to a common set of questions. One could even say that the differing kinds of questions asked by various philosophers provide a more important means of differentiating than do the answers proposed. In any event, this short although incomplete chart ( it leaves out, for example, such currently popular designations as existentialism and logical positivism) is complex enough to discourage the overly simple classification schemes that students like to record in their notebooks. Basically, philosophy is not taxonomic as, say, the early science of zoology or mineralogy. Philosophy is much concerned with analysis, so it does group and name. But its reason for being resides in its synoptic procedures. One studies philosophy in order to improve the soundness of his general view. One studies philosophy of education in order to attain a sound, general view of education. The use of simple, air-tight systems for classifying people and ideas is likely to hinder more than to help, for it violates all three dimensions of philosophic-mindedness: comprehensiveness, penetration, and flexibility.

## Suggestions for Additional Reading*

Students enrolled in a first course in philosophy of education typically bring to the class an unusually varied background of experience.

* The closing section of each chapter of this book presents suggestions for additional reading. More complete bibliographic notations for all books mentioned in these sections and in footnotes will be found in the Bibliography.

# CHAPTER 2

# What Is Education?

DURING DISCUSSIONS about the nature of education it is easy to forget what a wide range of meanings cluster around the term in ordinary conversation. For example, sometimes by education we mean a formal or deliberate process of schooling, other times our intention is to refer to a much larger context. In the expression "education goes on whether school keeps or not," we call attention to the fact that people learn many things before starting school, they continue to learn outside the schoolroom, and they keep on learning long after their formal education is terminated. Even during the hours of formal schooling, much is learned that is not part of the planned curriculum. On the other hand, the schoolroom is not the only place where deliberate teaching occurs. The home, the church, the political meeting, or the union hall is frequently a scene of planned teaching and, of course, magazines, newspapers, radio, and television are frequently employed as means of "educating" the public.

Within a process of formal schooling, the term *education* is sometimes used to refer only to that part of the formal instruction that is thought to be liberal or general in nature. Thus, people sometimes speak of vocational or technical *training* in contrast to *education*. Or again, education and training may be differentiated in terms of the intended outcome of teaching. Where the inculcation of skills, habits, attitudes, or beliefs is intended, the process of teaching is called training (or sometimes indoctrination or orientation), in contrast to teaching designed to increase the student's ability and inclination to employ critical, independent, and creative judgment.

23

It follows that the verb-form of the term is similarly ambiguous. What does it mean to say, "I shall attempt to educate him?" In addition to the confusion noted above concerning setting, content, and intent, there is widespread disagreement as to whether the verb to educate should be viewed as basically transitive or intransitive. A farmer speaks of "growing corn," yet we all recognize this as just a manner of speaking. Is the situation the same with "educating students"? Involved here, of course, are questions concerning the nature of learning and teaching, and we soon realize that the ambiguity and vagueness surrounding the basic term spreads like wildfire throughout the conceptual neighborhood, infecting even what one would suppose would be technical and precise expressions such as curriculum, course of study, and school program.

It is clear that the question "What is education?" is really many questions. From the standpoint of philosophy of education, the many questions seem to cluster around four central issues. *First,* what is the nature of the process that one undergoes as one becomes educated? There appears to be general agreement that such a process is basically a matter of personal development or growth. But, of course, these words are themselves infected with equivocal meanings. Still, we must study the nature of this process if we are to make any progress toward understanding the nature of education.

*Second,* what is the nature of education when it is viewed as a social or political or governmental undertaking—particularly as an institutionalized undertaking? Without exception, as a society becomes less primitive and more complex, it makes some sort of provisions, usually institutionalized ones, for providing a special, more or less artificial environment for the young. The purpose of such an environment is to provide a somewhat simplified and logically organized cultural setting in which the immature members of the society may be influenced in a more efficient manner than would otherwise be the case. We must, therefore, consider the nature of education as a sociopolitical institution.

*Third,* from the standpoint of the teacher, education is a practice, an art, a daily occupation. To what extent may education be compared with the practice of medicine or engineering? What are the foundational disciplines for education and how do they stand in relation to the practice of education? In short, what is education when viewed as an applied behavioral science or, at least, as a profession?

*Finally,* in whatever way we view education, the question of ends or aims arises. And one cannot dig very deeply into this question without confronting the difficult problem of the relation between means and ends. Indeed, the very nature of education, whether as a process of personal development, a sociopolitical institution, or an applied behavioral science, may change radically as one adopts differing sets of aims or holds various ends in view. And, of course, prior to the question of what should be the aims of education is the question of how one should decide upon aims. We must, therefore, introduce the problem of aims for education.

It should be clear that no final, or even tentatively authoritative, answers to any of these questions will be found within this chapter. After all, the entire book is designed to be only an introduction to the study of such problems.

## EDUCATION AS PERSONAL DEVELOPMENT

When one asks teachers, or teachers of teachers, what in its most general terms they are trying to accomplish, the most common answer is to the effect that they are trying to help each student develop his own peculiar talents and capabilities. This answer is as old as history and as modern as tomorrow's textbook on education, but what does it mean? We have noted that Plato viewed education as drawing out or bringing to consciousness truths that lay hidden within the student. Two thousand years later, Rousseau was advocating the natural development of the child's impulses toward the good, the true, and the beautiful. According to Rousseau, the teacher should protect the child from the corruptive influence of adult society—a society characterized by ugliness and perversion—until the student develops, in unstunted fashion, the latent powers implanted in him by nature. Rousseau was confident that the products of the schooling he advocated would be able to plunge into society and sweep it clean, thus realizing the social perfection intended by nature.

An interesting development of such educational ideas occurred at the hands of Froebel, who launched the kindergarten movement. He believed that the enfolded or sleeping seeds of perfection within each child could be awakened by the presentation of certain symbols. For example, in Froebel's kindergarten, children were arranged in a circle, not for convenience but because a circle was the symbol of divine perfection. Froebel believed that a ball was a most suitable gift for children for the sphere was a symbol of the unity of the universe. The same kind of loving care and nurture should be lavished upon children by a teacher as a rose-fancier bestows upon his plants. And just as a gardener must provide the proper kinds and amounts of soil and climate if his plants are to attain the perfection enfolded in the seed, so must an educator provide the environment that calls forth and develops the potential perfection divinely implanted in each child.

In America the kindergarten movement soon departed from some of the more mystical ideas of Froebel while retaining many of the practices. Certain disciples, principally those trained in Germany or by Germans in America, resented this departure from orthodoxy and, to protect the kindergarten from imitations and perversions, formed organizations such as the California Kindergarten Union and the American Froebel Union. Actually, since the development of the kindergarten movement in America paralleled the development of the child-study movement, it was probably inevitable that the more mystical and poetic ideas of Froebel would be modified or replaced by the advance of a more empirical approach. By the beginning of the twentieth century when John Dewey organized his experimental school at Chicago, he avoided using the term "kindergarten."

Under the more penetrating analysis of John Dewey, the idea of education as personal development underwent fundamental transformation. Dewey saw that beneath this sentimental and mystical glorification of childhood lurked a negative approach that, in effect, denied its positive values. Why should childhood or immaturity be viewed primarily as the absence of maturity and adulthood? Surely the potentialities which a child possesses are positive forces, not merely dormant or quiescent phenomena. It seemed to Dewey that the marvelous thing about a human being is his capacity for continuous development and this is a positive force or power at any age.

. . . when we say that immaturity means the possibility of growth, we are not referring to absence of powers which may exist at a later time; we express a force positively present—the *ability* to develop.

Our tendency to take immaturity as mere lack, and growth as something which fills up the gap between the immature and the mature is due to regarding childhood *comparatively*, instead of intrinsically. We treat it simply as a privation because we are measuring it by adulthood as a fixed standard. This fixes attention upon what the child has not, and will not have until he becomes a man. This comparative standard is legitimate enough for some purposes, but if we make it final, the question arises whether we are not guilty of an overweening presumption. Children, if they could express themselves articulately and sincerely, would tell a different tale; and there is excellent adult authority for the conviction that for certain moral and intellectual purposes adults must become as little children.

The seriousness of the assumption of the negative quality of the possibilities of immaturity is apparent when we reflect that it sets up as an ideal and standard a static end. The fulfillment of growing is taken to mean an *accomplished* growth: that is to say, an Ungrowth, something which is no longer growing. The futility of the assumption is seen in the fact that every adult resents the imputation of having no further possibilities of growth; and so far as he finds that they are closed to him mourns the fact as evidence of loss, instead of falling back on the achieved as adequate manifestation of power. Why an unequal measure for child and man?

Taken absolutely, instead of comparatively, immaturity designates a positive force or ability—the power to grow. We do not have to draw out or educe positive activities from a child, as some educational doctrines would have it. Where there is life, there are already eager and impassioned activities. Growth is not something done to them; it is something they do.[1]

As a central feature in his conception of education as growth, Dewey recognized the importance of acquiring effective habits and dispositions. He undoubtedly recognized the validity of Aristotle's observation:

> The virtues come neither by nature nor against nature, but nature gives the capacity for acquiring them, and this is developed by training. . . .
> But the virtues we acquire by doing the acts, as is the case with the arts too. We learn an art by doing that which we wish to do when we have learned it; we become builders by building, and harpers by harping. And so by doing just acts we become just, and by doing acts of temperance and courage we become temperate and courageous. . . .
> But habits or types of character are not only produced and preserved and destroyed by the same occasions and the same means, but they will also manifest themselves in the same circumstances. This is the case with palpable things like strength. Strength is produced by taking plenty of nourishment and doing plenty of hard work, and the strong man, in turn, has the greatest capacity for these. And the case is the same with the virtues: by abstaining from pleasure we become temperate, and when we have become temperate we are best able to abstain. And so with courage: by habituating ourselves to despise danger, and to face it, we become courageous; and when we have become courageous, we are best able to face danger.[2]

But Dewey's conceptions have an open-ended flexibility that is very difficult if not impossible to achieve under an Aristotelian ontology. Aristotle's simple observation that we learn by doing is transformed by Dewey into the cornerstone of a dynamic theory of education. Noting first man's remarkable ability to learn from experience, Dewey observes, "Still more important is the fact the human being acquires a habit of learning. He learns to learn."[3]

A habit also marks an intellectual disposition. Where there is a habit, there is acquaintance with materials and equipment to which action is applied. There is a definite way of understanding the situation in which the habit operates. Modes of thought, of observation

[1] John Dewey, *Democracy and Education*, Macmillan, New York, 1916, pp. 49-50.
[2] *Ethics* II, 1, 1.
[3] Dewey, *op. cit.*, p. 54.

and reflection, enter as forms of skill and of desire into the habits that make a man an engineer, an architect, a physician, or a merchant. In unskilled forms of labor, the intellectual factors are at a minimum precisely because the habits involved are not of a high grade. But there are habits of judging and reasoning as truly as of handling a tool, painting a picture, or conducting an experiment.[4]

Dewey noted further that a simple excitation-reaction psychology is inadequate for understanding habit.

Any habit marks an *inclination*—an active preference and choice for the conditions involved in its exercise. A habit does not wait, Micawber-like, for a stimulus to turn up so that it may get busy; it actively seeks for occasions to pass into full operation.[5]

Finally, Dewey stated:

Above all, the intellectual element in a habit fixes the relationship of the habit to varied and elastic use, and hence to continued growth. We speak of *fixed* habits. Well, the phrase may mean powers so well established that their possessor always has them as resources when needed. But the phrase is also used to mean ruts, routine ways, with loss of freshness, openmindedness, and originality. Fixity of habit may mean that something has a fixed hold upon us, instead of our having a free hold upon things. . . .

Habits reduce themselves to routine ways of acting, or degenerate into ways of action to which we are enslaved just in the degree in which intelligence is disconnected from them. Routine habits are unthinking habits: "bad" habits are habits so severed from reason that they are opposed to the conclusions of conscious deliberation and decision. As we have seen, the acquiring of habits is due to an original plasticity of our natures: to our ability to vary responses till we find an appropriate and efficient way of acting. Routine habits, and habits that possess us instead of our possessing them, are habits which put an end to plasticity. They mark the close of power to vary.[6]

It turns out then that, for Dewey, "education means the enterprise of supplying the conditions which insure growth, or adequacy of life, irrespective of age."[7] And,

since in reality there is nothing to which growth is relative save more growth, there is nothing to which education is subordinate save more

[4] *Ibid.*, p. 57.
[5] *Ibid.*
[6] *Ibid.*, p. 58.
[7] *Ibid.*, p. 61.

education . . . the purpose of school education is to insure the continuation of education by organizing the powers that insure growth. The inclination to learn from life itself and to make the conditions of life such that all will learn in the process of living is the finest product of schooling.[8]

## EDUCATION AS A SOCIOPOLITICAL INSTITUTION

Dewey held that education should be subordinate to nothing save more education and hence that education as such (i.e., as an abstract process) can be said to have no aims. He recognized, however, that students, teachers, parents, in short, all who support organized education, do have aims.[9] Wherever schools have been organized, there have been purposes in the minds of the organizers. Peoples or societies or governments establish and support schools because there is something they wish the schools to accomplish.

In Plato's ideal Republic, for example, schools were to perform a central and twofold basic function. It was through the process of public education that each member of the society would discover his own abilities, inclinations, and limitations. Each would thus learn where he belonged in the society—where he would be most happy and best adjusted, where he could make the greatest contribution to the general welfare. It was also in the schools that each would receive the proper amount and kind of education to equip him to take his proper place in the Republic.

On this score, Aristotle was in essential agreement with his teacher. He believed that support and control of public education is the single most important function of government.

But of all the things which I have mentioned, that which most contributes to the permanence of constitutions is the adaptation of education to the form of government, and yet in our own day this principle is universally neglected. The best laws, though sanctioned by every citizen of the state, will be of no avail unless the young are trained by habit and education in the spirit of the constitution, if the

[8] *Ibid.*, p. 60.
[9] *Ibid.*, p. 125.

laws are democratical, democratically, or oligarchically if the laws are oligarchical. For there may be a want of self-discipline in states as well as in individuals. . . . In democracies of the more extreme type there has arisen a false idea of freedom which is contradictory to the true interests of the state. For two principles are characteristic of democracy, the government of the majority and freedom. Men think that what is just is equal; and that equality is the supremacy of the popular will; and that freedom and equality mean the doing what a man likes. In such democracies everyone lives as he pleases, or in the words of Euripides, "according to his fancy," But this is all wrong; men should not think it slavery to live according to the rule of the constitution; for it is their salvation.

. . . virtue and goodness in the state are not a matter of chance but the result of knowledge and purpose. A city can be virtuous only when the citizens who have a share in the government are virtuous, and in our state all the citizens share in the government; let us then inquire how a man becomes virtuous. . . .

There are three things which make men good and virtuous; these are nature, habit, reason. . . .

Now the soul of man is divided into two parts, one of which has reason in itself, and the other, not having reason in itself, is able to obey reason. And we call a man good because he has the virtue of these two parts . . . in the world both of nature and of art the inferior always exists for the sake of the better or superior, and the better or superior is that which has reason. The reason too, in an ordinary way of speaking, is divided into two kinds, for there is a practical and a speculative reason. . . . The whole of life is further divided into two parts, business and leisure, war and peace, and all actions into those which are necessary and useful, and those which are honourable. And the preference given to one or the other class of actions must necessarily be like the preference given to one or the other part of the soul and its actions over the other; there must be war for the sake of peace, business for the sake of leisure, things useful and necessary for the sake of things honourable. All these points the statesman should keep in view when he frames his laws. . . . For men must be able to engage in business and go to war, but leisure and peace are better; they must do what is necessary and useful, but what is honourable is better. In such principles children and persons of every age who require education should be trained. . . .

No one will doubt that the legislator should direct his attention above all to the education of youth, or that the neglect of education does harm to states. The citizen should be moulded to suit the form of government under which he lives. For each government has a peculiar character which originally formed and which continues to preserve it. The character of democracy creates democracy, and the character of oligarchy creates oligarchy; and always the better the character the better the government. . . .

That education should be regulated by law and should be an affair of the state is not to be denied, but what should be the character of this public education, and how young persons should be educated, are questions which remain to be considered. As things are there is disagreement about the things to be taught, whether we look to virtue or the best life. Neither is it clear whether education should be more concerned with intellectual or moral virtue. The existing practice is perplexing; no one knows on what principle we should proceed— should the useful in life, or should virtue, or should the higher knowledge, be the aim of our training; all three opinions have been entertained. Again about the means there is no agreement; for different persons, starting with different ideas about the nature of virtue, naturally disagree about the practice of it. . . .[10]

The disagreement about the proper content and methods of education has erupted again and again, down through the ages, but there has been general acceptance of the classical principle that educational institutions should be compatible with the form or spirit of the society that supports them. Education, as a process of schooling, is, then, a sociopolitical undertaking. Where the social and political climate has been dominated by strong religious doctrine, education has been dominated by the same principles. Where the climate has been characterized by nationalism and the importance of the state, in contrast to the importance of the individual, education has taken on these same characteristics.

In America, schools have been established at various times and in various parts of the country for a curious mixture of reasons: secular, religious, cultural, civic, and, no doubt, many times by reason of a more or less vague faith in the general efficacy of "book learning." But, by the time the people of the original states decided to give up state sovereignty and band together "in order to form a more perfect union, establish justice, insure domestic tranquility, provide for the common defense, promote

[10] Condensed from the Jowett translation of Aristotle's *Politics*, Clarendon Press, Oxford, 1885, vol. 1, pp. 168-245.

the general welfare, and secure the blessings of liberty," there was only minimal disagreement among the leaders of the day on three fundamental points concerning education as a sociopolitical institution.

First, it was acknowledged that, if popular government were to succeed, there must be an informed, educated public. Second, if the separation of church and state were to be maintained, then education must not be dominated by a single religious organization. Third, if men are to remain free, then the education of children must not be controlled by a central bureaucracy.

There were interesting disagreements, of course, as to just what these principles meant in practice, and generally it was only the first principle that was explicitly formulated as a guideline to action. Consequently, education developed slowly and unevenly, largely as a local affair, with intermittent federal interest and support. It was not until well into the nineteenth century that state governments assumed general control and authority over education. And to this day we are still struggling with the problem of what constitutes proper support and control of education, as a sociopolitical institution, at each level of government.

Many complex questions are involved in this general problem. Consider, for example, the following:

**1. Who shall be educated?** For many years the tradition has been growing that society should provide public education for all the children of all the people. For some time, however, public education was thought of as a few years of elementary schooling. Gradually the number of years was extended to include three and then four years of high school.[11] Public kindergartens began

[11] The first public high school was opened in Boston in 1821. By about 1850 a number of other school districts in several states had extended public education beyond the elementary school and a number of friendly suits at law were brought to test the legality of city school districts collecting taxes to support high schools and to pay superintendents. The most famous of these suits is the Kalamazoo Case of 1874. The decision, written by the Chief Justice of the Michigan Supreme Court, was an eloquent review of the history of public education. It was pointed out that the legislature in establishing both the common schools and a state university must have

to appear and still more recently many communities have established public junior colleges. In addition, our states have supported public institutions of higher education wherein the tuition or registration fees charged students have represented only a small fraction of the cost of building and maintaining the institution. The underlying idea seems to be that society should make available to all youth a number of years of substantially free public schooling with the quality and quantity of schooling depending on what society feels it can afford to offer. Compulsory attendance[12] has always been limited to somewhat less than society has offered and it has generally been agreed that attendance at parochial or other private schools (including private tutoring) will satisfy the compulsory attendance law.

On the other hand, large numbers of citizens have always favored the notion that, in a democracy, society should provide pub-

---

intended a complete system of schools and that no limitations had been placed on the common schools in regard to either the number of years of schooling involved nor the kinds of school officials required for the proper functioning of the system.

[12] The history of compulsory school attendance laws is complicated and spotty affair. Toward the end of the nineteenth century many states passed such laws and the courts upheld them. At first the principle was that the welfare of minors is important enough that states have the right to interfere with the liberty of parents for the good of the child. Later, however, courts generally upheld such laws on the principle that the state may demand school attendance, not for the benefit of the child, but in order to safeguard the welfare of the community and the safety of the state. By the turn of the century, compulsory school attendance was well established in many states, but it was generally recognized that such laws should not interfere with the establishment and growth of parochial and other private schools. In 1922 in the state of Oregon, a law, strongly supported by the Klu Klux Klan, was passed requiring that all children between the ages of 8 and 16 attend the public schools whenever these were in session. The law was immediately challenged in the courts and in 1925 the United States Supreme Court denied the right of the states to prohibit private schools, although they might inspect and reasonably regulate them. The Court declared that the Oregon law "unreasonably interferes with the liberty of parents and guardians to direct the upbringing and education of children under their control. . . . The child is not the mere creature of the State. . . ." It is worthy of note that Justice Oliver Wendell Holmes dissented from this decision and argued that the Constitution does not deny the right of a state to require all children to attend public schools and that, indeed, in a democracy, such a system of education may eventually be necessary if we are to retain the republican form of government guaranteed to the states.

lic education that will vary in both amount and kind according to each individual's aptitude and talent. Under such an approach it is clear that, for the same amount of money it would take to provide, say, ten years of schooling for all, graduate education could be provided for a few with decreasing amounts provided for others with lesser ability. In practice, the first notion has provided the basic structure for public education in this country, with the structure modified by practices stemming from the second notion. For example, in many parts of the country compulsory attendance laws have been only selectively enforced. Fees and other expenses involved in attending public schools have increased while public money has been used to provide scholarships for students with special abilities. Public institutions of higher learning are increasingly adopting stricter admission or readmission policies. All such practices modify the basic structure of public education in the direction of the second approach to the question of who shall be educated.

2. **Who shall decide what, concerning public education?** At each level of sociopolitical organization, questions arise concerning the proper spheres of lay decision and of professional decision. In this country there is virtual consensus that the *over-all purposes* of public education shall be a matter of *public decision.* Perhaps this is a correlate of the view that the final control of the military should rest in civilian hands. Unfortunately, local school boards have generally assumed that this consensus means that they, as the representatives of lay opinion, should decide *what should be taught* while questions of *how to teach* may be left to the professionals. Many superintendents and even teachers have encouraged school boards and the public in general to adopt this attitude.

Even a little analysis of the situation should make it clear that the content of education is itself a means of education. We select this or that content in an attempt to accomplish some purpose. A layman, being a layman, may be forgiven if he avers that "One of the purposes of public education should be to teach American history and the U.S. Constitution." It should not be so quickly forgiven when a professional talks this way or when he encourages the public thus to confuse a statement of purpose with a discussion of the best way for accomplishing the purpose.

Actually, much of the argument about so-called purposes of education is not about the over-all purpose at all. Such public confusion about professional questions might not be especially serious except that it perpetuates confusion about who should decide what. The over-all purposes of public schooling are generally not discussed at all, for there is substantial common-sense agreement that the purpose of public elementary schooling is to develop the skills of oral and written communication (including basic computational skills) and to develop an understanding and an appreciation of the physical and cultural environment requisite for citizenship in American democracy. The purpose of secondary schooling is to broaden and deepen the skills and understandings developed in elementary school and to provide college preparatory studies and whatever vocational training can be agreed upon by the community.

Such broad statements, of course, do not solve our problems. Even if they were to be accepted as official public expressions of the purposes of public schooling, they would not provide the answer to borderline questions of who should decide what. They would, however, give us a clearer indication of the location of the boundary between lay and professional decision that can presently be gleaned from public discussion.

The lesson to be learned from the history of the development of professions is that the public grants professional autonomy not as a privilege, but as a responsibility, in order that the public may, in the long run, be better served. And history also teaches that the public is not likely to grant autonomy to any professional group until the group has demonstrated that it is willing and able to accept such responsibility. Oddly enough, the group must usually demonstrate its readiness for professional autonomy by a long and determined fight for autonomy. It is as if the public were a great awkward giant who needs an agile professional to fight his battles for him, but who will not allow a professional to fight for him until the professional has first won a fight against him.

**3. What social role should the school play?** When it is said that one of the purposes of education, as a sociopolitical institution, is "to develop an understanding and appreciation of the physical and cultural environment requisite for citizenship in American democracy," it should be obvious that in a free society reasonable men may disagree as to what constitutes a proper understanding and appreciation of our cultural environment. As a sociopolitical institution, the school always reflects the culture of which it is a part. But in a society that is neither totalitarian nor static the culture is not all of one piece—it does not rigidly conform to some one doctrine or ideology concerning what is worthy of being valued, what are the most desirable directions for change, what are the most worthy operational meanings of "citizenship," and "appreciation." It follows that in a free society one of the most fundamental and crucial questions of education is: "In what manner should the schools reflect the culture of today and yesterday and thus influence the culture of tomorrow." Translated into the inadequate but suggestive language of political argument, the question becomes, Should the schools merely drift with the times, or should they consciously promote a conservative interpretation of the culture and of citizenship or a liberal interpretation?" In more adequate language, John Dewey discussed the problem as follows:

. . . The existing state of society, which the schools reflect, is not something fixed and uniform. . . . Social conditions are not only in process of change, but the changes are going on in different directions, so different as to produce social confusion and conflict. There is no single and clear-cut pattern that pervades and holds together in an unified way the social conditions and forces that operate. . . .

The fact that it is possible to argue about the desirability of many of the changes that have occurred, and to give valid reasons for deploring aspects of the flux, is not relevant to the main point. For the stronger the arguments brought forth on these points, and the greater the amount of evidence produced to show that the educational system is in a state of disorder and confusion, the greater is the proof that the schools have responded to, and have reflected, social conditions which are themselves in a state of confusion and conflict. . . .

There are three possible directions of choice. Educators may act so as to perpetuate the present confusion and possibly increase it. That will be the result of drift, and under present conditions to drift is in the end to make a choice. Or they may select the newer scientific, technological, and cultural forces that are producing change in the old order; may estimate the direction in which they are moving and their outcome if given freer play, and see what can be done to make the schools their ally. Or, educators may become intelligently conservative and strive to make the schools a force in maintaining the old order intact against the impact of new forces.

If the second course is chosen—as of course I believe it should be— the problem will be other than merely that of accelerating the rate of the change that is going on. The problem will be to develop the insight and understanding that will enable the youth who go forth from the schools to take part in the great work of construction and organization that will have to be done, and to equip them with the attitudes and habits of action that will make their understanding and insight practically effective. . . .[13]

## EDUCATION AS TEACHING

When education is viewed from the standpoint of teaching, it has generally been recognized that the practice of education is basically an art. The same may be said, of course, of the practice of medicine or of engineering. It is also generally recognized, however, that if physicians today are better physicians than those of a hundred years ago it is not because they are more artful, but are more scientific. To what extent may the practice of teaching become scientific? Is a true science or technology of teaching possible, and, if so, what would it be like?

A further comparison with medical practice may be instructive. But first it may be useful to differentiate *the application of scientific knowledge* from *the scientific application of knowledge*. In the case of medical practice, it is clear that today's physician has the advantage of greater scientific knowledge of disease. This has come about largely through developments in the sciences of

[13] Condensed from John Dewey, "Education and Social Change," *The Social Frontier*, May, 1937.

biology, chemistry, and the like. When we speak of progress in medical science we usually intend reference to developments in these basic scientific disciplines. And when we say that today's physician is more scientific, we usually mean that he is in command of more comprehensive and scientific knowledge that may be applied to the prevention, cure, or alleviation of disease.

It is also true, although not quite so obvious, that today's physician is more scientific in the application of his special knowledge. This is to say, for example, that his diagnosing is more scientific. Indeed, most of his activities, from his bedside manner to his participation in professional and governmental organizations and programs, are generally more scientific than were the activities of his counterpart of a hundred years ago. In other words, the modern physician is more inclined to formulate his problems consciously on the basis of accurately made observations, to develop and explore hypotheses for their solution in the light of scientific medical knowledge, to check his tentative solutions in a plan of action that resembles an experimental design. Thus, the expression *scientific medicine* or *medical science* properly refers to both the scientific knowledge to be applied and the scientific application of that knowledge.

In order to facilitate the comparision let us provisionally define education (as teaching) as the science and art of the elimination of ignorance. We see immediately that as education becomes more scientific this means that educators gain command of greater scientific knowledge concerning the nature and elimination of ignorance and also that educators become more scientific in the application of that knowledge. Again, as in the case of medicine, a gain in scientific knowledge depends largely on developments in the foundational disciplines. For education, foundational disciplines are psychology, sociology, cultural anthropology, and the like—in short, what are usually called the behavioral sciences. To the extent that the foundational sciences of education are less well developed than the foundational sciences of medicine, one would expect education to be less scientific than medicine.

Although again not quite so obvious, the question of the scientific application of the best knowledge we have of the nature and elimination of ignorance is crucial for the development of a science of teaching. On the one hand there is still a widespread belief that teachers are born not made—or at least that the essential preparation for teaching is the mastery of the subject matter to be taught—and on the other hand there is confusion in our teacher education institutions about both the importance of and the means of creating scientific practitioners. There is very little in either the preservice or inservice education of teachers that is well calculated to develop a scientific spirit or habit of mind and action and the typical methods-course is oriented toward the use of specific techniques and tools of teaching rather than specifically toward the scientific use of the knowledge developed in the foundational disciplines. To the extent that society in general and medical schools in particular have a greater understanding of the importance of and the means of preparing scientific practitioners than is the case in teacher preparation, one may again expect education to be less scientific than medicine.

When we conceive education as an applied behavioral science, an additional problem arises due to the fact that any practice, such as education, medicine, or engineering, always involves something more than the scientific application of basic scientific knowledge. There is a value dimension in every practice. In the case of medicine, questions of value do not usually create much disturbance. It is generally recognized that a physician's knowledge of drugs could be used to commit murder as well as to save lives and, further, that his scientific skill in the application of his knowledge would give him a better-than-average chance of committing the perfect crime. The point to be noted, however, is that when a physician deliberately destroys life his action is generally recognized by society as a crime. There is widespread agreement as to what ought to be the value orientation of medical practice. We have generally accepted the proposition that good health is better than poor health and that life is better than death.

Now, of course, there are times when the value dimension

becomes controversial in the practice of medicine, ranging from questions of birth control to questions of merciful death. It may well be that in the not-too-distant future society will insist upon a more organized and systematic study of this value dimension. Even now there are questions concerning the use of scientific knowledge, falling within the value dimension of the various professions, that are causing public concern. Still, at the present time, as far as medical practice is concerned, most of us are not encouraging physicians to take time off from cancer research or from administering to the sick in order to ponder these philosophic matters.

What is the present situation with respect to the practice of teaching? In many communities, perhaps most, we could not obtain general agreement on even the basic proposition that knowledge is better than ignorance. In connection with many topics it is believed that ignorance is bliss and that a little knowledge is a dangerous thing. Rather than being encouraged to strive for the elimination of ignorance, prejudice, superstition, wherever it be found, schools are frequently urged (indeed legislatures pass laws and school boards set up rules) to instill loyalty and commitment to ideas which would never be accepted if thrown unprotected into the open market place of free inquiry.

It is unrealistic then, when viewing education as an applied behavioral science, to assume either that education is value free or neutral, or that a sufficiently clear value dimension will automatically be supplied by a plural society. And what is true of education in general permeates its various subdivisions. It is unrealistic, for example, to suppose that an adequate theory of educational administration can be developed apart from a systematic consideration of the value dimension. Or to look at another kind of subdivision of education, it is unrealistic to assume that a theory of learning developed to further the aims of a neutral research-discipline, such as psychology, can automatically serve as an adequate base for a theory of teaching.

This last point is not so obvious. Perhaps a further comparison with medicine may prove helpful. When a physician looks to his foundational disciplines he does not find any of them talking about a theory of health—or shall we say "healthing," that is, the attaining, maintaining, or regaining of good health or the absence of disease. Medical science, therefore, has always recognized that, if it is to get on with its business of preventing, curing, and alleviating disease, it must build for itself a theory of healthing. This it has done, even though until very recent years its theory has been little more than some more or less systematic empirical generalizations. Furthermore, even if one of the foundational research-disciplines, say biology, were to announce something called "a theory of organic health," medical science, while looking toward it hopefully, would immediately suspect that the biologists were using the term "health" in a more restricted and specialized sense than it is used by physicians and their patients.

It turns out then that an educator would be indulging in a dangerous naïveté were he to assume that the research disciplines of behavioral science will supply him with an adequate theory of learning (as the correlate of "healthing") or an adequate theory of any subordinate phenomenon such as group dynamics in the classroom, decision making in educational administration, or the like.

A recent promising development in education has been the attempt to build a theory of teaching based on careful observation and analysis of the teaching act, in contrast to assuming that a knowledge of the nature of learning somehow automatically provides a theory of teaching.[14]

On the other hand, one of the blocks to development of an adequate theory of teaching has been the attempt to use overly simple models. For example, a misunderstanding of the selling-buying relation as a model for viewing teaching-learning has frequently led to unfortunate results. In the first place, the analogy is of course not perfect. For example, teaching-learning is, in one sense, a three-element relation whereas selling-buying involves

[14] See B. Othanel Smith et al., A Study of the Logic of Teaching, University of Illinois, Urbana. 1963.

four or more elements. Both involve a vendor or teacher, merchandise or content, and a buyer or learner. In addition, selling-buying involves a transfer of ownership and a reverse movement of "one dollar or other valuable consideration." In this sense, giving-receiving is a closer analogy, especially when the giving is "miraculous loaves and fishes."

On the other hand, as a model for viewing teaching strategy (which is what Dewey intended)[15] it can be quite useful. It suggests, first of all, that there is something dogmatic and ridiculous about any teacher who insists he is doing his job even though his students are consistently failing to learn. In other words, both teaching and selling are activities that need continual evaluation in terms of results. Moreover, good teaching, like good selling, requires a sensitivity to the multiplicity of factors that contribute to success or failure. For instance, good selling frequently consists primarily of creating the kind of situation in which the potential buyer will "sell himself." At the very least, the salesman endeavors to enlist the cooperation of the customer toward culminating the selling-buying act. Unpleasant, argumentative situations in which the customer sees himself as somehow being in competition with the salesman are assiduously avoided. It is rather amazing how so many teachers permit competitive, even antagonistic, situations to develop vis-à-vis their students. To an observer it sometimes appears that the teacher must feel so insecure that he thinks it necessary to drop all of the usual rules of courtesy in order to make the students realize who is boss. Finally, of course, the astute salesman endeavors to learn enough about the prospect's situation that he will not lose the sale by trying to sell either too much or too little. The comparable aspects of good teaching are obvious.

[15] While discussing the art of teaching Dewey said, "Teaching may be compared to selling commodities. . . . There is the same exact equation between teaching and learning that there is between selling and buying. The only way to increase the learning of pupils is to augment the quantity and quality of real teaching." He then discussed such problems of teaching as arousing and maintaining curiosity, stimulating reflection, keeping classroom discussions on the track, etc. (see *How We Think*, rev. ed., Heath, Boston, 1933, chap. 3).

Anyone who has earned his living as a salesman knows, however, that good selling correlates well with actual sales only in the long run. It is not unusual for a salesman to do a first-rate job of selling, only to have the selling-buying process frustrated by the prospect's financial inability to close the deal. On the other hand, occasionally a customer will simply walk in, lay down the money, and demand the salesman's product. In such cases we frequently say that the customer had already been "sold," perhaps "sold himself," before he came in. Nevertheless, slogans appropriate for a salesman's convention, catchy phrases such as "There is no selling without buying" and "Let's sell our customers, not just merchandise," do call attention to important factors in successful salesmanship.

Nevertheless, such slogans, however useful, are never an adequate substitute for carefully developed theory. And, until educators develop a theoretical foundation for teaching practice, an essential element will be missing in the movement to lift teaching to the level of a profession.

It turns out then that to view education as teaching is another important way of understanding the meaning of education. And a science of education, as the science of medicine or the science of engineering, involves three major elements: First, it requires a body of scientific knowledge developed within its foundational research disciplines. Second, it requires a theory of practice concerned with the scientific application of the best knowledge available. Third, it requires an over-all theory (some may prefer to call it a philosophy) that includes systematic development of the value dimension.

## AIMS FOR EDUCATION

We have noted, with Dewey, that all who are involved in education have aims. Parents and citizens in general as well as students, teachers, and school officials have purposes and objectives in mind as they make proposals for school policy and practice. Individuals and groups frequently bring considerable pressure to bear upon school officials and, although it is sometimes said that teachers and administrators should offer leadership to lay groups in formulating goals for education, more frequently the educational leader finds himself playing the role of mediator or adjudicator in the midst of such a welter of proposals that it hardly seems expedient to encourage groups to formulate additional statements.

There are so many ways of conceiving education that it is probably unreasonable to expect an orderly discussion by any group whose members have not persevered in a program of rigorous study. Careful exploration of the nature of an educational aim is likely a minimum preparation for discussing aims for education.

Dewey has pointed out the following:

An aim implies an orderly and ordered activity, one in which the order consists in the progressive completing of a process. Given an activity having a time span and cumulative growth within the time succession, an aim means foresight in advance of the end or possible termination. . . . It is nonsense to talk about the aim of education—or any other undertaking—where conditions do not permit of foresight of results, and do not stimulate a person to look ahead to see what the outcome of a given activity is to be.

In the next place the aim as a foreseen end gives direction to the activity; it is not an idle view of a mere spectator, but influences the steps taken to reach the end. The foresight functions in three ways. In the first place, it involves careful observation of the given conditions to see what are the means available for reaching the end, and to discover the hindrances in the way. In the second place, it suggests the proper order or sequence in the use of means. It facilitates an economical selection and arrangement. In the third place, it makes a choice of alternatives possible. If we can predict the outcome of acting this way or that, we can compare the value of the two courses of action; we can pass judgment upon their relative desirability. . . .

The net conclusion is that acting with an aim is all one with acting intelligently. To foresee a terminus of an act is to have a basis upon which to observe, to select, and to order objects and our own capacities.[16]

[16] John Dewey, *Democracy and Education,* Macmillan, New York, 1916, pp. 119-120.

This suggests that an aim of education involves not only some-where to go but some idea of the purpose for going. Dewey speaks of "the means available for reaching the end." There is a sense in which the number of acceptable alternative means for a given end tend to diminish in proportion to the clarity of the pur-pose. I can hardly decide, for example, what mode of transporta-tion to use in going to Chicago unless I am clear about my purposes in going there. The more clear and detailed under-standing I have of my anticipated business in Chicago, the less likely it is that alternate modes of transportation will appear to me to be equally acceptable. Indeed, strictly speaking, in any situation in which the choice of one alternative rather than another makes no difference, the alternatives are, practically speaking, one and the same. It turns out, then, that an aim is not merely an end or goal or objective, an aim is a means-end process.

Inasmuch as formal education is normally a long-drawn-out affair, spanning a number of years in the life of a student, all who are concerned about the work of the schools tend to break down the over-all aims of education into more manageable interme-diate steps. Learning to read, or learning the multiplication tables, becomes an aim of education during elementary-school years. There is nothing wrong with seeing a long, complicated means-end process as a series of steps or activities. Indeed, this must be done if one is to think in operational terms. Difficulties arise because it is so easy to start thinking of some stage in the total process as the *end in view* and then eventually as the *end in itself*. When this happens, we forget the purpose of this step or end in view and we are likely to select what appears to be the most efficient or economical means for attaining the end. We forget that at every step along the way our selection of means progressively determines the total means-end process and thus the over-all aim of education.

Does it make any difference, for example, what means are used in teaching the multiplication tables or in teaching a child

to read? Or consider more complicated situations such as teach-
the United States Constitution or American history. When learning the Constitution becomes an end in itself, simple drill
procedures suggest themselves as the most promising means. It
is not a very difficult undertaking to have students memorize the
preamble and then learn to recite the main points of each article.
Many students will consider this to be a reasonable and relatively
easy assignment. But what is the purpose of learning the Constitution? If we continually (or even frequently) ignore over-all
purpose as we select means for attaining intermediate goals, the
total means-end process veers off in some unpredictable
direction.

Such deviations, with the resulting compartmentalization of
information and lack of articulation, might not be so serious were
it not for the fact that specific subject matter is, in the long run,
one of the least permanent and least important things learned in
school. Students learn habits, attitudes, dispositions that remain
operative long after they complete their formal education. No
doubt this is one reason it is sometimes said that education is
what is left after one has forgotten all the things he learned in
school. And the crucial point is that some of the habits that are
learned (good or bad habits as the case may be) are habits of
study, of learning, of relating and utilizing subject matter. And
some of the attitudes and dispositions are concerned with ways of
conceiving science, history, art, and all the subject matter of
formal education.

After pondering this sobering situation, it is no wonder that
men such as John Dewey have concluded that "the aim of education is to enable individuals to continue their education—the
object and reward of learning is continued capacity for
growth."[17] Or again, as we noted earlier, ". . . the purpose of
school education is to insure the continuance of education by
organizing the powers that insure growth. The inclination to

[17] *Ibid.*, p. 117.

learn from life itself and to make the conditions of life such that all will learn in the process of living is the finest product of schooling."[18] Dewey thus brings together the aim of education as a process of personal development, its aim as a sociopolitical institution, and its aim as the science and art of teaching.

Whether or not one agrees with Dewey, we recall that he also pointed out that it is nonsense to talk about aims when conditions do not permit us to foresee the results of this or that course of action. Surely all will agree with that! It follows then that until education becomes more fully developed as an applied behavioral science it will be very difficult for teachers, to say nothing of laymen, to speak with much assurance about the results of alternative educational policies and practices. We have no choice, however, but to start where we now are and develop a disciplined body of educational theory and practice using present insights as springboards to progress. Recognition that any educational aim should always be viewed as a means-end process gives us a bench mark for introducing order into the present welter of claims and counterclaims. But there is no substitute for careful, persistent effort to understand the nature of education in its various aspects. And the ways of viewing education discussed in this chapter are intended to be illustrative rather than exhaustive.

It turns out then that, although the proper aims for education are a matter of central importance in philosophy of education and should logically be introduced early in any systematic study of the discipline, conclusions about aims should be *conclusions*— not premises—and, therefore, should not be attempted until after at least a preliminary study of the sort of questions that makes up the chapter headings of this book. The question of aims will, therefore, turn up again and again as various topics are pursued and, indeed, if the reader will strive to see each topic in relation to its possible bearings on the question of aims of education he will have found a method for preventing philosophic analysis and discussion from becoming merely academic.

[18] *Ibid.*, p. 60.

## SUGGESTIONS FOR ADDITIONAL READING

The classic statement of education as a process of personal development will be found in Dewey's *Democracy and Education*, chapter IV. The reader should be warned, however, that Dewey's conception of education as growth is not easy to understand. It would help, of course, to read the three preceding chapters and at least the four or five chapters following it. In any event it should be remembered that in this chapter Dewey is concerned primarily with education as a process of personal development rather than with education as a sociopolitical institution or as the science of teaching.

A very useful book for improving one's understanding of education as a sociopolitical institution is William O. Stanley, and others, *Social Foundations of Education*. Part I of this book is titled "The School as a Social Institution." The sociopolitical approach to education has been a favored one in recent years and many excellent books are available. For example, there is V.T. Thayer, *The Role of the School in American Society*.

Utilizing a more sociological approach is B.R. Clark, *Educating the Expert Society*. This book, available in paperback, is a "must" for those students who have not had the advantage of course-work in educational sociology. One may also consult such books as Havighurst and Neugarten, *Society and Education*, or a book of readings such as Meltzer, and others, *Education in Society*. And for an historical approach to American education with special attention to the value dimension, Mason, *Educational Ideals in American Society*, should be helpful.

Typically, students in a first course in philosophy of education are weak in their grasp of the historical dimension of the problems encountered. This is, no doubt, due in part to the fact that, frequently, courses in American history are taught with scant attention to the development of educational institutions. And even courses in history of education are sometimes oriented toward questions of educational administration and finance rather than toward the development and reconstruction of educational ideas and ideals. In addition to Mason's book on American education, students may, therefore, find it helpful to consult books that dip into the European background of our educational ideas. Two such books written with special attention to the philosophic dimensions are Thut, *The Story of Education*, and Brubacher, *A History of the Problems of Education*.

Finally, anyone involved in education as a profession should become familiar with the nature and operation of the various teachers' organizations, especially the NEA (National Education Association), the AFT (American Federation of Teachers), and the AAUP (American Association of University Professors). A critical analysis of *Education as a Profession* has been written by Myron Lieberman. More recently he has written a much shorter and perhaps more provocative book called *The Future of Public Education.* And, of course, various publications and journals of these organizations are available in most libraries.

# CHAPTER 3

# What Is Philosophy of Education?

IF THERE ARE many ways of conceiving philosophy and many ways of conceiving education, it follows that there must be many, many, ways of conceiving philosophy of education. It might prove interesting and rewarding to develop systematically the possible permutations. For example, if we think of philosophy as a content or body of speculation concerning the nature of reality, the nature of knowledge, and the nature of value, and of education as a sociopolitical institution, then the philosopher of education could be viewed as having the task of delineating the system of schools that would best embody the fundamental philosophic posture of the state. Under this approach one would immediately face Aristotle's question concerning the compatibility of education and the Constitution.

In recent times this approach has gained significance due to the development of modern totalitarian forms of social organization. Hegel was not unaware of the importance of the state providing an education based on the principles of Absolute Idealism and the question was not overlooked by Nazi Germany and Fascist Italy. Hitler discussed education in *Mein Kampf,* and in Italy, Giovanni Gentile, a professional philosopher, was commissioned to explore dialectically the meaning for education of the principles of Fascistic social organization. Still more recently many persons have been concerned with the development of education as a sociopolitical institution under Communism. This, in turn, has impelled many to attempt a formulation of the correct forms of education for a democratic state.

On the other hand, suppose we conceive philosophy primarily as an activity and education as a process of personal development. The philosopher of education is then confronted with the task of bringing to bear upon such problem areas as curriculum, discipline, evaluating and reporting student progress, and the like, the kind of analysis and synthesis that has characterized the activity of the philosopher throughout the ages. Or what would be the problems of the philosopher of education if he conceived his job as being primarily a matter of exercising philosophic-mindedness in developing a theory of education as an applied behavioral science?

In order to reduce the number of topics to be considered, let us group the possible combinations, albeit somewhat arbitrarily, into four main categories: philosophy *and* education, philosophy *in* education, philosophy *for* education, and philosophy *of* education. Considering each of these in some detail should help us gain an over-all view of philosophy of education as an emerging area of systematic study in our institutions of higher learning.

## PHILOSOPHY AND EDUCATION

The idea that philosophy and education are intimately related is certainly not new. From at least the time of Plato many outstanding philosophers have been concerned with problems of education. When we remember that philosophy has traditionally studied the nature of reality, knowledge, and value, we see a number of obvious connections with education. For example, speculation concerning what can be known, what is most worthy of being known, and what is the manner of knowing is only a step away from consideration of the proper goals of education and the nature of teaching and learning. Or again, when the chief emphasis of philosophy has been "The Good Life," or when, with John Dewey, it has been an examination of "The Problems of Men," the intimate connection with problems of education is evident.

When such connections between philosophy and education are

emphasized, it has appeared to some that a specific philosophy of education is a derivative of a particular philosophy. Were not Plato's proposals for education derived from his philosophy—that is, from his views concerning the nature of reality, knowledge, and value? If this is so, then to the extent that a philosophy differs from that of Plato, one would expect that from it differing proposals for education could be derived. It thus becomes possible for the philosopher of education to devote himself to careful study of the great philosophers, noting what they have said about education and, wherein the philosopher has neglected to do so, supplying the kind of educational proposals that seem to be consistent with the basic philosophy. The philosopher of education thus becomes a specialist or expert in the meaning for education of the world's great systems of philosophy.

When one actually undertakes such a specialized study, however, certain difficulties arise. In the first place, philosophers who have discussed problems of education have generally not been very explicit about just how their educational proposals are derived from their philosophy. What are the rules for deriving a statement about education from a series of statements about the nature of reality or of knowledge or of value? If philosophies were constructed as deductive systems, as, for example, a system of geometry, then one could explore the question of what new or different theorems would follow from a change in one or more of the basic postulates. But this is not the case. So the philosopher of education is not able to say, with any great assurance, just what this or that philosopher would have said about certain problems of education had he decided to consider such a topic.

A second difficulty underlies the first. The various philosophies are not really alternate isomorphic systems presenting differing answers to a common set of questions. On the contrary, it is frequently the case that philosophers may be differentiated in terms of the different questions they select for emphasis or the differing ways they formulate the basic problems. And, of course, individual philosophers have been only more or less comprehensive. Some have devoted themselves primarily to metaphysics, others have written largely on questions of social or political philosophy, still others have concerned themselves mainly with, say, esthetics. It is impossible, therefore, to select a representative list of the great philosophers and show *systematically* how differing philosophies of education may be derived from their work.

It has occurred to many persons that it might be more promising to explore the meaning for education of the various *schools of philosophy* rather than the educational bearings of the work of individual philosophers. In cases where a philosopher has written in detail about education he could be viewed as a spokesman for the school of philosophy with which his views in philosophy are usually identified. Such an approach would thus, at least partially, remove the second difficulty mentioned above. Under this approach a new difficulty arises, however. Schools of philosophy span the ages but observations about education frequently have a time-and-place quality to them. This is true not only because the philosopher is more likely to be thinking about specific problems of his own age and culture when discussing education, than when discussing philosophy proper, but also because his educational proposals usually include much more than his basic philosophic posture. Discussion about education, in addition to reflecting one's philosophic orientation, generally reflects one's understanding, or misunderstanding, of matters that fall within the province of psychology, sociology, cultural anthropology, and the like. Thus it is that educational proposals frequently become "dated" in a way that more fundamental philosophic discussion does not.

Many interesting illustrations of this point could be cited. For example, in discussing the meaning for education of modern idealism, many scholars will select the writings of W. T. Harris, who was an influential and articulate spokesman in both philosophy and education in this country at the end of the nineteenth century. In discussing school discipline, Harris, taking his lead from Kant, spoke of "four cardinal duties in the schoolroom— regularity, punctuality, silence, and industry." He went on to say:

The general form of all school work is that of obedience. The will of the pupil comes into relation with the will of the teacher and yields to its sway. The will of the pupil inhibits its own wayward impulses, suppresses them, and supplants them by a higher rational will. In the act of obedience to a higher will the pupil becomes conscious of responsibility. Responsibility implies a sense of freedom. The child becomes conscious of its ability to accept or refuse—to obey or disobey. It becomes conscious of its power to originate actions and to give a new form to the chain of causation in which it finds itself. The great fact in the schoolroom is that the pupil is held responsible at each and every moment for all that he does. If he forgets himself and uses his voice, if he whispers, if he moves from his seat, if he pushes a book off his desk by accident, all these things are brought back to him at once by the presiding teacher. He is responsible not only for positive acts but also for neglect. Whatever he does or whatever he leaves undone is his business; this is justly regarded as the most potent means of ethical instruction."[1]

Some twenty-five years later, Professor Horne, who would certainly be classed in the same general school of philosophy, probably found these remarks about discipline at least a trifle embarrassing. Horne had this to say about "breaking a child's will."

It is better not to join this issue, not to conquer a child. Anticipate the issue; if the matter be important, decide it yourself in advance before allowing the child to reach or state his decision; if the matter is not over-important, leave him to decide for himself; even at some risk. If in an important matter the child's will is fixed, do not so much cross as circumvent him. Children raised in abject submission to parents become tyrants as adults; those whose wills were never broken, whose spirits were never crushed within them, make forceful and resolute characters. If you would make weak and irresolute men and women, break their wills as children.[2]

In less than another thirty years, Professor Butler, speaking from the same general philosophic orientation, and recognizing the importance of the same basic concerns about free will, moral

[1] W. T. Harris, "School Discipline," *The Third Yearbook of the National Herbart Society*, University of Chicago Press, 1897, pp. 65-66.
[2] Herman H. Horne, *Idealism in Education*, Macmillan, New York, 1923, p. 139.

responsibility, and the like, nevertheless urged greater "permissiveness" when dealing with children.

All of these considerations regarding the relation of axiology and education seem to me to point in the direction of an educational institution which is predominately permissive in relation to the value decisions of growing children and youth. The schools should freely provide opportunity for value consideration, decision, and realization; they should not withhold consideration, predetermine or force value decisions, and then expect realization to go on within this predisposed framework. . . .

While of course there are many decisions about the education of their children which must be made by parents, by elected authorities, by administrators, and by teachers, there are also many decisions to be made by pupils which are an essential part of education and apart from which genuinely educative activity cannot go on. I am often surprised at the number and extent of decisions it is commonly assumed that parents, teachers, administrators, and school officials must make. Many of these decisions, it seems to me, are going to be remade by the pupils. And I believe that most decisions which call for review by the pupils are rightly pupil decisions in the first instance anway. The value concerns of growing children and youth call for such indigenous decisions by them, and regarding these our schools should be more permissive than dominant. . . .

The teacher must never feel his own importance, but at the same time he can never underestimate his relation with his pupils. . . . It is the free response of the learner which is sought throughout the process. Imitative activities, if not abused, provide one channel through which this initiative may struggle into realization; interested application and effortful application are other means; and on occasion an externally imposed discipline may be a necessary reinforcement of these means to the birth of true initiative.[3]

It is clear, of course, that, although these quotations are not directed to precisely the same pedagogical points, nevertheless there are striking differences in the kind of classroom situations they cause a reader to visualize. The point to be noted is that the words of each man reflect not only the basic idealist position but also reflect the social-psychological insights of the time, namely,

[3] Donald Butler, *Four Philosophies and Their Practice in Education and Religion*, rev. ed., Harper, New York, 1957, pp. 578-582.

nineteen hundred, the nineteen twenties, and the nineteen fifties.

Many other difficulties are involved in a study of philosophy *and* education. If one is to explore the meaning for education of various schools of philosophy what particular classifications should be used? For example, in a standard handbook in the *History of Philosophy*[4] there is an appendix that presents "Schools of Philosophy and Their Adherents." More than fifty major classifications are offered, running from absolutism, agnosticism, altruism . . . to . . . transcendentalism, utilitarianism, voluntarism. Most of the important philosophers are listed several times. Which listing is the important one for education? Hegel, for example, is said to be an adherent of absolutism, of evolutionism, of idealism, and of rationalism. As an absolutist, Hegel appears in the company of men such as Plato, Thomas Aquinas, and Fichte. But as an evolutionist, these three companions drop out, being replaced by men such as Comte, Spencer, and Nietzsche. As an idealist, Hegel is rejoined by Plato and Fichte, but Aquinas, Comte, Spencer, and Nietzsche are now all absent. Room is thus made for Berkeley and Royce. Finally, as a rationalist, all of the former companions, save Plato, are missing and Hegel is now in the company of such diverse thinkers as Aristotle, Descartes, and Duns Scotus.

This is a confusing situation. Typically, specialists in philosophy *and* education have employed such blanket classifications as idealism, realism, and pragmatism, adding occasionally, scholasticism and naturalism, and more recently, logical empiricism and existentialism. Such an approach appears rather arbitrary, to say the least, and one wonders whether this manner of classifying results in more harm than benefit, especially with beginning students.

In order to avoid the oversimplification that almost inevitably accompanies the use of blanket labels, some students of philosophy *and* education have posed one or more basic questions

[4] Albert E. Avey, *Handbook in the History of Philosophy*, Barnes & Noble, New York, 1954.

whose relevance for both philosophy and education can be quickly demonstrated. For example, "What is the nature of mind?" Philosophers may then be grouped according to their theories of mind. Such classifications as the following might occur: Mind as Substance; Mind as Process; Mind as Function. The bearings of a theory of mind upon the proposals made for education may then be carefully explored.

A somewhat similar approach in philosophy *and* education is to select some question such as "What is the sociopolitical function of education?" Group the answers that have been made over the years into, say, conservative, liberal, reactionary, and radical, then study the ontological, epistemological, and axiological underpinnings of each group of answers. Such an approach can be very interesting, if for no reason other than that it forces students to rethink all the nice classifications to which they have grown accustomed under other approaches. In such a study it turns out, however, that many of the traditionally important questions concerning the nature of reality, the nature of knowledge, and the nature of value tend to blur while historical classifications emerge. It appears that reactionaries in educational theory are drawing their insights from ancient and medieval philosophy, conservatives draw from modern philosophy (beginning with, say, Descartes), liberals are inspired by contemporary philosophy (notably Whitehead and Dewey), and the radicals (that is, ultraliberals) draw from selected avant-garde thinkers (usually a curious mixture of pragmatism, positivism, and existentialism, plus some philosophically unidentified influences from social-psychology, cultural anthropology, and the sociology of knowledge).

Nothing that has been said should be construed to mean that philosophy of education as philosophy *and* education is a completely misconceived or unrewarding affair. In spite of the many pitfalls involved in this approach, the fact remains that many of the problems of systematic philosophy are intimately related to education. A systematic study of philosophy *and* education can, therefore, be a source of enlightenment to the serious student of either discipline. And, as a matter of fact, this is the most common approach to philosophy of education. Because of its tremendous complexities and subtle pitfalls it is doubtful, however, whether it is the most fruitful approach for the beginning student of either philosophy or education.

## PHILOSOPHY IN EDUCATION

When philosophy is viewed as philosophizing, then the philosopher of education is concerned with putting this activity to work in the field of education. Since, as we have seen, education may be viewed in various ways, philosophizing about education may take many forms. For example, philosophic analysis and synthesis may be directed primarily toward education as a sociopolitical institution. On the other hand, it could be concerned chiefly with building a comprehensive view of the nature of education as a process of personal development. Whatever the focus of attention may be, philosophy *in* education is the attempt to view education in the comprehensive, penetrating, and flexible manner that has characterized the philosophic approach regardless of the problem area.

Sometimes a course that attempts philosophy *in* education is taught through the use of a series of case studies. Problems that may typically arise in classroom, school, and community are presented, and the ways in which teachers A, B, and C dealt with the problems are described. Students are then encouraged to analyze these cases and speculate concerning the underlying assumptions of each teacher. This can certainly be a thought-provoking experience and can lead to valuable insights about both the causes and grounds for actual behavior. No doubt it can also contribute to development of the ability and the inclination on the part of students to be more thoughtful and comprehensive in their approach to similar problems when they confront them as practicing teachers or administrators.

This approach can, of course, be carried to absurd extremes. I have heard of college instructors who have taken their students on visits to nearby schools in order to observe various teachers in action. The students are then required to write "observation reports" in which they conclude that because teacher A did and said such and such she must be a realist, while teacher B is an idealist and teacher C a pragmatist.

In considering philosophy *and* education we noted that it is very difficult to demonstrate a one-to-one relation between a systematic philosophy and specific educational procedures. Even if, however, one could establish that a certain viewpoint in philosophy implies a certain educational practice, it would not be safe to assume that the presence of this practice necessarily indicates a commitment to that particular view in philosophy. It is one thing to point out that if, for example, mind is conceived in a certain way then such and such procedures in education would seem to be indicated. It is logically quite another thing to say that if such and such proposals for education are made they must be based on a certain conception of mind. This is known as the fallacy of affirming the consequent. If one believes that the mind is made up of faculties, such as reason, memory, and will, then it seems reasonable to anticipate a more or less automatic transfer of training. That is, if the faculty of reason were exercised or strengthened through a rigorous study of, say, mathematics, then one would expect an improved ability to reason about say, social problems. It is one thing to say all this; it is a formal fallacy, however, to say that because a person believes that under certain circumstances some transfer of training may take place he necessarily believes the mind is made up of faculties.

A more sophisticated approach to philosophy *in* education is the attempt to help students develop insight into the comprehensiveness, penetratation, and flexibility displayed by the philosophic-minded person as he attacks problems of education in contrast to the behavior of the person who attempts to solve the same problems on the level of tradition, expediency, or narrow common sense. Under this approach both case studies and actual observation may be used but no special attempt is made to classify, except perhaps in the sense of noting that various ways of dealing with problems exhibit more or less philosophic-mindedness.

One of the advantages of this kind of study is that it may spur students into reading much more widely than is typically the case among students of education. They may become interested in seeing how first-rate minds from Plato to Whitehead have analyzed educational problems. They may also, perhaps for the first time, become truly interested in the historical, political, and social aspects of certain of today's pressing educational problems in order to display some comprehensiveness, penetration, and flexibility in the analyses and proposals that they put forward and defend as class assignments. Thus it is that the same readings which may have appeared dull and academic under the philosophy *and* education approach may suddenly seem more alive and relevant when pursued in search of insight into an actual present-day problem that the student accepts as important to him.

At a more advanced level, philosophy may be put to work *in* education through courses that undertake an analysis of more complex problems. Such topics as the nature of reflective thinking or the meaning of democracy have frequently been selected. In any event, the attempt to bring the spirit and methods of philosophy to bear upon important present problems of education certainly falls within the finest traditions of the discipline. Moreover, since this tradition has never been content merely to analyze, but to analyze in order to develop a more adequate synthesis, this approach to philosophy of education is intended to make a difference *in the conduct of* education by helping preservice and inservice teachers attain a more adequate understanding of the problems of education.

## PHILOSOPHY FOR EDUCATION

Most articles or books that could be classified as writings in philosophy of education are made up of several types of observations and comment running from specific proposals for school practice and policy to a philosophic analysis of various educational problems. Such writing usually involves some comment upon the historical setting of the points at issue and frequently involves considerable logical, psychological, and sociological analysis and argument. All of this is commonly interspersed with some more or less philosophic observations about things in general—about the nature of man, of society, of democracy, or what not.

A little later we shall note that it is possible to differentiate among philosophy of education, educational theory, educational policy, and educational practice, and that it may be wise to do so and to note, more carefully than has generally been customary, what aspect is being talked about at each point in our reading, writing, or discussing of education. But for now let us note, first, that such distinctions are not usually clearly drawn and, second, that most who write about education, no matter what they start out to do, usually cannot resist making a number of proposals or suggestions for educational policies and practice. Whether the proposals are mostly about practice or about policy or about theory or about philosophy, if they are at all numerous and comprehensive, they are frequently referred to as "A Philosophy of Education," meaning, of course, a philosophy *for* education.

Some books discuss various aspects of philosophy, theory, policy, and practice frankly using such titles as *Philosophy for American Education* or more commonly a less direct title such as *Democracy and Education, Education and the Democratic Faith,* or *The Ideal and the Community.* Even in the case of books of more modest scope, addressed to a limited aspect of the field of philosophy of education, say, a study of certain philosophic systems and their bearing on education or an analysis of modern versus traditional practices, it is still common to include a last chapter entitled "This I Believe," or "An Outline for a Philosophy of Education," or "A Theory of Democratic Education."

Anyone who makes a careful study of education is likely to

develop ideas that seem good enough to pass along to others in the hope of contributing to the improvement of educational practice. This is as it should be. Trouble arises because having confused philosophy, theory, policy, and practice, we either forget (or have never fully grasped) that in a plural culture we should prize more highly the conditions that permit and encourage a diversity of philosophic opinion than any particular opinion, even one of superlative quality, or else we are likely to imagine that the only thing that prevents a certain set of suggestions being adopted as *the* philosophy *for* American education is that some people are still uninformed or stubborn about recent developments in the physical and behavioral sciences or else that they are simply antidemocratic.

Each of these charges obviously needs considerable exploration. Involved here are questions about the nature of science and the nature of democracy that will be discussed in Chapters 5 and 9 respectively, but the meaning of philosophy and of theory in contrast to policy and practice may now be explored.

## *Educational Theory*

We have previously noted that teachers as well as laymen frequently confuse ends and means in thinking about education, and often set up intermediate ends as ends in themselves. The basic difficulty is that educational policy and practice is not formulated in the light of any clear and comprehensive theory of education. What is a theory? Even within scientific discussion, no single meaning for this term is accepted by all. The basic or root meaning in all correct usage, however, involves the idea of a way of looking at something, that is, a point of view or a conceptual scheme. A theory is a plan for seeing, ordering, and speculating about various phenomena or experiences. Frequently a distinction is drawn between descriptive theory and normative theory. A descriptive theory is a scheme for seeing and thinking about what *is;* a normative theory is a scheme for seeing and thinking about what *ought* to be.

Later we shall see that such a distinction is overly simple.

When we consider the nature of science we shall find, for example, that even those theories that are deliberately constructed to be only descriptive nevertheless contain normative elements. But for the present the distinction may be useful for calling attention once again to an appropriate difference between theories designed for research disciplines, such as physics or psychology, and theories designed for the directing of disciplined practices, such as medicine or education. In the first case the theory is designed to enable one to understand certain objects and relations encountered in the field of study and to see how to go about extending and refining this understanding—in short, to push at the frontiers of knowledge. In the second case, theory that is appropriately designed for the practitioner should enable him to see how knowledge developed in the foundational disciplines relates to his problems and how to utilize this knowledge for moving *what is* in the direction of *what ought to be.* In other words, a theory of education must, by the nature of the enterprise, be normative as well as descriptive.

What should a theory of education be about, i.e., what sorts of things should be described and what manner of norms should be provided? Certainly a theory of education should describe education. It should provide a set of categories and classifications for seeing and thinking about education. But we saw in Chapter 2 that there is more than one appropriate and important way of looking at education. If we tentatively accept the ways discussed in Chapter 2, we could then say that a theory of education should provide a conceptual scheme for understanding education as a process of personal development, as a sociopolitical institution, and as the art and science of teaching. Moreover, the theory should enable us in each case to see and think about what ought to be as well as what is.

Such a theory cannot, of course, stand in isolation. The educator is not the only person concerned about processes of personal development, sociopolitical institutions, or behavioral science. Fortunately much is already known about these matters and the frontiers of knowledge are being explored in the light of theories developed in the various research disciplines that study human behavior, including processes of personal development and the forming and transforming of sociopolitical institutions. Hence, a theory of education should provide not only several systematic, and systematically related, ways of viewing education but it should also relate such conceptualization to the scientific knowledge developed by education's foundational disciplines.

It follows, of course, that an adequate theory of education will contain, or it will be the foundation for, various subtheories, such as curriculum theory, theory of educational administration, theory of educational economics and finance, theory of school plant construction, and so forth. It will also contain, or be the foundation for, subtheories of another type, such as theory of learning, theory of motivation, theory of personality development, and subtheories of still other types such as theory of teaching, theory of classroom control, theory of evaluating and reporting student progress, etc. It is clear that the way one divides and subdivides is more or less arbitrary, although it would seem less so if we actually had a well-developed theory of education that enabled us to see such relationships more systematically.

It also appears that certain of the subtheories should fall largely if not wholly within one or another of the foundational disciplines. For example, perhaps a theory of learning should be a part of psychology, and theory of educational economics and finance should be part of economics. If, however, we recall the discussion in Chapter 2 of education as an applied behavioral science we should hesitate before jumping to such a conclusion. In any event, a theory of education should be concerned not only with how schools may be financed but with how they *should be* financed, just as it must be concerned with what and how children *should* learn as well as with what and how they may and do learn.

To summarize, an educational theory is a systematic conceptual scheme that enables one to formulate descriptive and normative statements about education, about how scientific knowledge may be applied to educational problems and how conflicting proposals for education may be subjected to orderly inquiry and adjudication. How then does educational theory differ from educational policy and practice?

## Educational Policy

The term *policy* carries two somewhat conflicting root meanings both of which are involved in the meaning of *educational policy*. The first meaning has to do with displaying or making explicit what is involved in a contract or set of basic principles (as, for example, an insurance policy). The second meaning carries the connotation of agreement or compromise reached in the light of the exigencies of a particular situation, in contrast to an agreement based entirely on abstract principles. A policy is thus the means for giving contextually operational meaning to statements formulated on a theoretical base.

Without clearly understood policies, practice tends to be either paralyzed or impulsive. It takes time to think through the meaning of a theory for the various shifting circumstances that arise and, indeed, it is not to be expected that all practitioners will be well enough grounded in basic theory to accomplish such a task. A good policy thus serves the practitioner as a more accessible reference point enabling decisions to be made with greater dispatch and surety than would be possible were it necessary to refer every decision directly to basic theory. On the other hand, policy also prevents the singularities of the moment from running away with the decision. It prevents practice becoming chaotic or developing along tangents that are incompatible with basic principles.

Educational policy obviously exists on many levels, from pronouncements by national commissions to informal agreements at the local school or school district. In every case, however, a statement that is truly a policy statement will exhibit the characteristics of a mediatory instrument. It will reflect the influence of both educational theory and the pressing circumstances of specific time and place. Educational policy thus frequently involves a compromise between theoretical norms and what is thought to be presently feasible.

## Educational Practice

In contrast to both theory and policy, statements about educational practice should, ideally, be restricted to scientifically controlled descriptions and judgments about the various behaviors and experiences involved in the educational enterprise. It is such carefully controlled statements that, on the one hand, contribute to modification and refinement of educational theory and, on the other hand, enable one to make a more adequate assessment of what is actually feasible under a given set of circumstances. One of our present difficulties is that, lacking a carefully formulated theory of education, discussion of practice tends to be either a series of uncontrolled, nonsystematic (and hence doubtful and even confusing) empirical generalizations, or a series of exhortations and suggestions offered without empirical evidence. Many such suggestions develop wide popular support and therefore become one more complicating factor that must be considered as educational policies are formulated.

The expression "philosophy of education" (meaning philosophy *for* education) is frequently used in reference to any or all points of the theory-policy-practice system of discourse. The three most common uses, however, are at the point of normative theory, the point of "high level" policy, and in reference to that curious and truncated mixture of statements of theory, policy, and practice known as "a school philosophy." More disciplined usage would restrict the expression to the value assumptions (and their theoretical elaboration) of the normative theory. And in a democratic society there seems to be no good reason why any one occupational group such as philosophers or philosophers of education, should be privileged to dictate these value assumptions. On the other hand, because of their special competence, philosophers of education should be expected to develop a theory for the systematic understanding, in relation to education, of our free society's complex value structures. It is in this sense only that it is the special responsibility of the philosopher of education to tell us what education ought to do.

In any event, there appears to be an increasing disenchantment with philosophy of education as philosophy *for* education. In an age in which development of both theoretical science and technology are rapidly accelerating and in which the importance of education is increasingly recognized, it is to be expected that education, as a field of study, will become increasingly specialized and systematically disciplined. Nor is it likely, in such an age, that the term philosophy will be needed to lend either academic respectability or popular appeal to a serious and competent discussion of educational problems at any level of the theory-policy-practice spectrum.

## PHILOSOPHY OF EDUCATION

There is a growing tendency among philosophers of education to adopt the attitude and procedures of the philosophers of science. There are many reasons for this tendency. In the twentieth century, science has increasingly tended to dominate the intellectual and imaginative life of man. This corresponds roughly to a similar domination by commerce and exploration in the sixteenth century, theology and religion in the middle ages, and political organization in classical times. Throughout the ages philosophy has generally reflected the dominant interests and concerns of man. It is not surprising that in our time philosophy of science has emerged as an important discipline or field of study.

Philosophy of science is the disciplined study of the nature of science and this includes, of course, questions about the relation of science *and* philosophy, science *and* art, science *and* common sense, and the like. There is much disagreement and controversy in this field of study but there seems to be general agreement that it is not the business of this discipline to develop a philosophy *for* science. It is possible, of course, that such an approach could develop in the future, especially if the conduct of science should come under widespread public criticism. But for the present, philosophers of science, for the most part, limit themselves to a study of the nature of the enterprise.

As philosophy of science has gained greater emphasis in departments of philosophy, students studying philosophy as preparation for a career in philosophy of education have become increasingly impressed with the methods of this discipline. Moreover, as science has expanded its domination of all human affairs, including education, the philosopher of education, regardless of his formal preparation, has had little choice but to struggle to understand the nature of this dominating influence. Finally, as greater recognition of the importance of education develops (and in the next century it may be education rather than science that dominates the intellectual and imaginative life of man) there is growing pressure for the development of philosophy of education as a more or less independent disciplined area of study comparable to philosophy of science.

There are many reasons, however, why philosophy of science is an inadequate model for philosophy of education. In the first place, the various "philosophies of" (philosophy of science, philosophy of history, philosophy of medicine, philosophy of law, philosophy of education, etc.) are not parallel subdivisions of philosophy proper, and each has developed its own distinctive characteristics. The dissimilarities that exist are at least as great as the dissimilarities of the various sciences (that is, physics, biology, psychology, etc.). Moreover, since education is more nearly comparable to, say, medicine or law, one would expect, say, philosophy of medicine to provide a better model for philosophy of education.

What has actually happened, however, is that the development of philosophy of science has contributed to a changed conception of philosophy itself and thus, indirectly, philosophy of science is causing ferment and change within each of the various "philosophies of." It is this indirectly induced ferment in philosophy of education that accounts for the emphasis we may call philosophy *of* education.

One of the functions that philosophy *of* education may perform is the analysis of education into its most significant aspects as a basis for the development of educational theory. Moreover, philosophy *of* education may delineate the proper subdivisions and areas of specialization within the larger emerging discipline of philosophy of education. This is to say that it is philosophy *of* education that analyzes the total discipline into such divisions as philosophy *and* education, philosophy *in* education, philosophy *for* education, and philosophy *of* education.

In short, the first three chapters of this book may be considered an attempt at philosophy *of* education. But it is merely that—only an attempt. If our guess is correct, it is this approach that represents, at present, the most viable edge of the larger discipline. If it does develop, early attempts are destined to appear crude. And if they are not to appear foolish as well, they should avoid premature projections about what will or will not be included for study, how it should be studied, and what the value of such study will turn out to be.

### Suggestions for Additional Reading

Many of the standard textbooks in philosophy of education contain sections addressed to the general question of the nature and function of this discipline or field of study. Students frequently find the following especially helpful: Chapter I in Kilpatrick, *Philosophy of Education;* pages 11-19 in Broudy, *Building a Philosophy of Education;* chapter I in Brubacher, *Modern Philosophies of Education;* and pages 14-19 in Phenix, *Philosophy of Education.* For a brief review of the historical development of philosophy of education see chapter V in Brubacher, *A History of the Problems of Education.*

One of the ways to discover what philosophy of education is, is to study the articles written by present-day professionals in the discipline. In other words, one could say that philosophy of education is what philosophers of education do. The two journals devoted especially to this area of study are: *Educational Theory* and *Studies in Philosophy and Education.* Students will find it worthwhile to browse in these journals. There are also some books of readings available, for example, Joe Park (editor), *The Philosophy of Education* and Burns and Brauner (editors) *Philosophy of Education.*

While the beginning student will probably not read extensively in each of the four approaches to philosophy of education described in this chapter, a brief list of some of the better known texts may prove helpful. Remembering that the classifications developed in this chapter are post facto, that is, they were developed after most of the books to be listed were written, and remembering that most books are intended to accomplish more than one purpose or function, the following way of classifying these texts appears to be consistent with the discussion in this chapter:

## PHILOSOPHY *and* EDUCATION

Bode, *How We Learn*
Brameld, *Philosophies of Education in Cultural Perspective*
Butler, *Four Philosophies and Their Practice in Education and Religion*
Henry (editor), *Modern Philosophies and Education*
Morris, *Philosophy and the American School*
Wynne, *Theories of Education*

## PHILOSOPHY *in* EDUCATION

Brackenbury, *Getting Down to Cases*
Brubacher, *Modern Philosophies of Education*
Dewey, *Democracy and Education*
Dewey, *How We Think*
Hullfish and Smith, *Reflective Thinking: The Method of Education*
Mason, *Educational Ideals in American Society*
Thayer, *The Role of the School in American Society*

## PHILOSOPHY *for* EDUCATION

Bayles, *Democratic Educational Theory*
Berkson, *The Ideal and the Community*
Brameld, *Toward a Reconstructed Philosophy of Education*
Hansen, *Philosophy for American Education*
Kilpatrick, *Philosophy of Education*
Mayer, *Philosophy of Education for Our Time*
Sayers and Madden, *Education and the Democratic Faith*
Ulich, *Philosophy of Education*

## PHILOSOPHY *of* EDUCATION

Broudy, *Building a Philosophy of Education*
Kneller (editor), *Foundations of Education*
Phenix, *Philosophy of Education*
Scheffler (editor), *Philosophy and Education*
Smith and Ennis (editors), *Language and Concepts in Education*

# CHAPTER 4

# *What Is Knowledge?*

IT HAS BEEN SAID that education implies teaching and teaching implies knowledge. Many of us would not object to this. When it is said further, however, that knowledge implies truth and truth is everywhere the same,[1] then serious questions arise concerning the nature of truth, of knowledge, and, indeed, of teaching and education. We have seen that there are many ways of conceiving education so we may anticipate a variety of views concerning the truth and knowledge that education is said to imply.

## KNOWLEDGE AS INTENSE BELIEF

When we consider the ways in which we use expressions such as "I *believe* such and such is the case" and "I *know* such and such is the case," we discover that the things we believe lie along a continuum running from the extremely doubtful to the certain or indubitable. If we were to voice our beliefs in succession from the least certain to the most certain we might start with expressions such as "It is barely possible that . . .", and finally, at some point well beyond the middle of the range, we should find ourselves saying "I know that. . . ." Moreover, a little further analysis would reveal that the locus of dubiousness is usually subjective.

For example, I may say that I *believe* Mexico City is south of

---

[1] A statement made by Robert M. Hutchins, *The Higher Learning in America*, Yale University Press, 1936, p. 67.

Honolulu but I *know* Mexico City is south of Los Angeles. It is clear that I am no less certain about the stability of location in the case of Honolulu than in the case of Mexico City and Los Angeles. What I am uncertain about is the accuracy and extent of my own geographic information. It turns out then that what I call knowledge is simply my own state of believing, untroubled by doubt.

But what do I mean by a state of believing? It is clear that much more is involved here than linguistic expression or even "a state of mind." As I think about some of the things I know, it appears that many matters of which I am most certain are the very things I have never verbalized or even thought about. It now occurs to me, for example, that I am quite sure the back of my head is several inches behind my eyebrows. I am also reasonably certain that I have never thought about this before. Yet I have acted upon this piece of knowledge every time I have combed my hair. It seems, therefore, that believing is physical as well as mental—believing is willingness to act.

How do such psychophysical states come about? When we observe the human infant we note its helplessness and its aimless movements. There appear to be relatively few built-in responses. A light touch on the lips causes a sucking reaction, a puff of air on the eye causes a blink, and the like. In the case of a human infant there is evidently just about enough reflex action, sensorimotor schemata, or *programing* to provide for survival in a highly protective and beneficent environment and to serve as a base for the development, through transaction with the environment, of more complex responses which enable the child to survive in gradually less beneficent situations. The provisions that are made for the infant's survival not only set up what amounts to a classical conditioning situation, but they transform the original reflexive actions into more generalized, coordinated, and differentiated programs. In other words, the process consists not merely of adding something to original and fixed hereditary schemata which continue to function in their original form, but the initial patterns are, themselves, reorganized and reconstructed. Thus it is that in learning from experience the human child *learns how to learn*.[2]

It is likely, of course, that typical fond parents, watching every movement of their child, imagine and project considerably more purposefulness than is actually there. Nevertheless, it is clear that in even the early months the child does learn and that his development is more than simple maturation—more than an unfolding of preformed traits. The patterns or schemata or responses that are developed soon take on a dynamic and purposive (or at least intentional) quality so that long before the child is able to speak he may be said to *believe* many things. He is willing to act in certain ways rather than in others.

Sometimes people deliberately try to condition other people. Parents may consistently slap the child's hand and say "No, No!" whenever he reaches for one of those breakable prized objects that are found in most homes, and teachers sometimes bestow upon students certain unmistakable looks of approval or disapproval as reward or punishment for various types of classroom behavior. Even deans or employers have been known to try the same tactics in office or staff meetings. But for the most part we establish relationships of meaning, and hence beliefs, not as a result of formal conditioning but as the result of more complex transactions involving more or less thoughtful exploration of meaning. The nature of our physical-social environment is such that it is almost inevitable that we come to believe many things even though no one has deliberately tried to teach us. All about us we observe people behaving in certain ways and when we behave in similar fashion life runs smoothly. There is no occasion to doubt. Certain ways of acting thus become habitual.

Habits stand in a double relationship to belief. On the one hand, since a habit is willingness to act, it may be viewed directly as a belief—usually a rather complex belief. On the other hand, since a habit functions as a program or strategy for dealing with

---

[2] For a helpful review of what is now known about the way in which human intelligence develops through experience, see J. McV. Hunt, *Intelligence and Experience*, Ronald, New York, 1961.

the environment, it may be viewed as a set or screen that intervenes or mediates between past and present experiencing. It follows that habits may then be considered the structures that process, form, and make available for action the individual's beliefs. When a simple belief (say the belief that some particular item of information is true) remains in an isolated or peripheral state with respect to an individual's habits, the belief tends to be ephemeral. When a belief is processed, structured, and incorporated by and into one's habits, then we may anticipate that changes in behavior will occur and conclude that significant learning has taken place.

## KNOWLEDGE AS PATTERNS OF MEANING

We seldom talk about the things we *know* unless some person or situation casts the shadow of doubt on a belief. If life always ran smoothly on the level of nonverbalized patterns of belief, it is hard to imagine how language, beyond a few grunts of satisfaction, could ever have been invented. But, when our habitual ways of acting run into a snag, then we hesitate and, in effect, question the adequacy or truth of relevant belief patterns. Fortunately, a human being can *literally question* his beliefs, that is, he can verbalize beliefs and explore, through rational discourse, various combinations of meaning. He may thus avoid some of the errors that would attend a series of thoughtless, overt trials. Man is capable of constructing alternate hypothetical patterns of meaning and selecting only the most promising for overt test. Through language, men cooperate in the construction and testing of meaning and then they record and teach, formally and informally, what has turned out to be "the truth."

The dictionary says that knowledge is a clear perception of truth. So far, we have seen that each of us recognizes that our individual perception of various matters runs from the obscure to the very clear. As long as we remain at the level of nonverbalized beliefs, intensity of belief is a matter of effectiveness of the formal or informal conditioning processes we have undergone. When, however, beliefs (or knowledge or perceptions of truth) are verbalized and thus made available for thoughtful examination, it becomes possible to explore *why* we believe such and such.

We shall see that the question "Why?" is systematically ambiguous, referring (1) to the conditions that have caused the belief to form, and (2) to the evidence or argument that may be mustered in support of the belief. When patterns of meaning are organized or *caused* through a process of conditioning, or other processes that are uncontrolled by reflective activity, the person holding such a pattern of meaning is frequently unaware of any reason or grounds for such a belief. When confronted by a situation in which this pattern of meaning turns out to be inadequate, the feeling of doubt that arises is likely to turn into frustration or insecurity. This is the case because having never thought through the reasons or evidence for the belief he is at a loss to know in what way the pattern of meaning is inadequate. On the other hand, when patterns of meaning are constructed by thoughtfully controlled inquiry, then, when something goes wrong, the feeling of doubt may be experienced as intellectual stimulation and the inadequate patterns of meaning may be reconstructed to account for the new challenging experience.

Frequently, of course, our patterns of meaning are formed through a combination or mixture of reflective and nonreflective procedures and even those patterns which were originally organized largely by conditioning have later been at least partially rationalized so that we are seldom totally frustrated by the challenge of a new experience. Nevertheless, to the degree in which our habits and beliefs reflect a thoughtless organization of meaning we are likely to feel insecure or frustrated when experience proves them to be inadequate.

Regardless of how a pattern of meaning is formed, so long as it functions successfully there is normally no occasion for reflection concerning it. We go about our daily life, for the most part, *recognizing* the meaning of things rather than having to stop and think. This fact has frequently caused confusion concerning the nature of knowledge. We have said that many meanings are known or recognized immediately, that is, instantaneously or without hesitation. This has led some persons to assert that some knowledge is *immediate*. But in epistemology, the word immediate means nonmediated, that is, without inference or interpretation. When we view knowledge as patterns of meaning, however, we see that even though we frequently immediately recognize meaning it is not the case that such meaning has been grasped full-blown out of the blue. It is just because such meaning is part of a pattern that has been organized or constructed through past experience that we are able to recognize it without conscious inference or interpretation. This is why different persons with differing backgrounds of experience and hence differing patterns of meaning will, when confronted with an object or event, *recognize* differing meanings.

All this, obviously, has important bearing on education. It has long been recognized that students (of whatever age) can master new material only to the extent that it becomes meaningful to them in terms of their past experience. Moreover, since in a typical classroom there is a wide range of past experience, effective teaching has frequently been viewed as a matter of tying the new material to whatever patterns of meaning are held in common by the otherwise diverse personalities in the class. Under this approach, the more education the more alike the students will become, that is, the more they will hold meanings in common.

In a sense it is true that education results in commonality of meaning. Good education tends to reduce some of the prejudices and provincial outlooks that separate people and that block communication and mutual understanding. But it is equally true that good education enhances and strengthens some of the individual differences that exist in the classroom, so that the more the education the greater the range of individual differences. This is because education (as a process of personal growth) is, for the most part, a matter of thoughtful construction and reconstruction of meanings rather than unreflective organization of uniform patterns of meaning. Effective teaching, therefore, consists of confronting students with the kind of experiences that challenge their inadequate patterns of meaning and then helping each student to reconstruct his patterns toward greater adequacy. It is thus that individuality is enriched while at the same time meanings may be shared and mutual understanding and appreciation developed.

There is a further aspect of the process of reconstruction that is not so obvious, however. When a pattern of meaning is reconstructed it turns out that not only the meaning of present (and hence future) experience undergoes change but also the meaning or significance of one's past experience is altered. This may be understood by considering what takes place in a classical conditioning experiment in contrast to a situation in which meanings are reflectively created and tested.

Suppose that Pavlov had happened to use a "philosophic-minded dog." When the bell rang and food appeared, the dog, being accustomed to taking a comprehensive, penetrating, and flexible view of experience, would likely have pondered the question of why food should have appeared following the sound of the bell. In attempting to answer this question he would have *constructed* an hypothesis or theory (that is, a pattern of meaning) to account for his experience. During subsequent experiences, he would have refined this theory until it became the best possible explanation of this "bell-food invariant association" compatible with all the evidence he could obtain.

When the time arrived that the bell sounded and no food appeared, our philosophic-minded dog would, no doubt, salivate as an ordinary dog for whom a pattern of meaning had been organized by conditioning. Even for the most thoughtful persons a pattern of meaning or belief is still a willingness to act. But the philosophic-minded dog would view this new development not as a frustrating experience but as an occasion for further thought and inquiry. He would see immediately that his theory would have to be *reconstructed* in order to account for this new experience.

We have already noted that a theory is a *way of viewing* experience, so the point to be noted is that when the bell-food theory is reconstructed, the dog views differently (that is, understands differently) not just the present experience but the entire series of experiences. And, of course, his expectations about future experience will be correspondingly different. Thus it is that an education which proceeds by the reconstruction of experience enables one to lift himself by his own bootstaps, so to speak. It is this kind of education that enables one to overcome the restricting effects of a limited early environment or to use certain "unfortunate experiences" as building blocks for a comprehensive, humane view of life, while similar experiences condition others into developing merely antisocial attitudes. We noted that the dictionary reports knowledge as the clear perception of truth. But the truth is always mediated through the patterns of meaning that one holds.

## THE MEANING OF TRUTH

It is fascinating to observe in how many different ways we use the word *true*: The arrow went true to its mark. Give me 10 men tried and true. If you marry me I will forever be true. This is a true saying and worthy of all men to be received. A lizard is a true reptile. Is it true what they say about Dixie?

If we peel away the more figurative or poetic uses of the term, it appears that true is an adjective used to describe an assertion that conveys an accurate impression of some state of affairs. If this is approximately correct, then when the adjective is converted to a noun it presumably refers to a more or less exhaustive conjunction of all the correct assertions that could be made about a given state of affairs. If someone asks "Do you know the truth about Mary's divorce?" he is, in effect, asking whether you could frame a series of correct statements about the matter or, more practically, whether you can differentiate the true from the false statements that are being circulated about the affair. If teaching implies knowledge and knowledge is a clear perception of truth, it is no wonder that the true-false examination is a favorite evaluative device.[3]

Consider the following list of statements, most of which you have probably encountered at one time or another on a true-false examination:

1. The Battle of Hastings was fought in 1066.
2. Water is composed of oxygen and hydrogen.
3. By the twenty-first century the population of the United States will probably exceed 200 million.
4. The base angles of an isosceles triangle are equal.
5. A coronation is the act or ceremony of investing a sovereign or his consort with the royal crown.
6. The electrical current through a conductor is proportional to the electrical pressure between its ends.
7. You should do unto others as you would have them do unto you.

No doubt we should mark each of these statements true, indicating thereby that we believe each conveys an accurate impression of some particular state of affairs. *Why* do we consider such statements true? In the case of number one, we have all read about the Battle of Hastings and found the date 1066 presented, without controversy, as the year in which the battle took place. We have no reason to doubt the accuracy of the textbook accounts of this affair so we believe the statement to be true because authorities have said so. In spite of the fact that we lack personal acquaintance with the evidence, we feel sure enough about this item to speak of it as knowledge rather than belief.

When we consider the grounds for this belief, however, we recognize that, although the particular history textbooks that we have seen were based on earlier authorities and these in turn on still earlier ones, at some point this chain of authorities is grounded in eye-witness testimony. In other words, the truth of

[3] Difficulty arises, of course, because it is frequently very difficult to frame true-false questions that are both unequivocal and about anything that is very significant or important.

this statement rests on empirical grounds. People actually observed that the battle took place in 1066.

When we look at statement number two we find there are similar causes and grounds for belief in its truth. The textbooks tell us that water is composed of oxygen and hydrogen and we can verify this by our own observations in the laboratory.

In the case of the third statement, we see that it expresses a reasonable belief based on careful observation of population and population trends. The fact that it refers to a future state of affairs does not alter its basic empirical nature. It turns out then that all statements the truth or falsity of which can, in principle, be determined by empirical observation are called *factual assertions*. The question of tense is not involved in such designation and, indeed, such statements are called *factual assertions* even though they are thought to be or known to be false. For example, the statement "The moon is made of green cheese" is a factual assertion, although it is surely false. Its truth or falsity rests finally on empirical evidence.

Statement number four may appear to be similar to statement two in that both may be found in textbooks and the truth of both may be demonstrated in laboratory or classroom. But how do we demonstrate that the base angles of an isosceles triangle are equal? We can draw an isosceles triangle on the chalkboard, draw a line from the top of the triangle to the midpoint of the base, thus dividing the triangle into two congruent triangles, and then note that the base angles of the original triangle are now corresponding parts of congruent triangles. We thus see that the angles are equal. It appears that we have again grounded the assertion by observation.

If we remember more carefully the nature of plane geometry, however, we recall that one does not actually create a triangle on the chalkboard, one merely draws a representation of a triangle. Points, lines, triangles, circles, are all *conceptual entities*. They may be represented but are never actually presented. The figures we draw on the chalkboard help us think more clearly, but in the geometry class such expressions as "observe," "perceive," "see" carry figurative rather than literal meaning. In short, the truth of the assertion that the base angles of an isosceles triangle are equal is not a matter of empirical evidence. It is, rather, a matter of logical reasoning from the definitions, axioms, and postulates of geometry. Such statements may therefore be said to be *formally true*, in contrast to the first three statements which were found to be *factually true*.

Statement number five, as other dictionary definitions, confronts us with an interesting combination of formal and factual truth. Such definitions are empirical generalizations about usage. The lexicographer observes language behavior and records his generalizations, using procedures not unlike those used in any empirical science. Hence, his definitions are factual assertions. On the other hand, the truth conveyed by such assertions has to do with a relation of meanings and this is a formal affair. The truth that is perceived (again figuratively) when one consults a dictionary for the meaning of the word coronation is thus like the truth one gains from following a demonstration that the base angles of an isosceles triangle are equal. After such study one knows that a coronation may refer to the crowning of a consort as well as a sovereign just as one knows that the base angles as well as the sides of an isosceles triangle are equal. Moreover, there is no danger that some empirical evidence developed in the future will cause us to change our minds about the truth of these statements. Such statements may fall into disuse but they will not be shown to be untrue.

Thus far, we have seen that there are at least two distinct meanings of truth, a formal and a factual meaning. An assertion that is formally true conveys a correct impression about a relation of meanings within some given arrangement or scheme of ideas such as a mathematical, a logical, or a syntactical system. An assertion that is factually true conveys a correct impression about some existential state of affairs—affairs that exist in a space-time matrix. Or, more simply, factual assertions are about actual entities or conditions rather than about a relation of meanings.

Statement six raises questions about the status of such scientific entities as electrical currents and pressures and applied mathematical relations such as proportion. Are these actual entities or conceptual relations? This question is so complicated that we had best postpone discussion of it until Chapter 5 on the nature of science.

Statement seven, which asserts what is sometimes called a moral truth, is perhaps even more complicated. Do such statements convey factual truth, formal truth, or some third kind of truth? Or perhaps such statements are not intended to convey knowledge at all. Perhaps they are noncognitive and thus neither true nor false. Perhaps they are simply exclamations or exhortations. Again, we shall postpone discussion until Chapter 7 on the nature of value, for there remains much necessary preliminary exploration concerning the nature of knowledge.

## BELIEF AS IMPLICIT PREDICTION

To believe that a factual assertion is true is to hold a set of expectations. And this is the case whether the belief is mingled with some doubt or so firm that we say we *know* the statement is true. Every factual assertion implicitly amounts to a set of an indeterminate number of predictions about future experience. If we believe the assertion is true we expect that future experience will be somewhat different from what would be the case were the assertion false. This is why the state of believing is a willingness to act—a willingness to act in terms of expected future experience described by the set of implicit predictions involved in the assertion.

This is most noticeable in the case of assertions expressed in the future tense. For example, if I believe that it is going to rain tomorrow, it is obvious that my expectations about my future experience are different from what my expectations would be were I to believe we will experience a long dry spell. It is equally clear that differing sets of expectations will involve differing acts or cases of willingness to act. But the situation is the same with beliefs expressed in the present tense. If I believe it is raining at the present time I certainly hold a different set of expectations concerning what kind of experience, say, going home from work, will be this afternoon from what would be the case were I to believe it is not now raining. It is equally clear that the situation is the same concerning assertions expressed in the past tense, especially when they concern the immediate past. It is instructive to note that whatever we believe we believe here and now based on evidence presently available. If I believe that it rained during the night, surely I do so because I am now confronted with evidence of recent rainfall. In other words, we judge the truth or falsity of factual assertions about a past state of affairs according to whether the set of implicit predictions involved in the assertion correspond with the state of affairs that presently confronts us. If it rained during the night, then certain conditions exist this morning. It is the presence of these very conditions that causes me to believe it rained during the night. If the matter is serious enough to warrant more careful judgment, then, of course, I should investigate to see whether present conditions approximate those that could be expected *if and only if* it rained during the night.

In the case of assertions about a state of affairs in the more distant past, for example, "the Battle of Hastings was fought in 1066," I believe it because the world today, including the history textbooks, corresponds with what I expect the world would be like if the assertion were true. Or, more precisely, it is difficult to explain how the world could be as it is if the assertion were false.

There are two points to be noted: first, the possibility of error is obvious. Assertions about even a past state of affairs are never more than hypothetical and, as we shall see, hypotheses are never absolutely verified. It is always possible that some new evidence will develop that will cause us to change our minds about what was considered true in the past. The second point is that past, present, and future are always somewhat arbitrary designations. Where are the boundaries that set off the present from the past and the future? If we slice too thin, the present becomes meaningless. It turns out that grammatical tense is a man-made convenience for thinking and talking about a continuum of history and potential. All of our factual knowledge and belief are about a single infinitely complex state of affairs—a state of affairs *conceived* in a space-time matrix.

## TESTS FOR TRUTH

If man never held false beliefs, it is inconceivable that either philosophy or science could ever have arisen. But man is continually discovering that he holds mistaken ideas and this discovery tends to make him cautious and thoughtful, and he naturally wonders whether there is not some way of testing his ideas before instituting lines of action that will entail more or less irreversible consequences. If beliefs are to be dealt with thoughtfully, that is, dealt with as *ideas* rather than as overt actions or willingness to act, then, of course, they must be displayed for consideration as a series of artificial symbols that stand for the actual objects, qualities, activities, and relations involved in the belief. For example, if I believe that there are three maple trees just to the north of the mailbox that stands beside my driveway, I can examine this belief as an idea by expressing it in the following spoken or written symbols: *three maple trees—to the north of —driveway mailbox.* The particular symbols I choose are obviously a matter of convention. I could have expressed this belief, for example, by writing $3Tm-N-MBd$.

Once man displayed his beliefs as ideas for thoughtful consideration, a simple test for their truth must have very quickly occurred to him. If the content and arrangement of the symbols contained in an assertion *correspond* to the content and arrangement of the relevant actual state of affairs, the assertion is true; otherwise it is false. The expression $3Tm-N-MBd$ is true because it conveys an accurate (although highly stylized) picture of what I actually see when I look out the window toward the driveway.

If I were to dig up and remove one of the trees, then a true belief about the changed situation could be expressed as $2Tm-N-MBd$, and if I were to plant an oak tree to the south, my belief would then be $2Tm-N-$and$-1To-S-MBd$. It is a tremendous advantage to be able to sit in my study and deal with objects and relations *as ideas* rather than having to go to work and manipulate actual objects. And it is comforting to feel that I can check the truth of whatever beliefs I have, simply by noting whether they correspond with the relevant, actual state of affairs.

It turns out, however, that the act of noting whether an idea corresponds to an actual state of affairs is not so simple a matter as it seems. When I look out of the window at trees and mailbox, I gain an impression of their location. But the impression is itself a matter of visual imagery plus judgment about north and south, number, and the like. *The impression is made up of ideas.* Am I then really comparing an idea with an actual state of affairs or only with other ideas? There appears to be no way for me to get outside myself and take a look at both my ideas and an actual state of affairs to see whether they correspond.

To phrase the problem in another way, consider the fact that we sometimes make mistakes about what we think we see. We all know that illusion, hallucination, mirages are possible. We assume that they are infrequent but once we admit their possibility we cast some doubt on every experience. Philosophers have pointed out, therefore, that this means we accept an experience as veridical not in terms of itself but in terms of other experience. We strive for a coherent way of understanding experience as a whole, as an ongoing affair that is more than a summation of individual experiences. Hence, a given experience is taken to be veridical only if it is in harmony with the developing whole of experience.

It is conceivable, of course, that a person could be consistently and harmoniously wrong. As long as each experience is checked only against past experience in terms of coherence, one wonders how fact may be distinguished from fiction. A well-constructed novel may exhibit internal consistency or harmony and still not correspond with any actual state of affairs. We may acknowledge, then, that any system of ideas that lacks coherence is unsatisfactory, yet still insist that our ideas must be true to something beyond themselves. Perhaps some indirect test for correspondence can be made.

Recalling that factual assertions are always implicit predictions about future experience, a practical or pragmatic test for the truth of a belief suggests itself. It is certainly possible that the course of future experience is partially determined by what we believe, but unless we assume that it is completely determined by what we believe (and no one assumes this) we have found to what our ideas must be true if they are to be considered sound; namely, the course of *future experience*. And the way to apply this test is to take the actions indicated by our beliefs. Are the actions successful or do we encounter stubborn facts that indicate our belief to have been based on fiction—albeit even a beautifully consistent fiction.

A sophisticated person will, of course, employ a sophisticated version of the pragmatic test. He will not blindly convert every hunch or belief into immediate overt action in order to see whether it works. Beliefs may still be explored as *ideas* and may be imaginatively projected and tested, with only the most promising becoming the basis for overt action. By the same token, a person who is not overly self-centered or selfish will not judge the success of his actions (hence the truth of his beliefs) in terms of narrow or personal standards. Nevertheless, many persons object to the pragmatic test, insisting that it really does not escape the limitations of the correspondence and coherence tests. It is argued that the indirect test of correspondence which it provides is always a matter of interpretation from experience and, moreover, since experience (in *traditional philosophy*) is likely to be thought of as essentially subjective or personal, the criteria for success or workability are likely to be even more subjectively and narrowly conceived than under the coherence theory of truth.

In actual practice, most of us, not being very philosophic about the whole affair, are likely to use all three of these tests for truth with the emphasis shifting from one to another as the context of our thought and action changes. In daily affairs in which our beliefs are concerned with the objects, qualities, and relations that can be seen, touched, or heard, we tend to assume that a reasonably careful use of our senses does provide us with a direct-correspondence test for truth. Indeed, a laboratory scientist proceeds on the same general assumption even though he utilizes instruments that greatly refine and extend his natural sensory equipment. On the other hand, when we are concerned with formal problems dealing in conceptual relations, say, in mathematics, logic, or scientific-theory construction, we tend to rely on a coherence test for truth. And finally, when we are concerned about the truth or desirability of complicated practical judgments, dealing perhaps with sociopolitical arrangements or principles of right conduct, we tend to use a pragmatic test, judging the consequences of action in terms of the more or less well-established values or norms of our culture.

At the philosophic level, preference for one or another of the tests or theories of truth is usually made in terms of their respective underlying epistemological and metaphysical assumptions. Realists have generally assumed that a world of objective fact exists prior to and independently of its being known by a subjective knower. They are likely, therefore, to think of truth in terms of correspondence. Various forms of realism may be differentiated according to the way in which *correspondence* is conceived. Especially important is the way in which the problem of error is treated. For example, the notion that correspondence can be checked by relatively simple look-and-see procedures with errors corrected by more careful observations is known as *naïve realism*, or sometimes *common sense realism*. Even when the observation procedures are those of modern science (including advanced statistical treatment of data), if it is assumed that such observations disclose or discover objective facts existing prior to and independently of their being known, then, philosophically speaking, naïve realism is still present. On the other hand, it is sometimes said that all we can know is merely our own sensations of the outside world, but that these sensations correspond to (in the sense of representing) independently objective facts. Such a view is known as representative realism. Other variations are known as presentative realism, critical realism, neorealism, etc.[4]

In contrast to the basic assumption of realism, idealists generally argue that the mind and the objects of knowledge mutually implicate each other so that whatever is known is known only *as an object of knowledge,* not as an independent fact existing outside the knowing process. Again, there are several variations but, since ideas can be corroborated only by other more comprehensive and systematic ideas, truth is a matter of coherence.

Dissatisfied with the assumptions of both realist and idealist, a pragmatist denies the subjective-objective distinction as a starting point and turns to experience itself as the primitive, underived, or basic reality. Subjective-objective, self-environment, knower-known are distinctions that arise within experience; and all beliefs, whether about self or environment or about the knowing process itself, can be tested only as hypotheses are tested—that is, by using them as directive instruments for further thought and action and noting their relative success or failure in the process. Such a view is known as the pragmatic theory of truth.

Such philosophic differences have little direct influence on the conduct of schooling. Persons of various philosophic orientations may cooperate in the work of the schools just as they may and do work side by side in the scientific laboratory or field project. This is not to say that such differences make no difference; it is to say, first, that the influence of such differences is usually quite indirect and difficult to trace and, second, that most teachers, scientists, and people in general are not likely to be consistently

[4] Once again, labels are not the important consideration. What is important is the differing ways of posing and treating the problems involved in the nature of knowledge. Hospers, *An Introduction to Philosophical Analysis,* chap. 6, "Perceiving the World," should prove helpful in this connection.

clear about their own philosophic stance nor much concerned about the indirect influence on their work of whatever philosophic assumptions they may have. Nevertheless, it seems reasonable to expect that *differing degrees of understanding concerning the nature of knowledge and truth* will influence one's attitude toward inquiry and the sources of knowledge and *will make a difference* in the kind of intellectual climate that is generated in the classroom.

## SOURCES OF KNOWLEDGE

In the classroom the most common source of information is some authority—teacher, textbook, or other reference materials. Years ago, before printed materials were available to students, instruction in the great colleges of Europe was primarily a matter of lecturing, that is, reading a manuscript to a group of students so that they could make notes or copy what was said and thus come into possession of authorative information and judgment about the subject in question. This was a more efficient means of disseminating subject matter than attempting to pass the original manuscript from student to student. Even today when a teacher is in possession of important information and judgment that cannot be made readily available to students in printed form, such lecturing may still be an appropriate device. Our present concern, however, is not primarily with methods of teaching. It is rather with questions about the proper use of authority and the attitude toward authority that may be engendered in a classroom.

It is clear that, if everyone were unwilling to accept any statement unless he had personally verified it through direct, first-hand experience, civilization would be impossible and there would be little point in organizing a school. On the other hand, without reasonable skepticism about the pronouncements made by "authorities" we should become the gullible victims of every charlatan, quack, and confidence man that came along, to say nothing of the honest mistakes involved in reports made by the most competent specialists. One of the problems that confronts a teacher is how to help students develop respect for competent authority (so that they will not confuse the principle that everyone has a right to an opinion with the notion that one opinion is as good as another) and at the same time help the student progressively to develop an increasingly healthy skepticism about even the most widely accepted opinions of established authorities.

It is remarkably difficult to get even university professors to entertain seriously an idea that runs counter to standard textbooks. After years of schooling, in which statements are believed *primarily* because respected texts and teachers have said they were true and the so-called experiments and problems given to students have been in reality exercises in which whatever evidence is developed is not to be believed unless it agrees with the correct solution, it is no wonder that the graduates of such schooling are seldom inclined to strike out on their own with enough self-confidence to persevere in the kind of rigorous exploration of an idea that will enable them to see for themselves whether it has merit, regardless of what the authorities have said or have neglected to say. In an age of increasing specialization and interdependence, we must learn how to make more efficient use of expert judgment and at the same time devise better safeguards against the aura of infallibility that tends to surround certain authorities or groups of men, especially during periods of public crisis or anxiety.[5]

[5] During war, both hot and cold, governments find it necessary to make decisions in secret. By the nature of the case, such decisions are the very ones most likely to have a pervasive, profound, and irreversible influence. Consider, for example, the secret decision to develop an atom bomb and the decision to use the bomb against Japan. Any nation that does not employ and largely depend upon the decision of authorities in many different fields of specialization is doomed to be only a minor power in the world of today and tomorrow.

On the other hand, decisions that must be kept secret cannot be widely reviewed and it follows that decisions that require the most specialized competence are the least likely to be subjected to really adequate review. Our society can no longer afford the kind of carping criticism and myopic interference that, in the past, has frequently distracted our experts, our "eggheads," and our "brain trusts," yet we must never allow our lives to be

It turns out, then, that authority is our most common source of knowledge and, when it is open to free inquiry and question in the face of reasonable doubt, it is a legitimate source of belief or knowledge. It is clear, nevertheless, that authority is never a primary source. Whence the authority's knowledge? It is commonly said that there are three primary sources: sense experience, reason, and intuition. Let us examine each of these.

## Sense Experience

The view that all knowledge comes through the senses is known as empiricism. In the eighteenth century, John Locke argued that the human mind at birth is a *tabula rasa*, that is, a blank tablet. The mind registers impressions that come to it from the outside world through sense receptors. These impressions he called simple ideas. Under this view man is able to group and organize, and then reorganize, these simple ideas into complex ideas. All that man knows or can know directly is his own ideas, based on sense impressions. We generally assume that the simple ideas and even the complex ideas are reasonably accurate copies of what actually exists. We have already noted, however, some of the difficulties involved in establishing any test for truth at the philosophic level of analysis. We are now, however, concerned with sense experience as a source of knowledge, not as the ultimate test for the validity of a belief.

The fundamental problem that concerned Locke was whether man possesses any innate ideas. We all agree that the perceptions of an adult are influenced by his prejudices, his emotions, and his desires. Man tends to see what he wants to see and believe what he wants to believe. In Lockean terms, we could say that the complex ideas a man already holds tend to influence his perceptions. The fundamental question is whether man is born with a mental structure that influences his perceptions right from the beginning or with a mind that is essentially a

dominated by an elite group of scientific, economic, or social planning czars who make public decisions in secret. Surely one task of public education is to develop a generation of citizens who, at the very least, recognize the existence of this problem.

blank tablet as Locke argued. Again, we have already noted that, compared to other animals, it seems that man is born with relatively little instinctive or innate predisposition or willingness to act, hence few innate ideas, meanings, or beliefs. Indeed, human infants, unfortunate enough to be born without the major sense receptors of sight and sound, are very slow in developing any sizable fund of meanings or beliefs at all. In this respect, therefore, Locke's notions were evidently on the right track and sense impression surely plays an important role in the formation of belief and knowledge.

The more interesting part of Locke's view is the matter of complex ideas. How do we organize and reorganize simple sensory data into the complex ideas, the general ideas, the abstract ideas that function in even our most ordinary daily affairs. Consider, for example, the enormous complexity of the meanings involved in the following statement which you might make to a friend concerning a lecture you once heard, "I don't remember the details of what the man said, but my general impression was that he is a socialist." How does one form such a statement on the basis of the raw sensory data gained in a lecture hall?

*Reason*

The view that reasoning or thought is the central factor in knowledge is known as rationalism. A rationalist argues that the raw data of sensation must be organized by the mind into meaningful patterns before anything worthy of the name *knowledge* appears. What man *knows* is meaningful ideas, conceptions, and principles, albeit complex; not just raw sensations. Furthermore, if thought is a central factor in knowledge, then it might seem reasonable to suppose that thought alone (that is, thought divorced from sense experience) would be the source of at least some important knowledge. Consider statements such as "Nothing can both exist and not exist at the same time" or "Everything that exists is either 'A' or non 'A' (e.g., each thing that exists is either water or it is not water)." How do you know that such statements are true? Is such knowledge based on reason alone?

Or consider whether it is not the case that the knowledge gained about the interrelations among ideas or meanings within any formal system, such as logic or mathematics, are gained by taking thought or reasoning apart from sense experience. We have noted that one does not prove a theorem—in plane geometry, for example—by measuring lines and angles, but rather by *reasoning out* what must be true if one starts with certain definitions, axioms, and postulates. We sometimes draw representations of various geometric figures (just as we write out algebraic equations and transformations), but this is done only to help us concentrate and figuratively see the relationships involved. Surely we must all agree that reasoning is a source of some kinds of belief and knowledge. Like sense impressions, however, we recognize that reasoning may mislead us. We sometimes make mistakes in reasoning. It is not, therefore, an infallible source of knowledge.

The more controversial aspect of rationalism, however, has to do with the meaning of the expression *thought apart from sense experience*. In philosophic terminology, the question is usually posed as "What is the nature of a priori knowledge?" Traditionally, a priori knowledge was said to be gained by reasoning from self-evident principles without dependence on anything gained from sense experience. It was thus set in contrast to a posteriori knowledge which is attained by reasoning from the impressions gained through observations or other sense experience. Rationalists have generally argued that at least some statements which can be known to be self-evidently true are statements about the nature of reality or of matters of fact. For example, we believe that no thing can both exist and not exist at the same time and we believe this with a feeling of certainty that is quite different from the way we hold to empirical generalizations derived in a posteriori fashion. On the other hand, strict empiricists maintain that, since mind without sense impressions remains blank, all knowledge, including those self-evident principles that seem most certain, is fundamentally a posteriori.

In contemporary philosophy, the two views that are perhaps

the most influential (commonly known as logical empiricism and pragmatism or experimentalism) agree that the *truth* or validity of analytic assertions does not depend upon empirical evidence. But it follows that such assertions never can convey factual knowledge. In other words, these two contemporary views reject the idea of a priori, synthetic (i.e., factual) knowledge.

Perhaps all this can be better understood if we consider briefly the nature of *necessary* and *contingent* statements.[6] We have noted that assertions about some existential state of affairs are called factual or synthetic. We decide, on the basis of empirical evidence, that such assertions are either true or false (or are *probably* true or false). In other words, such assertions are contingent—their truth depends upon how the universe happens to be, and it is necessary to undertake empirical investigation in order to decide. In contrast, formal assertions, especially those usually called *analytic assertions,* convey only a relation of meanings. Since we may hold a particular way of relating meanings, regardless of how the universe happens to be or to become, such assertions are not contingent; hence, they are called *necessary.* Now, of course, investigation may reveal that certain ways of relating meanings are inept, clumsy, unnecessarily complicated, or the like, in the conduct of human affairs—including the human affair of trying to understand the universe. But, strictly speaking, such necessary statements can, at least in principle, be determined by a priori methods to be either valid or inconsistent without dependence on any empirical evidence.

With this new terminology before us we can now restate the positions thus far discussed: traditional empiricists hold that all statements are *contingent* (with the possible exception of obvious tautologies, such as "black is black") and, hence, there is no a priori knowledge. Traditional rationalists hold that there are both necessary and contingent statements and, moreover, that some necessary statements are synthetic. Hence, there is both a priori and a posteriori knowledge. Logical empiricists hold that

[6] For a detailed discussion see Hospers, *An Introduction to Philosophical Analysis,* esp. pp. 103-144.

all cognitive assertions may be divided into those that are contingent and synthetic, and those that are necessary and analytic. Hence, there can be no a priori "knowledge" of a synthetic character. Experimentalists or pragmatists agree to the inadequacy of both traditional empiricism and rationalism and, furthermore, demur at accepting, essentially intact, the traditional dichotomies on which these inadequate views were based. The experimentalist acknowledges the a priori and a posteriori aspects of all human knowledge but is less concerned to discover whether a given assertion *is* necessary or contingent and more concerned with the *function*[7] of the assertion in a specific context of communication or inquiry. Is it functioning *as if* it were necessary or contingent? We shall see later that under this approach the two-way division of analytic-synthetic seems unnecessarily restrictive and clumsy when one examines the complicated forms of knowledge developed systematically by science.

## Intuition

A common definition of intuition is "an immediate apprehension or cognition without recourse to inference or reasoning." When we examine the claims for intuition we discover many shades of meaning involved. Sometimes the term is used to denote an awareness of the indubitable and ineffable raw data of experience. For example, if I glance at my desk where there is a plain sheet of white paper, I am immediately aware, without inference or reasoning, of a datum which I might attempt to describe as "whiteness now." We have already noted that any attempt to attach meaning to the datum—to say, for example, that there actually is a sheet of white paper, or, strictly speaking, even to assert "whiteness now"—involves some degree of interpretation or inference and, therefore, the possibility of error. But the apprehension of the raw data itself may be said to be immediate or intuitive.

[7] See H. G. Hullfish and P. G. Smith, *Reflective Thinking: The Method of Education,* Dodd, Mead, New York, 1961, chap. 6.

In similar fashion it is said that each of us intuits the fact of self. We immediately apprehend not only the raw sensa of experience but also the fact of apprehending and the existence of an apprehending self.

The word *intuition* is sometimes used to describe a third step that is necessary to escape solipsism, or the subjective predicament. Solipsism is the view that the self can know only the fact of its own existence plus the variegated, meaningless flow of uninterpreted sensa which, for all the self knows, is entirely a creation of or a part of the self. No one actually believes this view even though he cannot logically refute it. Hence, it is said that we grasp by intuition that something more than self exists. Santayana, at this point, speaks of "animal faith" noting that even the most logical of human beings go right on living as if solipsism were certainly false, just as all animals do.

Intuition is frequently used to name the apprehension or grasp of formal relationships of meaning. Anyone who has taught mathematics, especially plane geometry, recognizes that there comes a time when the student either "sees it" or does not. In explaining a theorem or construction the teacher can break down the steps, go back through the material previously covered that is now needed to gain control of the problem at hand, and the like, but eventually the student must grasp for himself the logically necessary relationships. This grasp of the logic of a demonstration or argument is sometimes said to be by intuition and it is often the case that such an intuitive understanding appears to outrun our ability to set forth the precise steps of the logical argument involved. Many of us have learned by experience, however, that the feeling of certainty that accompanies these intuitive shortcuts may lead us astray.

The next use of the term intuition has to do with the basic drives or needs of human nature. It is sometimes said that man intuitively reaches toward the objects or experiences that will satisfy his basic need for nourishment, for love, and the like. The more elemental manifestations of basic drives are frequently called instinctive while intuition is reserved for the more complex behaviors. For example, Montague argues that intuition is the basic factor in romantic attraction.[8] One does not choose a sweetheart or even a friend on the basis of empirical analysis and logical reasoning. One is either intuitively attracted to another person or not, and questions of the reasonableness of the attraction do not normally enter the picture. And the same may be said concerning music and other art forms. There appear to be factors, intuitively grasped, that are not amenable to rational analysis. It should be pointed out, of course, that this sort of intuition frequently leads into difficulties—into situations that apparently do not, in fact, satisfy our basic needs.

Intuition sometimes refers to any kind of generalization that short-cuts conscious weighing of evidence or inferential reasoning. Persons with large backgrounds of well-digested experience are frequently able to go directly to the fundamental aspects of a problem situation in a way that is mystifying to the less experienced observer. No claim is made that such insight involves factors that could not be analyzed; the claim is rather that persons possessing such intuition can arrive at the conclusion without taking the time or effort to go through the process that less gifted individuals must follow. It is interesting that such a gift appears to be specialized and dependent upon previous experience, rather than generalized. It is the expert, experienced engineer who is most likely to have this intuitive grasp of what is at issue in an engineering problem. It is the experienced elementary teacher who is most likely to grasp intuitively what is troubling little Johnny. The experienced person, without thinking about it, has learned to pay attention to the important cues and to dismiss the irrelevant factors, with speed and surety that is sometimes quite difficult to explain.

There is a form of insight, also frequently called intuition, that does seem to be of a more generalized nature, and usually thought to be the mark of genius. Some persons have the knack or intuition which enables them to see situations in such a way

[8] William Pepperell Montague, *The Ways of Knowing*, J. H. Muirhead (ed.), G. Allen, London, 1925, p. 226.

that new Gestalten emerge and consequently new and usually rather different kinds of hypotheses or theories are created. At the present time not very much is known concerning the nature of such truly creative or original production although there is some agreement that such creative thrusts are much more likely to be made by men who have previously thoroughly mastered the fundamental facts and principles of the subject matter involved.

Finally, the term intuition is frequently used to describe what is sometimes called extrasensory perception.

This review of usage enables us to note two points: First, the term is used to refer to cognitive processes that are not well understood and which appear to be either more direct or more subtly complex than the better analyzed empirical and rational procedures, and, second, as a primary source of knowledge, intuition, like sense experience and reason, is not infallible.

## SUMMARY AND SOME CONCLUSIONS

We have seen that, from a psychological or personal point of view, knowledge is belief or willingness to act that has a settled quality. It is belief that has gone beyond reasonable doubt. Although much of knowledge appears, psychologically, to be direct or nonmediated, there are complicated mediating or interpreting processes involved that clothe the raw sensory data with meaning. This is to say that, although we do not have to stop and think in order to recognize the familiar objects, events, relations, and qualities of everyday experience, such familiar knowledge is not *immediate knowledge.*

When something doubtful arises, that is, when these instantaneous mediating processes fail to produce satisfactory recognitions, then it is necessary deliberately to control mediation and we say we are faced with a problem calling for reflective inquiry. Through an analysis of our problem-solving behavior we can learn something about the nature of the interpretations and inferences we make as we develop and test meanings for our sensory cues and conceptual associations. Reflective inquiry that eventuates in satisfactory solutions adds to our growing fund of knowledge or settled belief, and thus increases or extends our ability to deal with these matters on the level of recognition.

In addition to the patterns of meaning that are formed through reflective inquiry, many meanings are created by conditioning processes ranging from situations that resemble the classical conditioning experiments of Pavlov to the informal operant conditioning effect of the complex cultural milieu in which we are born and reared.

Thus it is that human knowledge is hypothetical. It is created and tested in and by experience. Sensory awareness, reason, and intuition are names given to complementary aspects of knowledge-producing experience. They are therefore frequently referred to as the *primary* sources of knowledge in contrast to such secondhand sources as tradition, custom, and the pronouncements of authorities. Since there are no infallible authorities and since authorities ultimately rely on primary sources, it follows that there are no infallible sources of knowledge. Or, put the other way around, since the inferences and interpretations involved in the mediating processes are always subject to error, there is no *direct* primary knowledge and hence no infallible authorities. Human knowledge is thus a constructed and reconstructed body of more or less tested hypotheses which dispose us to act with more or less surety.

When we consider the logical rather than the psychological aspects of knowledge, we note that when beliefs are expressed verbally they are of two types or functions, formal and factual. The formal function is assertion of a relationship of meaning, the factual function is assertion about an existential state of affairs (i.e., a state of affairs conceived in a space-time matrix). Factual assertions (sometimes called synthetic or empirical) are, therefore, implicit predictions about the content of experience and are recognized as false when the content of experience does not agree with what is predicted. Formal assertions are resolutions about how meanings are to be related.

Various schemes or systems of relating meanings and thus of

structuring experience have been developed and tested for long-range usefulness in the conduct of human affairs. Within such systems, statements that assert a correct relation of meanings are said to be valid or true in the formal sense. For example, within the usual system of arithmetic the statement "Two times two equals four" is formally true or valid whereas "Two times two equals five" is invalid or inconsistent. Or again, within a particular system of Christian ethics the statement "Thou shalt love thy neighbor as thyself" is a true saying.

An assertion of a relation of meaning that is valid in *every* rational system is said to be analytic. For example, "No thing can both exist and not exist at the same time." Such statements, because they apply to every conceivable thing, have no differentiating power at all. Assertions that perform the analytic function may thus be held *come what may in experience*. This is why they appear so certain. If it is inconceivable that they be incorrect it is simply because they partially define conceivability. They thus, so to speak, simply outline the empty space within which the edifice of human knowledge is constructed out of factual bricks and formal mortar.

Factual statements are said to be true if what they assert about existential affairs is actually the case. In our usual everyday experience this means that such statements are determined to be true or false according to whether or not what they assert corresponds with the *recognizable* existential conditions. As noted above, however, *what we recognize as being the present state of affairs* depends in part upon the patterns of meaning that have previously been developed through reflective inquiry and conditioning. Again, when something questionable arises so that we are unable simply *to recognize* whether a factual statement is true or false, then empirical investigation is undertaken.

Through a study of the way in which factual statements are investigated we discover that such statements amount to implicit predictions about the content of experience. A factual assertion that cannot be recognized as true or false is therefore investigated as an hypothesis. The hypothesis is refuted (and the factual assertion said to be false) if the implicit predictions do not correspond with what is recognized as the content of developing experience. An hypothesis is substantiated (and the factual assertion is said to be true) if the implicit predictions do correspond with what is recognized as the content of developing experience and all alternative assertions are recognized as false.

It turns out then that the edifice of human knowledge is a complex hypothetical structure constructed and reconstructed as the complementary tests of correspondence, coherence, and long-range usefulness are utilized. In the next chapter we shall examine some of the ways in which mankind has refined the knowing process into a developing body of content and methodology called science. Our present concern, however, has been to note the fallibility that pervades all knowledge and to recognize that each person acts in terms of his own beliefs. It follows that teachers should distinguish between the conditions or experiences that *cause* belief and the logical and methodological *grounds that warrant* a belief. To guide the education of students means essentially to help them develop the ability and inclination to construct and reconstruct patterns of belief that are *warranted* by a progressively expanding reflective experience.

## SUGGESTIONS FOR ADDITIONAL READING

In striving to understand the nature of knowledge and of the knowing process students frequently become discouraged because the problems encountered appear to involve, in a most confusing fashion, considerations from common sense, psychology, sociology, scientific methodology, and philosophy. And, when the additional task is imposed of understanding all this in its relation to the theory and practice of education, it is no wonder that some students give up in despair. It may help to remember that in an introductory study of a topic one should strive to grasp the most fundamental or general features. In order to do this it is frequently necessary to consider details, but such details should be treated as illustrative—that is, as a means to grasping the more basic and general idea or distinction, rather than as something of great importance on their own account. It may also be helpful to try to determine, at various points in one's reading, what aspect or level of the problem of the nature of knowledge the author is discussing. Is the intent of the writing to examine knowledge from a common-sense point of view or is it concerned with an analysis of the sociology or the psychology of knowing? Or perhaps the discussion is about some technical aspect, involving empirical evidence, such as the nature of perception. On the other hand, what may be intended is a conceptual or logical analysis.

Beginning students frequently find chapters 3, 4, and 5 in Titus, *Living Issues in Philosophy*, very helpful. A good alternate or addition to this reading is chapters 2 and 3 in Beck, *Philosophic Inquiry*. In addition, there are portions of a number of the standard works on philosophy of education that are generally helpful. For example, chapter XXV in Dewey's *Democracy and Education*; chapter 17 in Phenix, *Philosophy of Education;* chapter 5 in Broudy, *Building a Philosophy of Education*; chapters 5, 6, and 7 in Morris, *Philosophy and the American School*; and chapter 4, in Brubacher, *Modern Philosophies of Education.*

For a fuller discussion of knowledge in relation to thinking and of the formal and factual functions in inquiry, relevant chapters in Hullfish and Smith, *Reflective Thinking* should prove helpful. Many students have found Carl Becker's essay, "Everyman His Own Historian," very helpful in showing how we mediate our experience in an everyday sort of way. This essay may be found in chapter 3 of Madden (editor), *The Structure of Scientific Thought.*

Anyone desiring to delve more deeply into the nature of knowledge should begin reading some of the works in epistemology that have exerted major influence on modern thought. As a minimum one should consult the following:

Rene Descartes, "Discourse on Method"
John Locke, "Essay Concerning Human Understanding"
George Berkeley, "A Treatise Concerning the Principles of Human Knowledge"
David Hume, "An Inquiry Concerning Human Understanding"
Immanuel Kant, "Critique of Pure Reason"

After these one should then attempt such contemporary works as:

Bertrand Russell, *Human Knowledge: Its Scope and Limits*
C. I. Lewis, *An Analysis of Knowledge and Valuation*
Dewey and Bentley, *Knowing and the Known*

In addition to studying such primary sources most students find it helpful to consult one or more of the standard textbooks in philosophy that summarize, explain, and comment upon the primary sources. One such text, readily available in the College Outline Series, is Randall and Buchler, *Philosophy: An Introduction*; chapters VII through XI are devoted to the nature of knowledge.

# CHAPTER 5

# *What Is Science?*

WE LIVE in an age in which the term *scientific* commands much respect. The advertiser, extolling the merits of his product, is seldom content to point out that tests reveal his product to have certain advantages over its rivals; he informs us that scientific tests have been conducted. Presumably, if the product has been scientifically tested it has been *really* tested. Furthermore, this reference to science associates the product, in the public mind, with all the latest gadgets and conveniences in contrast to outmoded products of ten years ago.

All of this sounds a little ridiculous but, as is frequently the case, ordinary usage of a term may offer important insight into its most basic meaning. After careful study of the nature of science, many scholars have concluded that, fundamentally, science means simply the best systematic knowledge presently available in terms of the most perfected methods of inquiry. It follows that science is continuous with common sense and, when a scientific revolution occurs, what is overthrown is not anti-science not even nonscience, but an earlier science. In minor revolutions what was thought to be well-established knowledge is, so to speak, disestablished, and in major revolutions what was thought to be a reliable and valid conception or method of inquiry is replaced by new conceptions, new approaches, new methodologies. Literally, science means *knowing*. As a tentative first model, therefore, let us say that whenever, wherever, and by whatever means human knowledge is systematically growing, there is science.

104

## SCIENCE AND COMMON SENSE

All this is not to say, however, that there are no important differences between science and common sense. Science is a refinement of common sense and in its most refined forms, such as modern physics, scientific knowledge and the methodology that make it possible are so far removed from the objects and procedures of common-sense knowledge that it requires prolonged and disciplined study to understand the nature of the intellectual constructions involved and their relation to the objects and events recognized in everyday experience. Before attempting even a brief analysis of the nature of science, therefore, let us examine certain characteristics of common sense.

Titus mentions three characteristics of common sense.[1] First, since it rests largely upon custom and tradition it tends to be habitual and imitative. Second, since it is frequently only superficially grounded it tends to be vague and ambiguous. Third, inasmuch as common-sense answers or conclusions are thought to be a matter of what is obvious or self-evident or just plain sense, many unexamined assumptions are involved and, hence, common-sense opinion is, in considerable part, untested belief. Titus concludes:

> We never leave common sense belief wholly behind us, regardless of how far our education may carry us or how specialized our knowledge may become. And it may be fortunate that we never completely abandon common sense belief, since it may serve as a check against the "blind spots" some people develop through intensive specialization. But common sense belief, if it is to serve this useful purpose, needs constant and careful re-examination.[2]

Here, then, is an important cue for education. It is frequently thought that intensive study of mathematics or of a science such as biology or physics will automatically result in a gain in general or liberal education. It does seem plausible that after prolonged and disciplined study of a particular science a student will under-

[1] Harold H. Titus, *Living Issues in Philosophy*, 3rd ed., American Book, New York, 1959, pp. 34-35.
[2] *Ibid.*

stand the inadequacy of reliance on custom and tradition, will understand how to move beyond vague and ambiguous statement, and will grasp the logic and methodology of tested belief. In short, after a study in depth of a particular science the student should realize how common sense, in general, may be refined, and thus become generally educated or liberated from superficial, vague, unexamined, and untested belief in general.

Unfortunately, however, hope in this plausible road to general education, like similar hopes based on theories of mental discipline, is not supported by empirical evidence. Man is an expert at compartmentalization. Transfer of training (to say nothing of transforming training into general education) is not automatic. The "blind spots" of which Titus speaks are all too familiar and the spectacular advances within the specialized sciences, although having altered somewhat the content of common-sense belief, have not noticeably refined its methods. A direct attack upon the content, logic, and methodology of the common sense of a given age and culture likely remains, therefore, the most effective way of refining such common sense and, hence, such a direct approach is probably the most promising road to a general or liberal education.

A brief examination of a specific characteristic of common sense may be illustrative. Common sense is typically illogical. Its reasoning is fallacious. This is not to say that it is totally irrational or that its beliefs are totally unreasoned. A fallacy is a kind of middle ground between no reasoning and sound reasoning and, indeed, a person who consistently employed certain types of fallacious reasoning would likely move through life's problems with far more success than one who relied solely on unthinking habit and impulse. Consider *post hoc ergo propter hoc* ("after this therefore because of this") a typical common-sense line of reasoning. Here is the basis not only of many of the most ridiculous superstitions in our culture but, in refined form, was a foundational idea in science until well into the twentieth century. After repeated observations that thunder follows lightning, the common-sense conclusion is that lightning causes thunder. If, repeatedly, people get malaria *after* being exposed to the foul air of swamps or garbage-strewn alleys, the conclusion is that people get malaria *because of* bad air.

Over the ages, science (that is, the "best knowing") progressively refined this cause-effect reasoning—developing and testing stipulations and methodologies designed to keep superstition out of science. Yet during the so-called scientific revolution the notion of a world of cause-effect events running in a steady stream of before-and-after was retained; Newton's idea of force as a cause may perhaps be viewed as a projection of the human attribute of purposeful effort not essentially different from earlier projections that ascribed "will" to inanimate objects or that ordered all things according to their essences or ideal natures. Under twentieth-century relativity theory, however, time is no longer conceived as a strict sequence of before and after and the world is viewed not as a flow of events but as a complex of relations.

These developments in science gradually caused a remarkable transformation in the content of common-sense belief. To the man on the street the world that had been flat and the center of the universe became a spherical object moving in orbit around the sun. But in the conduct of his daily affairs, he still frequently reasoned *post hoc ergo propter hoc.* And in the middle of the twentieth century it is not uncommon to hear someone say: "Have you noticed in the last few years how the weather—all four seasons in fact—seems to be changed? It's just not like it used to be! Doesn't it seem more than a coincidence that this should have come about just after the series of atom-bomb tests?"

In other words, the feedback into common sense of the results of science gradually (or sometimes suddenly) changes the topics of conversation but with a much slower transformation of the way in which people reason about these topics.

It turns out then that, although the problem of providing our society with more and better-trained scientists is basically a problem of vocational education, the matter of helping all citizens (or as many as possible and certainly including our scientists) to attain a general or liberal education remains a problem of developing the ability and the inclination to refine both the content and the methods of their own common sense. And this seems more likely to be accomplished through a study of philosophy and the humanities, rather than through intensive study of one of the sciences.

## SOME CHARACTERISTICS OF SCIENCE

Although it is helpful to point out that science is a refinement of common sense and that there is no sharp break between the two, it would be more helpful if we could say specifically what is meant by *refinement*. We should note immediately that there is no such thing as a fixed set of rules or of method that will necessarily lead one to scientific discoveries or inventions, nor guarantee correct solutions to problems. Nevertheless, there are some general characteristics of science and its methods that set them off from common sense and, therefore, give an operational meaning to refinement.

1. **Systematic Knowledge.** The first such characteristic that one is likely to spot is the *organization* of scientific knowledge in contrast to the disorganized or conglomerate nature of common-sense beliefs. Yet, one could certainly organize his beliefs without thereby converting them into a science. It would be more accurate, therefore, to say that science is characterized by *systematic* knowledge, that is, by knowledge organized and classified in terms of underlying, explanatory principles that permit one to understand, in terms of the system as a whole, why the various parts of the system are as they are or even to predict what the condition of various parts will be when certain other parts are changed. For example, the science of astronomy enables one to understand why the orbits of the various planets are as they are, and to predict eclipses, return of comets, and the like.

It is interesting to note, however, that the expression "explanatory principles" is not entirely unequivocal and that the several modes of scientific explanation have undergone considerable change as science has developed. Auguste Comte, in the early nineteenth century, suggested that there had been three stages in the development of human thought and that each stage had its own notion of what constituted suitable or adequate explanation. In the early or theological stage of development, "the human mind, seeking the essential nature of beings . . . supposes all phenomena to be produced by the immediate action of supernatural beings." Lightning was caused by an angry god throwing bolts of fire. Storms, floods, disease, and death seemed frequently to occur in arbitrary fashion, as if they were caused by gods and demons whose actions were beyond human comprehension. After all, most early societies were organized as primitive, absolute monarchies, ruled by more-or-less capricious leaders, and it is understandable that men sought to appease the gods by the same sort of flattery and propitiation that proved effective in dealing with their arbitrary, human rulers.

Some five or six hundred years before the birth of Christ, however, the Greeks developed a society based on law and justice, and attempted to explain nature in these terms. They thus moved into what Comte called the second or metaphysical stage of explanation. The Greeks conceived of natural law and natural justice. Abstract forces caused the natural events that occurred, and the observable regularities of nature were considered evidence that natural forces and events "obeyed" the laws of nature. In a more or less refined form, this is the mode of explanation typical of common sense today. We say, for example, that objects fall to the ground "because of gravity," or that a certain man's death "was caused by an auto accident."

Comte called the third stage of development the positivistic or scientific stage. At this level, explanation returns more nearly to its literal meaning, that is, "to make plain or intelligible." Instead of emphasis on cause and effect, science is concerned with similarities and dissimilarities; with invariable relations and probabilities.

What is now understood when we speak of an explanation of fact is simply the establishment of a connection between single phenomena and some general facts, the number of which continually diminishes with the progress of science.[3]

Although not everyone today would accept Comte's definition of explanation nor interpret his views as a movement away from causal explanations, there is general agreement that one characteristic of science is that it organizes knowledge in terms of appropriate explanatory principles. The question of what principles are most appropriate for various subject matters is, of course, a question for further study.

**2. Special Language.** A second obvious characteristic of science has to do with refining away the characteristic of common sense noted by Titus—the traditional or habitual modes of thought. This is, in part, a matter of refining the language of common sense. Common-sense language is usually vague and indeterminate in two ways: first, the terms of ordinary speech generally lack any clear-cut, denotative range and, second, the customary distinctions of ordinary speech tend to reflect man's immediate day-to-day problems rather than the needs of a systematically organized body of knowledge. For example, in a culture in which snow only infrequently plays an important role in man's daily affairs the ordinary language contains just the one word "snow" to denote the whole range of "newly fallen, light, crisp, old, dirty, mushy, wet, snow." The Eskimo, on the other hand, has a rich vocabulary at this point because the various types of snow that he confronts from time to time are matters of considerable practical importance to him.

In somewhat less obvious fashion much of our ordinary language carries the imprint of the more practical, provincial concerns of an earlier day which render it unsuitable for scientific discourse that seeks to make experience intelligible in terms of underlying explanatory principles. A further complicating factor, of course, is the fact of lag in the reconstructing feedback of science into common sense. Ordinary language thus reflects not merely a nonscientific posture but, perhaps worse, the ways of

[3] Auguste Comte, *The Positive Philosophy* (1830), Harriet Martineau (trans.) John Chapman, London, 1853, vol. 1, p. 2.

posing and answering questions of an outmoded science. Our language contains many vestiges of Comte's first stage of the development of thought, and indeed the very subject-predicate structure of the languages of Western culture reflect early developments in the second stage. This is one reason, incidentally, why communication becomes a critical problem when reading such philosophers as Dewey or Whitehead. Philosophy depends largely upon ordinary language. When one tries to make this language express a radically different conception of the universe and of experience than it has done for two thousand years one must expect some communication difficulties.

Francis Bacon once noted that, although men may assume that reason governs the use of words, in reality it is often the other way around. And so science has found it necessary to develop special vocabularies and systems of notation to facilitate concise distinctions and quantification and to enable problems to be stated with precision. And this, of course, promotes in turn the systematization of knowledge.

There is an aspect of this characteristic of science that is of special interest to education as an applied behavioral science. It is the matter of developing operational meanings for terms in the language of education. Consider, by way of illustration, the science of metallurgy. As this science developed out of common sense it was necessary to make more precise many of the terms of ordinary language dealing with the properties of metals. For example, for centuries common sense had recognized and utilized the difference in "hardness" that exists among various metals. But more exactly what is meant by "hardness." In common-sense language it means many things—resistance to scratching, to chipping, to bending, to penetration, as well as resistance to molding, to heating, and, of course, resistance to general wear and tear. A word with so many and so generalized meanings is much too vague for a science.

A number of specific tests for hardness were developed. One test, consisting of a carefully specified set of operations, measured hardness by noting how deep a metal surface was penetrated by a diamond point of specified size under a specified amount of pressure. Other tests were developed to measure exact resistance to other aspects of the common-sense meaning of hardness. Such tests are frequently known by the name of the man who developed them. Today one may hear a metallurgist say, "This piece of steel has a Rockwell hardness of 37 while that one is only 34," or "The hardness of this metal on a Brinell test is 52." Since each of the various tests for hardness measures different but related characteristics, there are high correlations among the tests but not perfect ones. There are thus several different operational meanings established for "hardness" within the science of metallurgy.

This situation is somewhat similar to the operational meanings given to the common-sense word "intelligence" within the science of psychology. But, unfortunately, within education we have generally not disciplined ourselves to careful use of operational language. We go part way by glibly saying that Johnny has an IQ of 113. But there are many tests of intelligence and, again, the correlations are fairly high but not perfect. Moreover, there are considerable differences in reliability, so that to report that Johnny has an Otis Short Form of 113 is rather different from reporting that his IQ has been measured at, say a Wechsler 113.

We have noted earlier that, within education as an applied behavioral science, statements about practice should ideally be scientifically controlled descriptions and judgments about the various behaviors and experiences involved in the educational enterprise. We now see that this requires an operational language. For example, at the present time one hears teachers arguing about statements such as "ability grouping leads to a better learning situation." What is the argument about? If operational language were employed, one could at least tell what is at issue. In *a science of education* such a statement might become "A Ross ability grouping, under such and such circumstances, will lead to significant improvement on the Conway-Arkansas Placement Tests." To know that such an assertion is true or false will, of course, not automatically answer questions of educational policy, to say nothing of questions of theory or philosophy. Yet, without the scientific control that such operational language would facilitate, there can be no sound empirical base for education as an applied behavioral science.

**3. Depersonalized or Dehumanized Knowledge.** It is sometimes said that science (especially academic or pure science) is depersonalized or even dehumanized. We noted above that one reason why ordinary speech tends to be unsuitable for science is that such language reflects man's immediate concerns rather than the needs of a systematically organized body of knowledge. When generalized, this fact enables us to see one of the reasons why we would not refer to astrology as a science, in contrast to astronomy.[4] Astrologists certainly have made careful observations of the same objects in the sky that have interested astronomers. Moreover, a great deal of rather complicated organizing and classifying of material has taken place within the subject matter of astrology. But the system of beliefs engendered by this study has not been ordered systematically, in terms of underlying explanatory principles. An astrologist is not interested in explaining why Saturn is in the ascent during a certain period, he is interested rather in what effect this may have on the lives of particular people. It is revealing to note that an obsolete definition of astrology is "practical astronomy."

It is in this sense, then, that science is characterized by depersonalized or dehumanized knowledge. In order to develop systematic explanation, inquiry must be pursued in a way that holds at bay the normally pressing desires and concerns and values of the various individuals involved. Again, in its most generalized sense, this means setting aside the typically human or anthropocentric approach to experience. Even in the applied sciences where systematic knowledge and inquiry are put to work to accomplish human goals, problems have to be viewed objectively.

[4] The reader should, of course, be able to think of other reasons why astrology should not be called a science.

This striving for objectivity that characterizes science does not mean, however, that science has developed a set of rules which guarantee that all personal bias or human error will be eliminated if the rules are carefully followed. Operationally, scientific objectivity means simply the control of inquiry and judgment by the procedures presently deemed the most likely to lead to warranted assertions in the subject matter under discussion. Various sciences have developed various procedures. One should be careful, therefore, not to overgeneralize from the methods and procedures developed within a particular science. For example, if one should attempt to characterize all science by generalizing from the methodology of physics, one would likely conclude that very little other than physics is worthy of being called science. Or if one becomes provincial about the role of statistics in educational research he may find himself arbitrarily dismissing all other research as nonobjective.

**4. Stipulations and Methodology.** Even a brief commentary upon the nature of science would be incomplete without discussion of some of the stipulations or methodological assumptions that are said to characterize the enterprise. Perhaps the most basic of these stipulations is the one frequently referred to as the *uniformity of nature*. At the level of philosophic analysis a number of troublesome questions arise concerning this stipulation, ranging from how man can possibly justify this assumption when every procedure that might appear to justify it has already assumed it in advance to whether the Creator of the universe operated according to the laws that science has discovered. This last question is sometimes phrased, "Is God a mathematician?"

In the nineteenth century the philosopher looked at the world described by science and concluded that God must be a mathematician; now the philosopher looks at mathematics and concludes that the mathematician must be a Godlike creator.

For the mathematician said:
Let there be numbers such that the first number is one
And the next number is one more
And the next, still one more, and so forth.

And there were numbers without end.
And the mathematician beheld what he had made
And saw that it was good.

And then the mathematician said:
Let $x$ be any number and $y$ be any other number,
And let $x$ plus $y$ equal $y$ plus $x$.
And let $x$ times $y$ equal $y$ times $x$.
And addition and multiplication became commutative.
And the mathematician beheld what he had made
And saw that it was good.

And then the mathematician said:
Let $z$ be still any other number
And let the sum of $x$ and $y$ times $z$ equal the sum of $y$ and $z$ times $x$
And let the sum of $x$ and $y$ plus $z$ equal the sum of $y$ and $z$ plus $x$
And addition and multiplication became associative.
And the mathematician beheld what he had made
And saw that it was good.

And then the mathematician said:
And now let $z$ times the sum of $x$ plus $y$, equal the sum of the
   products of $x$ and $z$ and $y$ and $z$
And addition and multiplication became distributive.
And the mathematician beheld what he had made.
And he rested, for he had made mathematics.

From a methodological standpoint, however, it appears that science, as an enterprise, assumes simply that experience is orderable, that it is worthwhile to attempt a systematic organization of knowledge and that such an approach has, in fact, been pragmatically justified—that is, it has turned out to be helpful. As a stipulation that *characterizes* science, the notion of the uniformity of nature may then be construed to mean that any collection of statements that are not ordered in terms of some uniformities of nature are not to be considered part of the corpus of scientific knowledge. This does not mean, of course, that every investigation that fails to produce conclusions that are accepted into the corpus of a science is thereby unscientific.

Another stipulation is that science requires public verifiability. The uninitiated may interpret this stipulation in a too literal fashion, imagining that science requires a "team approach" in which one's observations and calculations are checked, step by step, by one's colleagues, with all procedures carefully recorded and described so that other scientists may duplicate the work and thus attest to its "public verifiability." It is true, of course, that, in striving for objectivity, scientists exercise great care to avoid "personal errors," but this is usually more a matter of proper training in the use of procedures and equipment than a literal checking of one another's work. Public verifiability runs deeper than this. What is stipulated is not that work *be* publically verified, but that it *could* be.

The case of a scientific test for color is frequently cited in this connection. There are persons who are color blind. A typical case of color blindness is inability to distinguish between certain shades of pink and greenish-blue. Such persons may be said to have a built-in or permanent personal error, or illusion. This being the case, it is said that science cannot utilize the usual observations about color as experimental evidence, for such observations could not be verified by the color-blind segment of the public. In other words, in the matter of shades of color, public verifiability seems impossible.

It turns out, however, that public agreement can be obtained on shades of color by introducing certain indirect tests. In the case of pink in contrast to greenish-blue, for example, public agreement can be obtained by viewing these colors through ruby-tinted glass. Through the tinted glass, pink and blue objects appear different to both color blind and normal vision. Pink appears light red; blue appears dark red. And, of course, with more complicated laboratory equipment, colors can be translated into a range of wave lengths concerning which public agreement can be obtained.

Sometimes a person will report that he sees or feels or hears something that others nearby cannot observe and, since science does not wish to be arbitrary in what it excludes as evidence, such a situation sometimes calls for serious investigation. Such investigations are undertaken in light of a point already noted, namely, that belief is willingness to act. In the case of a person who is willfully lying, "tricks" of some sort can be devised that will cause his actions to reveal the lie. Even in the case of a sincere report, the fact of illusion or hallucination will usually come to light through application of the principle that belief is a willingness to act.

There is always the possibility, of course, that an individual will truly believe (i.e., will consistently act upon) an observation that others conceive as a mistaken one. In such a case, society, more or less arbitrarily, pronounces the individual insane. In terms of our earlier discussion of the nature of knowledge such a situation could be explained by noting that an individual could allow a factual assertion to perform an analytic function in experience. For example, the story was once told of a certain individual who concluded one morning that he was dead. When his friends could not persuade him to give up this notion, they arranged for him to see a psychiatrist. The doctor, having no greater success than the man's friends, finally took a scalpel and cut the patient's arm so that blood appeared. As the patient observed the blood the physician asked, "There! Now doesn't that prove something?" The patient replied, "It certainly does. If I hadn't seen this I would never have believed that a dead man could bleed."

Finally, at least one more stipulation should be noted that is usually referred to as the *law of parsimony*. It has been said that science should not needlessly multiply conceptual entities or hypotheses. It is this stipulation that has kept science minimally metaphysical. Science has not endeavored to develop elaborate speculations concerning what might conceivably be true; it strives, rather, to find the simplest explanation for what may be publically observed. When alternative hypotheses, theories, or explanations are advanced, *ceteris paribus* (i.e., other things being equal) the more simple is taken to be the better.

Simplicity should not be confused with familiarity or with other common-sense tests of plausibility. Science strives for *systematic simplicity* which, as already noted, is the attempt to order the widest possible range of phenomena in terms of the fewest possible explanatory principles. This is why, frequently, what seems simple to a scientist seems complicated to a layman, and even the other way around. For what seems like a simple, straightforward explanation to common sense (e.g., that the sun, moon, and planets revolve around the earth) may seem unnecessarily complicated to the scientist when he attempts to build a systematic explanation.

## SCIENTIFIC LAWS

It has frequently been observed that science is the study, par excellence, the results of which may be expressed in the indicative mood, since it is this mood that is used to represent or indicate objective fact. Inasmuch as the grammatical tenses, moods, and syntax of our language were invented a long time before the development of modern science, it seems unlikely, on the face of it, that grammatical distinctions would have any direct correspondence to the sort of classifications that may emerge in an analysis of the controlled inquiry of the present day. Nevertheless, there is a very persistent common-sense notion that science is concerned primarily with discovery of "facts," that the facts are "out there" waiting to be discovered, and that the hypotheses and theories of science are merely shrewd guesses, later to be replaced by "true facts" once these have been discovered. From what has already been said concerning the characteristics and stipulations of science, we can see that this common-sense notion about science goes wide of the mark. Just how wide can be better understood if we examine the nature of the laws formulated by science.

A scientific law is an assertion of an invariable association of independently defined variables or properties. Various kinds of associations have been noted, and one of the kinds first noted by inquiring man was the association of properties that define a type or class of objects. For example, iron is a type of object that is strongly attracted by magnets and that will rust quickly in moist air. Silver is very malleable, capable of a high polish but will tarnish, especially if exposed to stifling fumes. Much of early science was concerned with refining such taxonomy as had been developed by common sense; and, as might be expected, many unfruitful classifications were made, based on associations that were thought to be invariable but which later broke down under more careful analysis.

A very brief review of the development of the science of chemistry may illustrate this matter.

At about the beginning of what Comte called the metaphysical stage in the development of human thought, the notion became widespread that the world is formed of four basic elements: fire, air, earth, and water. With various modifications, this basic notion dominated man's thinking into the Middle Ages and, mixed with various magic rites and formulas, gave rise to the pursuit of alchemy. Transformed into hotness, dryness, coldness, and fluidity, the same basic notion exerted considerable influence on medical practice.

In 1702, the German chemist Stahl invented the term *phlogiston* to name "the fiery element present in all substances." The notion of phlogiston, though still carrying the traces of the early developments of human inquiry, nevertheless stimulated a series of experiments that tied in with the industrial revolution and brought on the development of modern chemistry. For, in 1775 as a result of such experimentation, Lavoisier isolated and named oxygen as an element. In a short time air was shown to be about one-fifth oxygen and nearly four-fifths nitrogen, and water was discovered to be a compound of oxygen and hydrogen.

In the next century, chemists in various countries continued analyzing substances into compounds and elements. By the middle of the century, some sixty distinct elements had been identified, with each one's primary characteristics established. As compounds and elements were studied, it became possible to develop a number of chemical recipes, so to speak, even though the fact that certain elements could be joined in certain ways and not in others was not yet explainable in terms of then-formulated principles.

But the basic conception of atomic weights was already in process of development. In 1804, John Dalton, a Quaker schoolmaster, working in the light of Newton's idea that gas could be considered as made up of tiny, solid, elastic spheres, proposed the theory that each chemical element was made up of atoms, each of a distinct kind, and each having a particular weight that could be denoted by a number. Within about fifty years, the Italian Avogadro conceived the *molecule* as two or more atoms joined to form a single unit of matter. Using hydrogen—lightest of the known elements—as a base and assigning it the atomic weight of 1, the other elements could be compared with it and each assigned its appropriate atomic weight. For example, oxygen turned out to be 16.

As the various elements were studied and their atomic weights determined, some sort of underlying order seemed to be suggested. In 1870, the Russian, Mendeleev, showed that, if the elements were arranged in ascending order of atomic weights, they fell into periodic groups having similar characteristics. Mendeleev left blank spaces in his table for unknown elements and predicted the approximate weights and densities for many of the elements later discovered.

In the meantime, Sir Edward Frankland proposed the *valence theory* to explain how elements combine to form compound molecules and Kekule introduced the idea that molecules may be arranged in various ways by their atoms being formed into chains, rings, and the like. By the end of the nineteenth century, this work merged with the work of physics through the discovery of the X ray, radium, and the high-energy particles called electrons.

Early in the twentieth century, the atom was conceived as a miniature solar system with the nucleus made up of a dense core of protons and neutrons and various numbers of electrons orbiting around the center. As this conception was refined, it led to reexamination of the chemical periodic table and it turned out that the table of weights could now be explained in terms of the number of electrons, protons, and neutrons that form the atoms of the various elements. For example, the hydrogen atom with an atomic weight of 1 is composed of 1 proton and 1 electron. The next element, helium, has an atom of 2 protons and 2 electrons (with 2 neutrons also in the core) and uranium, the heaviest element then known, has a core of 92 protons plus many neutrons, with 92 electrons orbiting about the core. And, of course, the work has continued, with the latest findings and refinements of conceptualization resulting in the spectacular present-day developments within subatomic technology.

The points to be noted are these:

1. Grouping and naming, or ordering things on the bases of similarities, is a fundamental characteristic of human thought. This is actually a creative process even though its results appear to be merely cases of discovering traits implanted by nature. Newton's insight concerning the similarity of the fall of an apple and the movement of the moon around the earth was certainly more than a "discovery" in any obvious sense of the word. He saw (i.e., conceived) a likeness that no one else had seen. In the case of conceiving of the atom as a miniature solar system, here was a likeness that literally could not be seen. It turns out that grouping and ordering is basically a conceptual rather than a perceptual[5] activity and, although the manifest intent of such theoretical construction is descriptive, it is also normative, suggesting that subsequent inquiry *should* view relevant phenomena in one way rather than another.

2. Starting with the familiar kinds of objects and events of common sense, scientific development consists of both analysis and synthesis. On the one hand, it breaks down such common-sense "elements" as fire and earth, showing that they do not represent an invariable association of properties. On the other hand, it puts together, in a way that frequently violates common sense, such unusual combinations as the fall of an apple and the movement of the moon. In the first process, science starts with

[5] We have previously noted that even perception involves more than a passive receiving of uninterpreted sensa. As Norwood Hanson has remarked, "there is more to seeing than meets the eyeball." See *Patterns of Discovery*, Cambridge, 1961, pp. 6-7.

the simple associations or "laws" of common sense, analyzes them and shows that they are not laws at all, then explains common-sense objects and events in terms of a few simple underlying associations that really do appear to be invariant. In the second process, science starts with simple laws that define types of objects, discovers additional invariant relations among these types, and thus arrives at new more general laws. At a given time in the development of a given science, one or the other of these processes may be more in evidence, but both processes are necessary for full development.

3. We have said that a scientific law is the assertion of an invariable association but our brief review of the development of chemistry enables us now to see that what is thought to be invariant, and hence a law, at one stage in the development of a science may later turn out to be too gross a generalization. In other words, the process of refinement is continuous. If yesterday's science was a refinement of common sense, today's science is a refinement of yesterday's science. In any event, in even the most advanced sciences no one today would assert that the limits of analysis have been reached or that present laws assert invariant associations that are absolute. This again shows that at any given time science may be viewed as the best knowledge or the best warranted assertions in terms of the best methods of inquiry then available.

There are, of course, types of invariant association other than the association of properties that define kinds of objects. From a common-sense point of view, perhaps the most obvious kind of invariant association is the *invariable sequence* that is usually called cause-effect. We have already noted that the notion of cause-effect is an unusually vague and tricky one so a little further analysis of the idea may be in order. Common sense is inclined to say that if and only if event B is invariably preceded by event A, then A is the cause and B an effect. A little thought about the matter enables us to see, however, that not every such invariant sequence is considered cause and effect. A man will die if and only if he has first been born. The day is invariably followed by the night, or, for that matter, night is invariably followed by day. The common-sense notion of cause-effect is obviously something different from the notion of invariable sequence.

Does science have a more refined conception of cause-effect? Actually, this question is somewhat controversial today, but it appears that physical science is in the process of so refining the idea of cause-effect that it is refining it away, at least as an ontological category. In our most advanced physical sciences, it is becoming increasingly awkward to maintain that there are laws that assert cause-effect relations. The conception of effect is essentially teleological. In the behavioral sciences, therefore, since man may be viewed as the cause of the effects he produces, cause-effect may continue to be a fundamental idea.

Our most highly developed sciences are increasingly characterized by *numerical laws,* for example, the assertion that one magnitude is proportional to another. In Chapter 4 we considered a list of various types of true statements and number six of the list was "The electrical current through a conductor is proportional to the electrical pressure between its ends." This is known as Ohm's law. A slightly different type of numerical law is well illustrated by Galileo's law for freely falling bodies in a vacuum: d equals $gt^2/2$, where d is the distance, t the duration of fall, and g the acceleration due to gravity. Still another type of numerical law is increasingly becoming characteristic of modern science, namely, statistical laws—laws concerned with percentage or probabilities of aggregate behaviors (whether of physical particles or human beings) in contrast to assertions of invariant associations that enable one to predict the occurrence or behavior of particular events or of individuals.

What does it mean to say that the assertion of a scientific law is a true assertion? Is it factually true, or formally true? Or is there involved here a third meaning of truth that should be distinguished from the formal and factual meanings of truth, identified under our discussion of the nature of knowledge? In order to answer this question, we must first consider the nature of scientific theories and their relation to laws. But before proceeding we may note that, by the time a science has reached a stage of development that permits formulation of such general laws as we are now considering, it has moved away from expressing itself in the indicative mood. The moods, the tenses, and all the grammatical forms of ordinary speech remain just what they are —forms of common-sense expression. If one insists upon using grammatical distinctions to point to a characteristic of science, then it would be approximately correct to note that the laws of a well developed science assert not "facts" but *subjunctive conditionals*. Galileo's law, for example, does not "indicatively assert" that nature contains bodies freely falling in a vacuum but rather that *if there were* such freely falling bodies then d would equal $gt^2/2$.

## SCIENTIFIC THEORIES

As a science in its early stages proceeds with refinement of the taxonomy of common sense, it is likely to be largely empirical. This is to say that its laws are developed and refined through observations that are much more precise and carefully controlled than are those of common sense. It is necessary to keep in mind, however, a point developed in our consideration of the nature of knowledge, namely, that both formal and factual functions of thought are operative in every assertion of matters of fact. Hence, no matter how obviously empirical a science appears to be, its assertions always involve some formal relation of meaning. As long as a science emphasizes refinement of the observing procedures of common sense and largely takes for granted the implicit ideational patterns, the laws that are discovered are said to be *empirical* ones. We noted, for example, that very early in Greek thought the idea or theory was developed that all the material of the universe is made up of four basic elements in various combinations. By the Middle Ages, this theory or way of viewing experience became thoroughly incorporated into common sense. By improving observation, the developing science of chemistry analyzed what common sense took to be the four basic elements and empirically discovered the invariant associations of properties that defined a series of elements and compounds. This work went forward, without much explicit consideration of the underlying idea or theory that the material of the universe was made up of basic elements in various combinations.

Eventually, however, chemistry became more consciously *theoretical*. This is to say that the notions of elements, compounds, atoms, molecules, atomic weights, and valence were entertained as ideas or theoretical constructs. Explicit attention was now given to the formal function involved in chemistry's factual assertions, and attempts were made to construct theories that would explain or account for the empirical laws that had been discovered. A successful theory, when rigorously formulated, *implies* the known relevant empirical laws. That is, the laws may be deduced from the theory. Furthermore, *additional laws* may be deduced from the theory or from a slightly modified or extended form of the theory. Such additional laws must, of course, be empirically justified, or the theory will be rejected or modified. Nevertheless, once a theory is well accepted the laws that are deduced from it are generally known as *theoretical laws*, in contrast to *empirical laws* which are not yet explained by a consciously formulated theory.

The more developed a science becomes the more likely it is that its new laws will be first deduced from theories rather than discovered empirically. Nevertheless, any law that has been established empirically retains a certain independence even though it is later systematically explained by a theory. This is why certain laws may be retained after the theory that originally explained them may be modified or rejected. It thus appears that science is basically empirical, with its theoretical superstructure standing or falling in terms of the degree of confirmation that may be discovered through empirical-experimental procedures. But such a conclusion is not entirely accurate. It turns out that, although a law that is established empirically does enjoy a certain independence from any particular theory that explains it, it is not independent of all ideational structuring. If nothing else, the terms employed in stating the law are a part of some common-sense pattern of meaning.

For example, largely through careful observation, a number of laws were discovered concerning the behavior of any gas when confined in a vessel: the pressure is inversely proportional to the volume; at a constant volume the pressure increases proportionally with the temperature. Other laws were discovered that state the relation between pressure and the conducting of heat, and so on. Very early in this work, Isaac Newton proposed that such gases might be thought of as made up of tiny, hard, elastic, spheres or particles that move about, continually colliding with each other and with the sides of the container. It was not necessary, however, to adopt this theory or "way of viewing" a gas in order to establish experimentally the various empirical laws about pressure, volume, and conduction.

Early in the nineteenth century a more elaborate version of Newton's idea, known as the Dynamical Theory of Gases, was created to explain the various laws of gases. When such a molecular theory of gases was rigorously formulated it was found that from it the known laws of gases could be deduced. Thus, the science of thermodynamics was developed. Still later, it was found that by introducing certain statistical procedures the laws of thermodynamics could be related to the general laws of motion developed in the science of mechanics. In other words, the empirical laws of gases are experimentally meaningful and verifiable, whether they are viewed more or less in isolation, as part of classical thermodynamics, or as part of modern physics. And, presumably, they would continue to stand even in the unlikely event that all our present theories that explain them were to be discarded.

But, epistemologically speaking, the notion that such laws are "experimentally meaningful and verifiable more or less in isolation" is misleading. Generally speaking, when a law or any factual assertion appears to be meaningful *apart from any theory*, we should suspect that it is a part of some implicit common-sense theory that is so widely accepted that it escapes notice. Actually, in the case of the laws of gases, many of the ideational structures or ways-of-viewing experience involved in their assertion are not even very deeply buried in common sense. Except, perhaps, in the case of the pressure cooker, we do not normally have much occasion to think about volume, pressure, and temperature in connection with gases. When we consider Boyle's law, which states that the pressure of a gas is inversely proportional to the volume, we discover that it is not really very meaningful unless understood in the light of a common sense that has already been somewhat refined and extended by classical physics. And, in the case of Gay-Lussac's law that states "if the volume of a gas is held constant the pressure increases proportionally to the temperature," there is involved in it an operational meaning of temperature that is different from our usual or everyday use of the thermometer. So it turns out that such empirical laws are not fully meaningful independent of theory, even when "theory" is construed to include the implicit theories of *unrefined* common sense.

The point of all this is that science can never be more independently empirical than common sense, and actually it is considerably less so. Many of the factual assertions of common sense appear to exhibit an independently empirical nature simply because the implicit ideational structures are taken for granted. This is to say, epistemologically, that the assertions are about *recognizable* objects, events, and relations. Knowledge about them gained through careful observation appears to be immediate knowledge.[6] Hence, such assertions are believed true or false on the basis of observation or experimentation conducted independently of any explicitly formulated theory. When such assertions are about invariant associations, they may be called *empirical laws*.

But, as a science refines the empirical generalizations of common sense, it introduces new ideational structures and modifies

[6] *Ante,* pp. 76-77.

many of the implicit ones of common sense. For example, as empirical procedures are refined, many ideas receive new or refined operational meaning even though the old linguistic expressions are retained.[7] And, since individual scientists are, quite properly, more concerned with advancing knowledge within their own specialty rather than with carefully observing and reporting their own thought processes, they continually pour new conceptual wine into the old linguistic bottles. It may well be that Newton believed that the basic concepts of his system such as space, time, mass, acceleration, and force were thoroughly empirical, being directly derived from experience by abstraction, yet developments in modern science (particularly relativity theory) have made it increasingly difficult to maintain such a view. There is now a widespread recognition of the role of what Einstein and others have called *free invention* in the development of the basic constructions of science.[8] This growing recognition is a correlate of the recognition of the formal or analytic nature of the postulates of mathematics.[9]

All of this would seem to suggest that the usual distinction between empirical and theoretical laws is of doubtful value. Nevertheless, the distinction may be useful on other grounds. A theory, in addition to explaining laws in the sense that the laws may be deduced from the theory, frequently explains in the sense of providing a common-sense model or analogy for understanding the laws or generalizations that are empirically justified. This is especially noticeable in nineteenth-century science. One could, for example, through a series of careful observations, arrive at the conclusion that the pressure of a gas is inversely proportional to the volume, without having any feeling that he understood why this was so. One could even construct a series of propositions from which this law and other laws about gases

[7] For a discussion of how, for example, the operational meaning of "length" has undergone change see P. W. Bridgmen, *The Logic of Modern Physics*, Macmillan Paperback, 1960, pp. 3-25.

[8] See Albert Einstein, "On the Method of Theoretical Physics," Oxford, 1933, reprinted in Edward H. Madden, *The Structure of Scientific Thought*, Houghton Mifflin, Boston, 1960, pp. 80-84.

[9] *Ante*, p. 82.

could be formally deduced, and one would still not feel that he understood very much about the behavior of gases. When, however, a theory "explains" that gases are made up of molecules that are continually bouncing against each other and against the sides of the container, then one is likely to feel that he understands why it is that as volume is decreased the gas exerts greater pressure on its container. Or again, when it is suggested that the atom may be viewed as a miniature solar system, such a theory elicits the feeling of "having explained," in a sense more satisfactory than the most beautiful set of mathematical equations.

In twentieth-century science, however, the usefulness of explanatory models, especially common-sense mechanical models, has been subjected to review and it appears that frequently such models tend to explain too much. There are evidently two points at issue here. The first has to do with the age-old difficulty of reasoning by analogy. It has often been observed that no analogy is perfect and, indeed, if it were perfect it would be of no use since it would merely reproduce exactly the original problem-situation. Any analogy or model, therefore, will always suggest either too little or too much or both, and since, as we have noted, models tend to elicit a "feeling of understanding," it is always appropriate to raise the question whether a model is dulling more than sharpening sensitivity to the nature of the phenomena that it explains.

The second point turns on the question of the so-called *indeterminacy* that has become so incorporated in recent science. From a programatic standpoint, science has always operated under a deterministic approach and it still does. By the beginning of the twentieth century, science had become so dominated by classical mechanics that it had, in effect, erected its deterministic approach into a kind of determinism. For example, it was assumed that, given a finite, self-contained system of mass points (our solar system may be thought of as approximating such a system), if at any given time every mass, position and velocity were known, then by the laws of force from classical mechanics it would be possible to calculate the state of the system for all points of time forward or backward. This was so firmly believed that whenever such formal calculations were not closely approximated by empirical work the conclusion was that either the observations were inaccurate or that the system being observed was not properly bound—that is, that there were additional forces at work that had not been included in the calculations. In other words, the principle of determinism performed an analytic or a priori function in inquiry not unlike the way in which a system of geometry functions in relation to problems of mechanical engineering.

In contrast to all this, there was proposed early in the twentieth century the principle of Uncertainty Relations that said in effect (as it relates to our last paragraph) that, first, it is in principle impossible to determine with exactitude both position and velocity of a mass at a given time, and that, second, repeated applications of the same force on the same mass point cannot be observed to be invariant. What is invariant, given a large sample, is the mean variation from the calculated velocity. Thus, the shift from mechanical models based on a Newtonian conception of absolute space and time to a statistical analysis of events in a relativistic space-time matrix.

Actually, however, long before development of these twentieth-century ideas, what might be called little pockets of indeterminacy had been incorporated into science. For example, consider games of chance involving, say, dice. It has long been held that the results of the next throw are nonpredictable. One could argue, of course, that the dice obey the laws of motion and that if all the forces affecting their movement were calculated the results of the next throw would be determinable. But this overlooks the analytic function of the definition or the way of conceiving "true dice" and "free throw." If in any particular case one could actually predict the next throw (even with the slightest accuracy), then we would say that either the dice were loaded or the throw was rigged. In other words, the way in which the matter is conceived imposes limitations. In this case it creates an indeterminacy that requires statistical treatment if the deterministic program is to be carried forward.

Now, in the case of subatomic physics, we should note that the original conception of the atom as a miniature solar system has undergone radical modification in order to make it square with experimental phenomena that have been developed. One might say that, at first, electrons were conceived as little thingamabobs moving in orbits. Now their "thingness" has largely disappeared, leaving only "bobs" that may jump about obeying statistical rather than mechanical laws. Again, the way in which these matters are conceived simply rules out a determination of the data that would permit prediction under traditional mechanical models.

If the question now arises as to whether, underneath these conceptual limitations, all events (whether involving dice, electrons, or human behavior) are *really* determinant and could be predicted if we just knew enough, we should recognize it as a metaphysical question beyond the reach of science. In any event, we should not confuse metaphysical doctrines (such as determinism and free will) with questions about the usefulness of various models in the several sciences. Science tries to understand, in one way or another, what can be publically observed. In order to do this, it employs various conceptual models even though it may be that every such model imposes both too much and too little on what it explains. But this may be just another way of saying that any system of human thought cannot be both consistent and complete (or even completable) at the same time.

So it is that the question of what constitutes an adequate or appropriate mode of explanation remains a controversial one. And it is conceivable that a new answer to this question could mark the beginning of a fourth stage in human thought, beyond the three stages noted by Comte.

It turns out then that the "truth" of a scientific law may be usefully differentiated from *formal truth*, which is a correct assertion of a relation of meanings, and *factual truth*, which is an assertion that conveys a correct impression about some existential state of affairs. For, if a fundamental characteristic of science is its systematically organized knowledge, then the truth of a law within this system (in contrast to a formal assertion about a relation of meanings within the system, or a factual assertion about the existential affairs that have been lawfully ordered) depends upon systemic considerations involving both formal structure and factual content. And in actual practice the acceptance or rejection of a proposed law requires explicit consideration of both. More significantly, a reconstruction of an accepted law may be called for because of either a new way of relating meanings (such as a shift from Newton's absolute space and time to Einstein's relativistic space-time) or a new impression of existential affairs (such as may be gained by a new means of observation, say a radio telescope or an instrumented satellite in space). The decision to retain, reject, or ascribe new boundaries of applicability for the law rests on systemic considerations rather than on a true-false decision about either a clear-cut formal or a clear-cut factual assertion. The decision turns on the question of what is the most parsimonious or least disturbing adjustment to the science as a whole. *Systemic truth* is, therefore, a matter of *economy and power* in addition to logical consistency and correspondence with "fact."

## TEACHING SCIENCE

Inasmuch as it is philosophy of education, not philosophy of science, that is our primary concern, it seems appropriate to close this brief discussion of science by considering whether our analysis is suggestive for educational theory, policy, and practice. Do the characteristics, stipulations, and organization of science suggest any directives for education in general, and for the teaching of the several sciences in particular?

Such subjects as mathematics, physics, biology, geography—indeed, most subjects usually identified as academic in the high school curriculum—are frequently thought to perform a twofold function in education through at least the first two years of college. On the one hand, such subjects perform a vocational function, introducing the student to various areas of potential specialization and providing a foundation upon which many vocations may rest. On the other hand, such subjects are said to contribute to one's liberal or general education. Furthermore, it is frequently said that these two functions are not entirely compatible. A student preparing to become a specialist in, say, history, or physics, needs to master a range of detailed information and techniques that runs considerably beyond what is of interest or benefit to the student not planning to specialize in that area. Another way of posing the same problem is to note that a given course may be introductory and preparatory for some students while introductory and terminal for others. One of the most common general criticisms of course-work at the college level is that each course is taught by a specialist in the area and taught as if all students in the course were preparing to become specialists in that subject.

Curriculum makers have sometimes tries to remedy this situation by introducing special courses for the nonspecialist. Usually such courses have been known as survey courses at the college level or as broad fields or core curriculum at the high school level. As one would expect, two kinds of criticism have been directed at such attempts: It is said that this results in watered down versions of subject matter. The teachers who really know a given subject matter (i.e., true specialists) do not like to teach such broad surveys, hence such courses tend increasingly to be taught by people who have not themselves ever really mastered the subject. This produces further watering down and deforming of the subject. The other kind of criticism is directed at the idea that there is a real conflict between the general and the special education functions of a course. It is argued that there is only one way to attain an understanding of any subject—a sustained, rigorous, systematic study of the details of that subject. If the subject has any general educative value (and the proponents of the argument do not agree among themselves concerning which subjects do and which do not), then it should be pursued to some appropriate level, just as if one were expecting to specialize in it. The difference between a specialist's understanding of a subject and a general understanding of it is primarily a matter of how far one goes.

Now if fundamentally science is knowledge systematically organized in terms of underlying explanatory principles, it appears that a grasp of such principles should be of prime concern to both the student seeking a general education and the student seeking to prepare himself for eventual specialization in a given subject matter. The problem of curriculum and teaching methods, with respect to this question, then resolves itself into the question of how best to teach for a grasp of the basic structures or principles of a subject. Fortunately, the question of effectiveness of various ways of teaching is basically an empirical one and there is some evidence to suggest, first, that the basic structures of various subject matters can be at least partially understood (perhaps intuitively) by relatively young or inexperienced students, second, that a student need not plough through large amounts of detailed information in order to grasp such principles, and, third, that once the student has attained such insight it becomes much easier for him to master the details of the subject in meaningful fashion. If this turns out to be the case, then some sort of *spiral curriculum* would seem to be indicated.[10] This is to say that at whatever level a subject is first introduced, the prime objective should be to help students gain some understanding of its most fundamental principles. Teaching of the subject in subsequent years should be designed to expand this understanding by filling out the skeleton, so to speak, and putting meat on the bones. The kind of minute attention to esoteric detail that fascinates a specialist should be emphasized only in the advanced study of the subject, typically in graduate school.

Unfortunately, the question "What are the fundamental principles and structures of the various branches of knowledge?" is

[10] See Jerome S. Bruner, *The Process of Education,* Harvard University Press, Cambridge, 1960, esp. chaps. 2 and 4.

not merely an empirical one. A body of knowledge is not a physical thing that can be taken apart in order to see how it is constructed. In the next chapter, therefore, we shall take a preliminary look at some of the problems that arise when one undertakes to set forth the basic structures of knowledge.

## SUGGESTIONS FOR ADDITIONAL READING

Chapters 4, 5, and 6 in Beck, *Philosophic Inquiry,* chapters 6 and 7 in Titus, *Living Issues in Philosophy,* and chapter VI in Randall and Buchler, *Philosophy: An Introduction,* provide a good introduction to the nature of science. In reading Beck, special attention should be given to the Appendix to chapter 4 in which a very instructive illustration of scientific method is presented.

Three books in philosophy of education discuss the nature of science in relation to education:

Bayles, *Democratic Educational Theory,* chapters 5 and 6
Phenix, *Philosophy of Education,* chapters 18 through 21.
Scheffler (editor), *Philosophy and Education,* pages 143-198

Students desiring to pursue the subject further should consult some of the standard texts in philosophy of science. One of the best known of these is *Logic and Scientific Method* by Cohen and Nagel. There is a very readable collection of essays presented by Madden (editor) under the title, *The Structure of Scientific Thought.* Students interested in a more advanced study of the logic of scientific explanation may wish to consult Nagel, *The Structure of Science.*

There are available a wealth of paperback books on the nature of science. Here are a few of the titles students seem to find most helpful:

Bronowski, *The Common Sense of Science*
Burtt, E. A., *The Metaphysical Foundations of Modern Science*
Campbell, *What Is Science?*
Conant, *On Understanding Science*
Danto and Morgenbesser (editors), *Philosophy of Science*
Frank, Philipp, *Philosophy of Science*
Schrodinger, *Science, Theory, and Man*
Whitehead, *Science and the Modern World*

# CHAPTER 6

# What Are Structures of Knowledge?

ONE OF THE most pressing educational problems of our time is the so-called knowledge explosion. As knowledge expands and the rate of expansion accelerates, educators are faced with a frightful dilemma. Either the length of school day and year must be increased or old material must be deleted to make room for new. Moreover, either choice, or a combination of the two, can never be more than a stopgap measure. If, however, students can be taught to grasp the underlying principles and the basic structures of various subject matters without being required to master an ever-increasing body of detail, then it seems reasonable to hope that both the general and the preparatory functions of education may be accomplished, perhaps more effectively, in the same length of time now devoted to these functions.

Furthermore, if there are no sharp breaks between common sense and science nor between the various sciences, then it would seem likely that an emphasis upon basic structures and principles of a subject would provide the most promising base for both the integration of learning and the transfer of training. As students gain insight into some of the most fundamental structures that cut across many disciplines, a base would be established for that refinement of common sense which, as previously noted, may be the key to a truly liberating education.

There is nothing new about urging the schools to emphasize fundamentals. Difficulties arise when we try to translate this advice into courses of study and curricula. What are the fundamental principles and structures of the various subject matters or disciplines, how are these related to one another, and what are the relevant psychological and pedagogical considerations that should be taken into account? The development of courses of study runs beyond the proper domain of philosophy of education. Nevertheless, there are certain aspects of the problem that are in need of clarification, and that is a concern of the philosopher of education.

## ORGANIZATIONS OF KNOWLEDGE

Early in our discussion of science it was suggested that science may be viewed simply as the best established knowledge presently available in terms of the most perfected methods of inquiry. It would follow that science, as an activity, would be any sustained effort to arrive at such knowledge, and there would be no obvious limits to what science may study. On the other hand, our more detailed discussion of the characteristics and stipulations of science would seem to suggest that not all forms of serious inquiry should properly be termed "scientific." What then, may science study? No attempt will be made to answer this question in a definitively proscriptive or even prescriptive manner, for in doing philosophy of science any trace of dogmatic prescription is tantamount to denying one of the most fundamental characteristics of scientific inquiry, namely, that science is autonomous—it is self-regulating, and no doubt will continue, as it has in the past, to decide through its own activity, what it will study and how.

It is frequently asked why there are many sciences rather than just one big science. Two kinds of answers are usually given, one to the effect that science is so complex and far-reaching that more or less compartmentalized specialization is inevitable, and another that the range of objects and relations studied by the various sciences are so widely divergent that one should not expect that there would be any principles or methodologies applicable to the entire range. The first answer misses the point and the second answer converts an a posteriori question into an a priori assumption.

Although it is true that today no one man could thoroughly understand all of the sciences, it is likely also true that presently there is no man who thoroughly understands even all of physics. But such an observation says nothing at all about the "logical unity" of physics in particular or of science in general. And as for the differences that exist among the subject matters of the various sciences, the nature of such differences is one of the things that science is trying to determine—it is not something to be taken for granted.

It appears, then, that here is a kind of paradox. On the one hand, if a characteristic of science is an attempt to systematize knowledge in terms of a decreasing number of underlying general principles, then the unity of science (that is, the organizing of all sciences into one big science) is an obvious goal. On the other hand, if no system of thought can be both consistent and completable, then the unity of science is, theoretically, an unobtainable goal. And so it is that although, from time to time, many persons have attempted to arrange the various sciences or disciplines or forms of knowledge into some sort of organization chart or periodic table, today it is widely recognized that such attempts should be viewed only as heuristic devices with a very limited range of usefulness.

For example, in Book VI of *The Republic,* Plato developed a scheme for grasping man's attempts to attain knowledge. Plato divided all such attempts into four levels: conjecture, belief, understanding, and pure reason. *Pure reason* could grasp the "reals," that is, the Platonic "ideas," which, as we noted earlier, were thought to be more real than the imperfect copies of the material universe. *Understanding* was of "hypothetical ideas." These exist on the level of man's conceptual life. Translated into present concerns, hypothetical ideas could be viewed as a name for the theoretical constructs and laws of science. *Belief,* for Plato, was at the level of "things," that is, actual objects and events, while *conjecture* was concerned with "images." Such images suffered from double or compounded imperfection—they were partial and imperfect copies of actual things, which were, in turn, imperfect copies of "reals." At this lowest level nothing more than conjecture was possible.

Variations on Plato's way of organizing knowledge are still popular today[1] and may still be useful to the educator in that they encourage a comprehensive view that cuts across the traditional subject matter boundary lines. In the teaching of any of the sciences, for example, Plato's organization of knowledge should enable teacher and students to grasp both the hypothetical nature of scientific knowledge and the systemic aspect of the "truth" developed by the science. On the other hand, such a view does not appear to be very helpful when one tries to decide what are the most fundamental structures or principles of a given science or body of knowledge.

Aristotle divided the disciplines into three classes: "The Theoretical," "The Practical," and "The Productive." The aim of the theoretical is to know or to understand. The aim of the practical is to do, and the aim of the productive is to make or to create. Each requires special kinds of subject matter and special competence. For example, theoretical disciplines, such as mathematics and the natural sciences, require investigators who are able to reason logically, to deal with abstractions, to build comprehensive theories; and the objects of study must possess at least relative permanence and uniformity. Thus it is that, say, physics deals not with singular facts (particular events) but with general facts (invariant associations).

In contrast to the theoretical disciplines, the practical disciplines are concerned with subject matter capable of change or alteration. Such subject matters, for example, as human character and social institutions have the necessary characteristics. The chief practical disciplines for Aristotle were ethics, politics, and education. The practitioner obviously needs certain skills and abilities that differ from, or go beyond those needed by one undertaking theoretical investigations.

The productive disciplines, such as engineering, the fine arts,

---

[1] For example, see Mortimer Adler, *The Difference Between Knowledge and Opinion*, National Educational Television Films, No. 28.

and the applied arts, require material that is even more malleable and skills that are more specialized and distinctive.

If we look at the typical school curriculum from the standpoint of this Aristotelian framework, we note overwhelming emphasis on the theoretical disciplines and neglect of the practical ones. Or, perhaps, what has happened is that our schools are confused, having transformed theoretical disciplines into how-to-do-it courses. Perhaps we teach mathematics and science not to enable the student to know but to do. And, conversely, what little attention we do give to ethics and politics seems to be more concerned with knowing than with doing.

In any event, these classical ways of organizing knowledge appear strange to many public school teachers and administrators. This may be due, at least in part, to their stemming from what Comte called the second or metaphysical stage in the development of human thought. In the third or positivistic stage we have generally attempted to organize knowledge in terms of subject matter. Comte suggested the following arrangement: mathematics, physics, chemistry, biology, sociology. Such an organization, no doubt, seems much more familiar, and if we keep in mind the merely heuristic nature of any such attempt at organization, an expanded form of this arrangement may prove helpful for our purpose. Consider the following:

1. The formal sciences, such as logic and mathematics
2. The inorganic sciences, such as physics and inorganic chemistry
3. The biological sciences, such as zoology and botany
4. The hominological sciences,[2] such as psychology and sociology
5. The ideological sciences,[3] such as history and ethics

[2] I am indebted to Professor Elizabeth Steiner Maccia for the expression "hominological." She has pointed out that "social" has the difficulty of ruling out the psychological with its emphasis on the individual. "Psychological" suggests an exclusion of the social and in addition suggests "mind" as an entity in contrast to the biological body. Finally, "behavioral" generally includes studies of animal behavior that, perhaps, should be included under the biological sciences.

[3] The term "ideology" was popularized by philosophers of the French Enlightenment as the science that explores the origin and development of

When the sciences are arranged in this way, a number of observations arise. There appears to be a movement from the abstract to the concrete, from the general to the particular, from the more rational to the more empirical, and from the more advanced to the less well developed. And of course it is clear that our numbers indicate only noticeable stages in these movements rather than sharp breaks. There is, for example, only the thinnest of lines between inorganic and organic chemistry, and the science of physiology is both biological and hominological; indeed, so are large portions of modern psychology.

What about the characteristics of science that were discussed earlier? Is it the case that as we move from one through five in our arrangement of the sciences we find inquiry decreasingly characterized by systematic organization in terms of underlying explanatory principles, precise language, depersonalized objectivity, and careful adherence to such stipulations as the uniformity of nature, public verifiability, and parsimony? Possibly so, although it appears that such characteristics and stipulations may have a somewhat different meaning in the formal sciences than in the inorganic sciences, and perhaps still different in the biological sciences. If this is so, then one might expect them to undergo further modification in meaning in the hominological and ideological studies. Furthermore, as noted earlier, even

---

ideas. In the hands of such men as Helvetius and Holbach, ideological studies were an attempt to obtain objectivity by disentangling truth from the prejudices fostered by partisans of church, state, or social class. In more recent times some men have claimed that bias is universal and the term "ideology" has frequently been taken to mean the manner of thinking characteristic of a particular society or class (e.g. bourgeois ideology). In any event, "ideological" should not be confused with "ideographic." It has frequently been claimed that history is ideographic while science is nomothetic, i.e., history deals in particular events while science deals in general laws. But history is always both more and less than a simple listing of particular events. History should not be confused with the various sources (documents, chronicles, etc.) used by the historian. A meaningful, useful, history is always a structured account of the facts—structured by the historian in terms of the ideas and values that are intelligible to the society that is the intended reader. Since facts never speak for themselves, there is nothing necessarily unscientific or nonobjective about presenting facts in a meaningful way. History becomes nonscientific when the historian violates the canons of objective inquiry as he selects and establishes "the facts."

though a certain inquiry may not produce a body of knowledge that meets all of the requirements for inclusion in the corpus of science, it does not follow that the unsuccessful attempt must be classed as unscientific. In any event, our arrangement of the sciences suggests that it would be rather arbitrary to select any point in the list and maintain that the studies above it were scientific while those below were not.

On the contrary, it may well be the case that at any point in the arrangement one *could* pose questions that would not yield to scientific investigation because of such deficiencies as the lack of publicly verifiable evidence, the unavailability of precise language, failure to adopt a depersonalized objective approach, and the like. And, if this be so, then it follows that the less well-developed sciences may be less well developed not because (as is frequently alleged) they are more recent in origin and deal with more complicated subject matter that is less approachable through controlled inquiry, but because, in these areas, we may have been posing the wrong kinds of questions.

Unfortunately, it is much easier to note that we may be asking the wrong kind of questions than to point out how we may go about asking the right ones. Surely, however, a direct, sustained effort to make our inquiries exemplify the characteristics of science that have been discussed would have salutary results. Fortunately, our heuristic arrangement of the sciences suggests a more indirect approach that could also prove useful, namely, a deliberate shift in the less well-developed sciences toward concerns that are more abstract, more general, and less directly empirical.

Again we should note that it would be presumptuous for a nonspecialist in a given science to attempt a prescription for the shortcomings of that science. Nevertheless, a few illustrations may help us to understand some of the difficulties encountered in the less well-developed sciences. Consider what constitutes an appropriate degree of abstraction. In psychology, for example, is it possible that much of the conceptualization has proceeded at an unfortunate level? For instance, observable behavior is frequently described as aggressive, anxious, hostile, dependent, or the like. Such description may be too abstract and interpretive to permit reliable protocols (comparable to, say, reports of pointer readings in the inorganic sciences) yet too empirical or "behavioral" to encourage truly creative theoretical manipulation (comparable to, say, theoretical constructions using mass, energy, momentum, etc.). Or again, consider the general absence of idealized conceptual entities and conditions embodied in the subjective conditional mode of expression. It appears that the typical psychologist has shied away from any constructions that would compare favorably with "freely falling bodies in a vacuum."

We are not suggesting that psychology should necessarily follow a mathematico-deductive approach (as in the Hullian tradition, for example) that apes too closely the procedures of physical science. On the contrary, our plea is for the development and testing of novel structures and modes of explanation. If psychology is to remain distinct from biology, on the one hand, and sociology, on the other, then perhaps what is needed is the "free invention" and theoretical elaboration of a system of non-reified psychic constructs that would generate hypotheses for ordering observable behavior.[4]

Closely related to these matters is the question of whether sociology, for example, can ever hope to explain (and thus possibly to predict) human behavior in terms of some underlying uniformities or whether it must be content with the kind of statistical generalizations that are presently characteristic of this science. One cannot help but wonder whether much of the research in this science has not been motivated by the desire to obtain practical results rather than to develop and test underlying explanatory principles. What is sociology to be, in Aristotelian terms—a theoretical or a practical discipline?

One of the most perplexing problems of the hominological and ideological disciplines is the matter of how to deal with the

[4] See, e.g., Donald Snygg, "Another Look at Learning Theory," *Educational Psychologist*, vol. 1, no. 1, pp. 1-2, 9-11, October, 1963.

human values that are so centrally located in these studies. We noted that one of the characteristics of science is that it adopts a *depersonalized objective* approach to its problems. Can man be objective about human values—especially about his own values? Since our next chapter is about the nature of value, we shall once again postpone discussion of this question.

## STRUCTURES WITHIN A DISCIPLINE

Regardless of how one strives to organize knowledge as a whole, whether one regards science as an essential unity or as a complex of essentially distinct disciplines, regardless of where one draws the line between scientific and nonscientific disciplines, the question still remains as to what are the basic structures of any given discipline, say, mathematics or history. The curriculum maker may be more interested in seeing human knowledge as a whole, but the teacher and textbook writer is, understandably, concerned with determining the basic principles and structures of a particular discipline. Again we should note that this problem runs far beyond the domain of philosophy of education. Nevertheless, some of the questions involved are certainly worth consideration by anyone striving for comprehensive understanding of education.

What do we mean by "the basic structures of a given discipline"? The root meaning of discipline or subject matter is, simply, "that which is taught or presented for thoughtful consideration or study." The root meaning of structure is "to build, or to put together." When information, skills, ideas, or ideals are presented for study, they need to be put together or organized in some logical fashion.[5] One may then say that the structure refers to the way in which the parts have been put together—that is, the way in which they are interrelated and are meaningful as parts of a whole rather than as a collection of

[5] For a brief discussion of the meaning of subject matter see Smith, Stanley, Shores, *Fundamentals of Curriculum Development*, rev. ed. World, Yonkers, 1957, pp. 127-131.

independent items. And, of course, many subject matters are quite complex, containing many subgroupings, so that we more accurately speak of its structures rather than of a single structure.

Typically, in our culture, subject matter has been organized into research disciplines and, as we noted earlier, when a subject matter is organized in terms of underlying explanatory principles, we refer to it as a science. The various sciences differ not only in the different objects studied but, perhaps more significantly, they differ in the types of explanations and research methods that are employed. Indeed, where the modes of researching and explaining tend to converge, it becomes difficult to distinguish two sciences even though the objects studied are presumed to be quite distinct. Consider, for example, the presumed distinctiveness of mathematicals, physicals, chemicals, and biologicals, in contrast to the fused nature of theoretical organic chemistry.

Whether or not it may be called a science, any organized area of knowledge or discipline involves some basic conceptions and procedures that are the "organizers." It is these that are called the basic structures of that discipline and it is these structures that give the discipline its distinctiveness. If the discipline is a viable, growing one, it is these structures that largely determine what kind of questions will be posed and researched, what kind of data will be developed and how they will be interpreted. It follows of course that unless the discipline is dogma, the basic structures will be relatively stable rather than absolute. If the discipline is a scientific one, then the structures may be systematically reconstructed as an increase of knowledge developed under one conception permits the conceiving and testing of more powerful ideas.

It has long been recognized, at least theoretically, that it is important for the teacher to understand the structure of the discipline he teaches. Without such an understanding, how can he judge what is important as against what is trivial? Without such understanding, how can he judge what sort of preparatory exercises are necessary for students to grasp what he is trying to teach? Unfortunately, however, it has frequently been thought that almost any way of organizing is satisfactory, as long as all the material is covered. Actually, of course, the time has long since passed when it was possible to teach more than a fraction of any field of knowledge. But many teachers have evidently shrugged off this fact as something to worry textbook writers but not teachers. If a teacher "covered the book" he did his job. In similar fashion, if he understood the way the book was organized, this was all that was required. Under this approach, history, literature, even the sciences became *whatever was in the book* rather than dynamic fields of inquiry. And many books consisted of enormous quantities of facts and formulas, with little conceptual structure beyond superficial taxonomy.

Now that the knowledge explosion has become more obvious, we are coming to recognize not only that it is important for the teacher to understand the living structure of the field of knowledge (in contrast to the organization of standard textbooks) but also that this same living structure is the most important "fact" to be taught. In short, understanding of structure is of prime importance to student as well as teacher. We have noted, with John Dewey, that the aim of education is more education. It is the understanding of the structures of a subject that permits other ideas to be related to it meaningfully. It is the grasping of structure that adds most to the meaning of experience and increases control over the course of subsequent experience.

It is not surprising that it is in the formal and physical sciences that courses of study have recently been developed in terms of the structures of the disciplines to be taught. It is in these sciences that there is most agreement concerning basic structures and it is these same areas of study that, in the public mind, are most closely or most directly related to national security and, hence, in the best position to obtain financial support. A report of the American Association for the Advancement of Science[6]

---

[6] American Association for the Advancement of Science, Misc. Publication No. 63-66, *The New School Science*, Washington, D.C.

indicates that all of the new science curriculum projects have included the following features:

1. They have sprung from the minds mostly of professional scientists. . . .
2. They have involved, along with the scientists, professional educators. . . .
3. They have had the organizational strength and the prestige to attract substantial financial support, most of it from the National Science Foundation. This has enabled talented people to throw themselves into the problem completely on a full time basis as opposed to taking it on as a peripheral activity along with their regular jobs as is so often the case in preparing new curricula and in writing textbooks.
4. Their emphasis has been on basic science and not on engineering or technology. A student is asked to explore and discover, to develop an understanding of the big ideas in the science rather than to memorize large numbers of facts and formulas, many of which will be out of date in a few years.
5. Their approach has been a total one in which a complete kit of materials has been provided to help both students and teachers.
6. They have made provisions for the tryout of the new courses in hundreds of schools with many thousands of students. As a part of this phase, feedback information has been collected to aid in the evaluation of the courses and to guide their further development. In addition, special training programs for teachers have been conducted all over the country.
7. These programs have seemed to awaken interest in education by other professional groups and to stimulate others not directly connected with the schools to consider their responsibility in the improvement of education.[7]

In discussing the nature and organization of science, we noted that, although it would probably be unwise for workers in the hominological and ideological studies to imitate too closely the conceptions and procedures of the physical sciences, nevertheless, more rigorous efforts to exemplify in their work the fundamental characteristics of the more mature sciences would likely have salutary results. We may now suggest that teachers and curriculum makers in any field of knowledge may profit from

[7] *Ibid.*, p. 5.

close attention to the following statement of "New Goals for Science Education."

Modern science teaching should attempt to:

1. Provide a logical and integrated picture of contemporary science: the theories, models, and generalizations that show the unity of science.
2. Illustrate the diverse processes that are used to produce the conclusions of science and which show the limitations of these methods: the ways of inquiry and the structure of scientific knowledge.
3. Enable the student to reach at some point the shadow of the frontier: to experience the meaning of "we just don't know" and to become sensitive to the progress of science.

In science teaching efforts are made to avoid the fragmentation and discontinuity represented by the unit organization of traditional science courses. Coherence and conceptual structure are sought through integrative themes that provide a logical picture of the course. Series of learning cycles are established to allow for growth in understanding. The framework of the course is strengthened through continuing concern with the characteristics of scientific inquiry. Students are led to feel that science is more a verb than a noun; more a process than a product.

Those who would develop new courses in science must raise the quality of learning. Quality in science is sometimes defined as knowing the characteristics of a science, its methods of investigation, and the nature of its data. It is recognized in the student's ability to pattern the conclusions, processes, and theories of science. The student's understanding of the structure of science is revealed by his capacity for logical thinking within the subject.

Grasping the structure of a subject also means understanding it in a manner that permits other ideas and new knowledge to be related to it in some meaningful way. When ideas have been grouped and unified, a student is in an intellectual position to use his knowledge to attack new problems. Through the act of problem-solving, learning becomes more versatile and the student's capacity for thinking increases.

The emphasis upon ordering or structuring of knowledge seems to be the best way in which the common high school science subjects can be taught. It also places the learner in a favorable position for the harboring of new knowledge. It is the most efficient way for original learning to take place if understanding is the expected outcome and retrieval is the goal. Even more important, the capacity of the student to generate ideas, to attack old questions and to raise new ones is greatly enhanced.

The ideas expressed here are in contradiction to a teaching procedure which consists mostly of describing the phenomena of science, memorizing its nomenclature, and reciting its laws. They are in contradiction to courses organized into distinct units without thematic continuity in which students have little concern for what has preceded or what will follow.[8]

## STRUCTURES OF PRODUCTIVE DISCIPLINES

Even if we assume (as our organization chart of the sciences would suggest) that the problem of delineating the structures of the hominological and ideological studies is not essentially different from the problem of structure of the physical sciences, there still remains the question of the structures of literature and the fine arts. These *productive disciplines* do not appear in our organization chart, yet they are typically included in the school curriculum. In what sense do these disciplines convey knowledge? Are they included in the curriculum because of their cognitive content, or for some other reason? Are such disciplines structured in ways that are essentially different from the subject matters included in our organization chart?

In order to deal with such questions, let us develop three distinctions: (1) knowledge *within* versus knowledge *about* a discipline, (2) discursive versus nondiscursive symbols and meanings, (3) discursive versus nondiscursive purpose and function. (The reader will note, of course, that in order to structure this topic for our study or discussion we are proposing these distinctions as the "organizers.")

1. Very early in this book we noted that history of philosophy should not be mistaken for philosophy itself. We should also note that history of literature or music is not literature or music. What about literary criticism or art criticism? Criticism of philosophy may be philosophy and, of course, some literary criticism may be properly classed as literature. But criticism of music or painting

[8] *Ibid.*, pp. 6-7.

or sculpture or ballet, though it may on occasion attain the status of literature, does not thereby become music or painting or sculpture or ballet. Of course, it is possible that a composer could construct a musical composition that criticized music or a great painting could stand as a criticism of, say, a certain style of painting. But normally, both history and criticism of a given discipline convey knowledge and judgment *about* that discipline in contrast to conveying knowledge *within* or by means of that discipline. History and criticism of the arts, therefore, are ideological disciplines, rather than art, notwithstanding the undeniable fact that such "productions" (as is also the case in all sciences) frequently exhibit artistic qualities. Indeed, it may well be that artistic creation is more fundamental than either theoretical or practical (applied) discipline and may be the more basic or essential characteristic of human (in contrast to other animal) behavior.

To the extent, then, that courses in literature or other arts are courses in history or criticism, that is, courses that convey knowledge *about* such arts, there appear to be no special problems about the structure of such knowledge. Special problems do arise, however, because many such courses presumably are designed to do more than teach *about* the arts. What else are they intended to do?

It is generally maintained that courses in the arts are intended to accomplish one or both of two additional functions: the development of artistic skill, the development of artistic appreciation. What are the structures of skill and appreciation? Are skills and appreciation forms of knowledge? But first, let us continue with our proposed distinctions.

2. Susanne Langer has pointed out[9] that knowledge conveying symbols may be of two types: discursive and nondiscursive. Discursive symbols are always part of some conventional system or *language* having a vocabulary and syntax. This is to say that discursive symbols are, or may be reduced to, "elements" with conventionally fixed meanings out of which meaningful composite

[9] Susanne K. Langer, *Philosophy in a New Key*, Harvard University Press, Cambridge, 1942, see esp. chap. 4.

symbols may be constructed. For example, in the English language the elements are words,[10] having one or more fixed meanings, which may be combined into phrases, sentences, paragraphs, etc., to express discursively many complex meanings. In contrast, nondiscursive symbols, such as sounds, colors, shapes, movements, are neither elements nor made up of elements having conventionally fixed meanings.[11] Nevertheless, such symbols may be combined to *present* meanings. For example, a picture of an object or event conveys information about the object or event, sometimes more adequately than ten thousand words.

Now, of course, much of what is conveyed by nondiscursive symbols may be more or less adequately translated into discursive symbols—using, if necessary, more than ten thousand words. But, presumably, there is always some residue of meaning. Or, the other way around, when one "paints word pictures" there is more conveyed than the meaning that is carried discursively. If there is not a residue of nondiscursive meaning, then we have been dealing with less than a work of art—perhaps with some audiovisual aid. Our concern, then, is with the structure of the residual meaning—with meaning that is largely or wholly ineffable.

At this point one is likely to remember Wittgenstein's remark to the effect that concerning that about which one cannot speak it is best to remain silent. Nevertheless, here is the nub of the problem of art education and this is the reason, no doubt, why many have been willing to settle for apprenticeship training for

[10] Letters are, of course, still more basic units but, strictly speaking, since they are common to several languages they are not the elements of English. Some have argued that sentences are the basic elements and that single words, except they be used as one words sentences, have no clear fixed meaning in isolation.

[11] Sometimes, certain ways of *presenting* meanings may become stylized and conventionally fixed so that what was originally a nondiscursive symbol becomes an element in a language. One thinks immediately of certain hieroglyphic picture writing. Less obvious are stylized motions in, for example, the hula and parts of more complex ballet dancing. Interesting questions are to what extent choreography has vocabulary and syntax and, hence, to what extent (in Susanne Langer's terms) a certain dance *represents*, discursively, in contrast to a nondiscursive *presentation*.

the development of both artistic skill and artistic appreciation. And it may well be that we should frankly acknowledge that some form of nondiscursive teaching must always remain at the heart of any program of art education. Yet there is much that can be discussed.

3. One of the questions frequently discussed in courses and elsewhere, sometimes ad nauseam, is "What was the purpose or intent of the artist?" It is clear that many works of art convey both discursive and nondiscursive meaning, and although one can sometimes do no more than speculate concerning the intent of the artist, one can in more empirical fashion note the various functions which a work of art actually performs in a given setting or culture. One can, for example, discover to what use a given poem, painting, or musical composition is devoted in a school program. In addition to a number of more or less aesthetic functions, works of art are frequently employed to convey information, arouse emotions, build attitudes, reinforce moral commands, and the like.

It would be foolish and arbitrary to attempt to dictate that selection of artistic creations in a school program should be made only for certain purposes. But it is equally foolish for teachers to ignore or default the question of criteria for content selection, relying merely on custom or textbook writers. And, of course, we should realize that, when the discursive functions of aesthetic selections overwhelm or eliminate their nondiscursive functions, we are no longer engaged in aesthetic education.

What, then, is the nature of *aesthetic* education? One can certainly be trained or indoctrinated with respect to aesthetics, just as in any other field. But is this all that is possible? This question is part of the larger question of education for valuing, which must await considerations to be developed in the next chapter. But at this point we may review relevant ideas that have already been partially developed and perhaps further explicate their meaning by applying them to the problem now before us.

John Dewey once formulated the following definition of education: "It is that reconstruction or reorganization of experience which adds to the meaning of experience, and which increases ability to direct the course of subsequent experience."[12] Thus far we have seen that meaning may be rather thoughtlessly *organized* and *reorganized* by processes that resemble conditioning experiments, and meaning may be more thoughtfully *constructed* and *reconstructed*.[13] We may, therefore, define *learning* as any reconstruction or reorganization of experience which adds to the meaning of experience. But not all learning experiences are educative; some are dangerously miseducative, many are perhaps harmlessly noneducative. Only those learning experiences which increase ability to direct the course of subsequent experience are *educative*.

Now, certainly, nondiscursive meanings can be organized and reorganized, and, possibly, constructed and reconstructed. This second suggestion sounds absurd only to those who hold that all thinking is discursive—perhaps, indeed, subvocal speech. But surely meaning runs deeper than language[14] and it is possible to think with sensory qualities as well as with words.[15] This does not mean that we think with qualities that are *immediate* in an epistemological sense. What we hear, feel, taste, smell are not raw sensa, but more or less meaningful (thus mediated) qualities. We *recognize*[16] the sounds of a violin or the smell of roast beef. Surely it is obvious that such recognitions are based on past experience. Although it is true that most of us are not well educated with respect to nondiscursive meanings and, consequently, are not able to exercise much control over the aesthetic aspects of experience, this does not mean that we remain virginal with respect to nondiscursive meanings. We may find many nondiscursive symbols meaningless, that is, to us they may be nonsymbolic. But whatever meaning they do present is mediate, not immediate.

[12] *Democracy and Education*, pp. 89-90.
[13] *Ante*, pp. 76-79.
[14] See Hullfish and Smith, *Reflective Thinking: The Method of Education*, p. 134.
[15] *Ibid.*, pp. 38-41.
[16] *Ante*, pp. 76-77.

It is because nondiscursive symbols do not have conventionally fixed meanings that the problem of delineating and teaching aesthetic structures is so baffling. There is certainly as much difference among the various arts or media as among the various sciences, but more than that, since meanings are not fixed, there is a sense in which each artist (and even each consumer) is in a kind of Alice in Wonderland, where meanings are whatever you please. In this sense one may discuss not the structure of music, but the structure of a particular composition; not the structure of painting, but the structure of a particular picture.

On the other hand, artists, as scientists and people in general, live and work within a culture, and the symbols they use are seldom entirely private or esoteric. Various tempi, shapes, colors, motions have frequently become so closely associated with types of events, emotions, or qualities that they constitute a rudimentary form of language—a language that is more fluid and open than ordinary language and, hence, at the end of a continuum opposite from the precise language of science.

It is sometimes said that in abstract art or music the symbols are completely open, so that they suggest nothing at all or anything whatsoever. But we should note that there is more than one way in which the open-closed continuum may be construed. On the one hand, an open symbol is one that is vague or ambiguous; it stands in contrast to a symbol that conveys precise or unequivocal meaning. On the other hand, an open symbol is one that conveys private or esoteric meaning in contrast to public or exoteric meaning. And, of course, there are several modes of discursive meaning, as well as the whole area of nondiscursive meaning. Now a given configuration may convey more than one kind of meaning in more than one mode, and each may be more or less open or closed in either of the two meanings of open-closed. It seems reasonably safe to assert that the language of science is both relatively precise and exoteric in all modes. But, as we move through common-sense symbols into the domain of the arts, the possible permutations become rather staggering.

For example, without considering the question of what the

artist had in mind, we may note that a given abstract composition may convey to certain persons a relatively closed or determinate but highly esoteric meaning, whereas to others it may function as a kind of ink blot that calls forth a range of meanings of every conceivable kind and mode.

It has sometimes been thought that only emotion is expressed by nondiscursive symbols. Under this view, art is simply technique plus deep feeling. The artist expresses his feelings and the work of art is then capable of arousing similar feelings. Under this view, excellence is a matter of technique and composition, greatness is a matter of the comparative triviality or profoundness of the feelings expressed and/or aroused. It follows that aesthetic education is a matter of refining one's emotions or feelings.

But to many this conception appears inadequate. There is little doubt that aesthetics and emotion are intimately related, but it seems doubtful that the nondiscursive meanings and functions of aesthetics are merely emotional any more than discursive meanings are entirely rational. In the presence of the masterfully restrained exuberance of Dvorak's "From the New World" symphony, or the magnificently romantic second piano concerto of Rachmaninoff, or the passionately articulate fifth and sixth symphonies of Tchaikovsky, or the wizardry of Wagner, or the genius of Beethoven—in the presence of these does one find merely emotion plus technique? Or when the overwhelming technique and composition of Salvador Dali's "The Last Supper" is set aside, is what is left merely emotion? It seems more likely that to fail to see the nondiscursive cognitive meanings in art is as myopic as to overlook the aesthetic in mathematics or science. It follows that aesthetic education does not merely refine the emotions but, as is true of all education, it reorganizes or reconstructs experience (including the personality or self of the one experiencing) in such a way as to enhance the ability to control the course of subsequent experience. And since every particular experience is always a more or less arbitrarily *taken* segment of the continuing line of experience and since experiences do not come nicely sorted into emotional, rational, cognitive, aesthetic (these being distinctions made within experience), it follows that aesthetic education should increase control over subsequent *experience,* not merely "subsequent aesthetic experiences."

Finally, as for the structures of skill and appreciation, to the extent that each of the arts is a discipline, it has its peculiar forms and taxonomy which, of course, can be taught. Even though knowledge about, say, the structure of a symphony in contrast to the structure of an overture remains knowledge *about* music, it provides an entering wedge for the more intimate grasp of the cognitive content found *within* the discipline. This appears to be true of every discipline, whether scientific or aesthetic. Perhaps the essential difference between appreciation and skill is, simply, the difference between cognitive-emotional grasp and physical mastery. But there is no sharp break between the two. We think and know with muscle as well as with mind—we have noted that "believing" is "willingness to act."

Thus it is that to try one's hand at painting or composing and performing music deepens appreciation, just as experience in laboratory or field project facilitates the cognitive-emotional grasp of the structures of a science. In the new science education, the emphasis on basic structures appears to be fruitful. Let us hope that specialists in aesthetic education will explore just as rigorously the possibilities of using this approach in their fields.

## PSYCHOLOGICAL AND PEDAGOGICAL CONSIDERATIONS

Once a subject has been nicely structured, even if we avoid the mistake of treating it as a corpse lying in state rather than as a vital, growing organism, there is still grave danger that we may slip back into an Herbartian, normal-school approach to instruction.[17] Unfortunately, recent dramatic development of sophisticated electronic computers, furnishing, as they do, important insights into efficent processing and retrieval of information,

[17] For a very brief and critical presentation of the Herbartian view of education see Dewey, *Democracy and Education,* pp. 81-84.

may also encourage teachers to think of their students as machines to be programed. It is hardly a gain to bring subject matter to life only to treat the student as a lifeless mass of cells and circuits.

No doubt it is true that a considerable part of what we try to accomplish in the classroom does have significant similarity to the programing and reprograming of machines. We deliberately arrange for students to reorganize and reconstruct their patterns of meanings in ways that are calculated to increase the students' control over the course of subsequent experience. Moreover, much of this instruction can be facilitated and improved by the use of mechanical and electronic devices. Perhaps the limit toward which all this tends is a machine teaching at one end of a coaxial cable and a machine learning at the other end.

But, of course, this is not all there is to education.[18] Teachers and students can behave in ways that are rather machinelike and there may be times when such behavior is appropriate. Yet the very characteristics of the machine that command our respect— its efficiency and the antiseptic quality of its products—render it unsuitable as a model for the educative process. Human thought is rambling and gloriously contaminated with the yeast of irrelevancy. Consequently, human thought can be right for the wrong reasons and can make those fortuitous mistakes which, when insightfully grasped, may lead to truly original production. Indeed, it may well be that it is those deviations from "perfect operation" which are typical of this or that person that constitute his personality.[19] When machines develop personality we send them out for repair.

There are, then, some missing links between the structures to be taught and the education of students. One obvious link is the teaching act. Teaching is a productive and a practical discipline —an art and an applied science—having structures of its own.

[18] For two provocative essays on this topic see Harry S. Broudy, *Paradox and Promise*, Prentice-Hall, Englewood Cliffs, N.J., 1961, "Teaching Machines," pp. 149-154, and "Mirabile Dictu," pp. 74-85.

[19] See C. West Churchman, *Prediction and Optimal Decision*, Prentice-Hall Englewood Cliffs, N.J., 1961, p. 175.

Unless we grasp the fundamental principles, conceptions, and procedures of this discipline, we may erroneously assume that teaching consists simply of programed instruction.

For example, it might seem reasonable to assume that the basic task of teaching is the development of a sequence of presentations, demonstrations, applications, examinations, and the like that would maximize accuracy, clarity, retention, consolidation, integration, recall, transferability, etc., and minimize rote learning, proactive and retroactive inhibition, forgetting, compartmentalization, obliterative subsumption, erosion of meaning, etc. And a firm grasp of the fundamental structures of a subject matter certainly facilitates such programing. It follows that preparation for teaching consists of mastery, under the guidance of subject specialists, of the subject or subjects to be taught, plus mastery, under the guidance of specialists in the psychology of learning, of the principles and techniques of programing. But such preparation would be needed by only an elite group; the ordinary classroom could be managed by a trained mechanic who would use the programs prepared by the elite.

The trouble with all this is that the structures of teaching as a discipline are, very likely, at least as complicated as the structures of any of the disciplines to be taught. There is no reason to assume either that there is some quick and easy road to their mastery or that this discipline is some sort of exceptional case in which a grasp of fundamentals is unimportant. Once again, we should note that a theory of learning is not an adequate substitute for a theory of teaching, and an adequate theory of teaching can be formulated only in the light of a comprehensive theory of education. A proper preparation for teaching should, then, include a cognitive-emotional grasp of education as a process of personal development, as a sociopolitical institution, and as the science and art of teaching, as well as the physical mastery of instructional technology.

## SUGGESTIONS FOR ADDITIONAL READING

There are, perhaps, three lines of development that have converged to produce the current interest in the structure of subject matter. As a result of the cold-war emphasis on the role of science in national security, organizations such as the National Academy of Sciences, the American Association for the Advancement of Science, and the Carnegie Corporation have sponsored a "new look" at courses of study and methods of teaching mathematics, physics, chemistry, and biology. Many eminent scientists and educators have been involved and numerous materials have been developed—books, workbooks, films, etc. Many of these materials are available in School-of-Education libraries or curriculum laboratories. For a brief introduction one might read, *The New School Science,* which is number 63-6 of the miscellaneous publications of the American Association for the Advancement of Science.

Concurrently, a number of psychologists (e.g., the Harvard Center for Cognitive Studies) have been taking a new look at the "structure of cognition"—e.g., learning, thinking, problem solving, creativity. Some of this work seems to have been inspired by the studies of Piaget and some by recent developments in cybernetics. Piaget's book, *The Origins of Intelligence in Children,* or Inhilder and Piaget, *The Growth of Logical Thinking,* are well worth reading in this connection. For a brief, critical discussion of Piaget's work see chapters 5, 6 and 7 in J. McV. Hunt, *Intelligence and Experience.* A popular paperback on cybernetics is Norbert Wiener, *The Human Use of Human Beings.* A useful early report of the work of the Harvard Center for Cognitive Studies is Bruner, Goodnow, and Austin, *A Study of Thinking.* More recently, Jerome Bruner has brought together these two lines of development in a very readable brief book, *The Process of Education.*

The third development contributing to the interest in structure of subject matter has been the trend toward programed instruction and teaching machines. Presumably, in order properly to program material one should understand the structures of that material. Although many of the programs that have been developed are an improvement over the way the same material was organized in typical textbooks, unfortunately as yet the programers do not seem to have come to grips with the problem of delineating the fundamental structures of a subject, viewed comprehensively. It is one thing to improve the way a unit is organized and presented; it is more difficult to explicate the underlying conceptions that make a subject more than a collection of units. Finally, neither should be confused with a program for teaching these underlying conceptions.

While following these new developments one should be alert to the danger that education may once again fall into the errors of Herbartianism. The present generation of teachers and professors may have largely forgotten the good reasons for moving beyond the normal school and its programed instruction—its lesson plans based on Herbart's psychological associationism and his steps of instruction. The present generation of students may know little about this important period in the history of American education. As a propaedeutic to the study of structures of knowledge in relation to education, students should, therefore, review the ideas of Herbart. For this purpose pages 271-283 in Ulich, *History of Educational Thought*, may serve.

It would also be possible to confuse the new emphasis on structures of knowledge with the philosophic tradition of attempting to order or to organize human knowledge in terms of eternal principles. This tradition is as old as Plato and Aristotle and is still alive today. Students interested in a contemporary expression of this tradition should consult Martin, *The Order and Integration of Knowledge*.

Finally, this whole area of concern was recently the topic of a Phi Delta Kappa symposium reported under the title, *Education and the Structures of Knowledge*.

# CHAPTER 7

# What Is Value?

FROM THE BEGINNING of the scientific revolution many of the men who were conducting experimental investigations got into trouble with organized religion. This occurred in spite of the fact that, for the most part, these early scientists were not irreligious men. When, however, the results of their investigations appeared to conflict with the established theological cosmology of their day, these men were faced with difficult alternatives. Since religious orthodoxy was completely unyielding and since the new scientific spirit could not be completely suppressed, some sort of truce or compromise was indicated. There finally developed a tacit agreement (perhaps not unlike some of the balance-of-power or spheres-of-influence agreements reached by political leaders) to the effect that science could investigate questions of fact while questions of value, including of course all questions of religious and moral values, were to be marked "off limits" to science.

After several generations this agreement has become so taken for granted that it appears quite natural, in its literal sense—that is, the distinction between facts and values is assumed to be directly observable in experience, perhaps like the distinction between air and water. In any event, many people today look back upon this agreement as a great victory for science. Was not such an agreement the very thing needed to permit science to develop the objectivity, the public verifiability, the depersonalized approach that is essential to a scientific refinement of common sense?

Be this as it may, a result of this *fact versus value* bifurcation of experience has been that investigations into the nature of value have been largely cut off from the kind of systematic and cooperative inquiry developed in the sciences. While science has been involved in its search for *new truths,* value studies have generally been characterized by a search for, or adherence to, *eternal truths.* Nevertheless, there have developed some more or less widely accepted distinctions, classifications, and ways of posing problems in connection with the study of value. We shall need to consider some of these, therefore, as we attempt to investigate the nature of value.

## LOCUS OF VALUE

From a common-sense point of view each of us recognizes that man makes value distinctions. We like some things; dislike others. We consider some things beautiful; others ugly. We judge some actions good; others evil. Moreover, in the conduct of our daily efforts we tend to assume that the reason why certain objects are considered beautiful and others ugly is the presence or absence of certain properties or qualities in those objects. In much the same way we assume that an evil act exhibits certain characteristics that are distinctively different from the characteristics of a good act.

When one becomes more thoughtful about this situation, however, certain problems arise. For example, if beauty is in the object, that is, if what makes an object beautiful is the presence of certain objective properties, then why is it that we have such wide disagreements about beauty? One could answer immediately, of course, that a person unschooled in matters of aesthetics is not likely to recognize beauty when he sees it. Nevertheless, disagreements about beauty are not uncommon even among the experts. And the same thing can be said about other forms of value, ranging from questions about what foods are the best tasting to what kinds of behavior are moral or immoral.

More precisely, it appears that public verifiability or agreement is difficult if not impossible to attain concerning the alleged value properties of an object or an event. Men can agree about the physical properties of a work of art. They can even agree about certain of its qualities such as form, texture, color, and the like, and still not agree as to its beauty. Or again, men may agree about what the consequences of a certain line of action will likely be and still not agree concerning the morality of such action. In short, in the face of conflict or disagreement about values, the common-sense view of the locus of value appears inadequate.

## Value as Objective

The classical refinement of the common-sense view of value depends upon the rationalistic notion that truth is arrived at by reasoning. In connection with objects of art, for example, the rationalist points out that one should not expect to find the true principles of beauty entirely exemplified within any actual object. One should, through reason, attempt to arrive at the basic principles which, though imperfectly realized, are the common property of all beautiful things. For example, such ideational properties as harmony, proportion, balance seem to characterize all aesthetic objects, and, although not every man immediately recognizes those properties, it is clear that aesthetic sensitivity can be increased through proper training. Moreover, though even experts may not always agree concerning the exact extent to which a certain work of art exhibits such qualities, still all will agree that the absence of such qualities is the mark of ugliness.

It should be noted that this form of realism is a refinement of the "realism" of common sense. At first thought, we are likely to say that the most realistic painting or novel is the one that is most nearly photographic. But, if we adopt the position that value is objective, then the work of art that presents ideas and principles in a form more pure than their embodiment in usual objects and events may be said to be more realistic than life itself. In other words, painting, sculpture, literature, even music, may be used to present basic principles of reality, of beauty, truth, and goodness, in bold relief. Such aesthetic objects are thus more realistic than the objects and events of life that less perfectly embody these same basic forms.

In similar fashion, the objectivist in value theory may argue that moral value is as basic a category in the world as any truth discovered by science. Indeed, truth, beauty, and goodness may ultimately be different aspects of the same basic reality. Involved here is the old philosophic argument between realism and nominalism. Are such general or universal ideas as beauty, justice, goodness merely names (i.e., nominal) for man-made abstractions, or are they the actual (i.e., real) basic forms of the objective world? In classical objectivism, truth, beauty, and goodness are basic categories of an objectively real and rationally constructed cosmos. Man, being rational, may discover what is really valuable in much the same way that he discovers what is really true.

When such a classical objectivism is combined with theology, it may result in subordination of reason to revelation. In addition to the truths that man has discovered by reason, many religions claim a substantial body of revealed truths (as one aspect of revelation), especially with respect to what is truly valuable. The life of Christ, for example, may be viewed as a nondiscursive explication of value—a living illustration of the way the universe is structured with respect to value. It is said that religion thus provides turths that, on the one hand, although not necessarily in conflict with reason, go beyond what man could discover by reason alone, and, on the other hand, provide the basic premises from which man may reason to still further truth.

If moral values are objective, then it is possible that moral law enjoys substantially the same status in the universe as the laws discovered by science. Perhaps natural law includes moral law. Many persons have pondered the proposition that, if moral law is part of natural law, then attempts to ignore moral law should lead to disastrous consequences comparable to what follows the ignoring of other natural laws. For example, if I ignore the law of gravity by stepping out of a second-story window, I very quickly learn that regardless of my personal desires or convenience the universe is as it is and, if I am to continue living in it, I had best recognize necessity and discipline my conduct into forms that are compatible with natural law. Is it possible that flying in the face of natural moral law will, in the long run, lead to similar consequences?

## Value as Subjective

In spite of the obvious advantages of viewing value as objective, many have pointed out that, in fact, no one as yet has been able to find any specific, objective (i.e., publicly verifiable) standards of value that are binding on all men. It would be a fine thing if we could find an objective base for values, especially moral values, that would enable all men of every culture to agree in their evaluations in a manner similar to the way that intelligent men of various cultures can reach a single conclusion on a scientific question. Even if it were true, however, that a great majority of men of most cultures have agreed on certain moral evaluations, concerning, say, incest, murder, and the like, would it follow that something is objectively true because there is a consensus about it? In science, is a statement true because men agree to it?

Those who view value as subjective maintain, therefore, that value is a human category—a name given to certain kinds of experience in which human desires or interests are at issue. The question of what is *desirable,* in contrast to what is *desired,* can mean either "What, in the long run, will satisfy my desires in contrast to my present impulses?" or "What does a given culture designate as valuable, in contrast to the desires of an individual living within the culture?" Thus, value as subjective can be the basis for either personal relativism or cultural relativism.

Relativism should not be confused with either a recognition of the fact that desires differ from individual to individual and from society to society, or with various theories of relativity concerned with ways of understanding phenomena. As herein used the expression *personal relativism* names the belief that criteria for judgment are and should be ultimately individual and personal. *Cultural relativism* names the belief that criteria for judgment are and should be located within the culture of a particular society.

Some subjectivists hold an emotivist theory of values. They argue that, since values are nonobjective, value assertions are noncognitive and are neither true nor false. For example, if one asserts "Port wine is better than sherry" or "Murder is wrong," indirectly one may be conveying information about one's own feelings or about the culture's value viewpoint, but the assertion itself is merely an exclamation and, therefore, neither true nor false—perhaps similar to the "ooh!" or "ugh!" that one might hear in a picture gallery as various individuals view the paintings. An extreme emotivist is likely, therefore, to shrug off all value disagreements with "*De gustibus non est disputandum*" and concern himself exclusively with scientific questions that can, at least in principle, be settled on the basis of objective inquiry.

On the other hand, some subjectivists have maintained that a reliable basis for adjudicating value disagreements may someday be found through careful empirical study of the nature of man and of human society. Even though value is a human, subjective category, human beings are themselves a part of objective reality. As we attain a better understanding of *what man is* we shall likely gain greater insight into what man *ought to desire* if he is to realize his full potential. Even though man-made abstractions such as justice, morality, beauty, and truth are nominal rather than objectively real, it does not follow that they are entirely arbitrary. Man may be the measure of all things and still discover that some ways of measuring, rather than others, satisfy better his basic needs. Not because they can be known to correspond to what is objectively real but because they make experience more coherent or harmonious.

### Value as Relational

Because of the difficulties involved in viewing value either as completely objective or entirely subjective, a third theory concerning the locus of value has been developed. This third theory of value may be considered conceptualistic in contrast to both the realistic view that value is objective and the nominalistic view that value is subjective. Proponents of this theory maintain that, though objects and events do not have any value when viewed apart from human experience, values are not exclusively subjective or personal. The locus of value is thus the relation between a valuing human being and his environment. Value is a relational property.

This theory of value thus agrees with the objectivists that there are objective bases and conditions of value that are independent of the person experiencing value; it disagrees that any object has some inherent value apart from human experience. On the other hand, the theory agrees with the subjectivist that value is always dependent upon some person's interest or appreciation—some human need or desire is a necessary condition for value. It disagrees with subjectivism, however, in that it maintains that this necessary condition is not the sufficient condition for value; value also depends upon objective properties that remain stubbornly as they are in spite of human desires.

Under this view of the locus of value it is clear that science may aid in two important ways in enabling us to become more intelligent in our value choices. In the first place, since value is not an inherent property of things but rather a relational property, scientific investigation can help us understand more fully the consequences and ramifications of assigning value to one thing rather than another. Consider, for example, how helpful science may be in enabling us to deal intelligently with other relational properties such as color. Through careful investigation we have learned that the color of an object depends not only on the properties of the object itself but also upon the conditions of light under which it is seen and even upon the physical and psychological characteristics of the observer. In similar fashion, what may at first appear to be of great value may be judged quite differently when, through inquiry, one sees it in a different light; that is, when one becomes aware of how it would stand in relation to other contexts or situations. Such investigation does not automatically decide for us what is worthy of being valued, but it does make it possible for us to be more intelligent about such decisions.

Science may also enable us to be more intelligent with respect to the other side of the relation. The hominological sciences provide greater insight into what is worthy of being valued than can be gained by an individual working in the light of only his personal experience. Moreover, such studies help us to understand what is feasible in contrast to what is merely ideal. The intelligent man need not rest content with his present desires, striving only to satisfy them. By drawing upon science, he may expect to broaden and deepen his understanding both of himself and of the probable consequences of various value choices. One's desires may, thus, progressively be reconstructed toward the truly desirable. In an abstract sense, one could perhaps say that "the desirable" is that which eventually all intelligent men will desire.

## Value as Activity

At least one more alternative is possible and that is to reject the question of the locus of value and point out that the term *value* is basically a verb. It denotes an activity rather than an objective, subjective or relational property. As a noun, it is used figuratively to designate whatever happens to be the object of the valuing activity.[1] This activity is executed in a more or less spontaneous fashion toward objects that are dealt with on the level of recognition. From a personal or psychological point of view, valuing (or disvaluing) at this level appears to be immediate. As was noted in our discussion of the nature of knowledge,[2] however, such recognitions are immediate only in the sense of being without delay; they are highly mediated by our past experience. Such recognitions are built through prior reorganization, reconstruction, or a combination of the two.

When, for any reason, such recognitions of value or disvalue

[1] See, e.g., John Dewey, *Logic: The Theory of Inquiry*, Holt, New York, 1938, pp. 172-174.
[2] *Ante*, p. 77.

appear to be inadequate, then there is occasion for thoughtful investigation—we are faced with a valuation problem. At this level, to value becomes a matter of *evaluating;* that is, consciously striving for a judgment of what is worthy of being valued. We shall explore the nature of such valuation judgments a little later but first we should continue our preliminary study of the more traditional distinctions and views concerning the nature of value.

## EXTRINSIC AND INTRINSIC

Perhaps most of the objects or events that we value we approve and strive for, not for their own sake, but because we see them as a means or a step in the attainment of something else. Indeed, certain of these means, when viewed apart from some desired end, may be disvalued rather than valued. For example, we are willing to take unpleasant medicine and endure physical discomfort when they are seen as means of restoring good health. In other words, we desire the medicine for its instrumental or *extrinsic* value.

Suppose someone asks why you desire good health. One could say that it is desired extrinsically as a means to happiness or to enable one to accomplish his daily work. But more likely one would say that he values good health for its own sake. That is, good health is usually viewed as having *intrinsic* value. In any event, if good health is valued extrinsically, then some other goal, such as happiness, long life, professional accomplishment, successful parenthood, or the like, for which good health is a means, will be valued intrinsically. Moreover, it should be clear that what is valued intrinsically in one situation may be valued extrinsically in another and, of course, many things may be valued both intrinsically and extrinsically at the same time.

This distinction between intrinsic and extrinsic values is undoubtedly helpful in analyzing certain valuation problems, but it also raises a number of perplexing questions. For example, is it possible to view all values as fundamentally extrinsic? Does not every object or event that is valued always stand in relation to other objects and events? Perhaps we never value something simply for its own sake, apart from some actual context in which the act of valuing or disvaluing will have divergent consequences. Perhaps one could hold to a kind of general theory of relativity with respect to values.

On the other hand, if there are no intrinsic values how could anyone ever develop a sustained value interest in anything? For if A is valued only because it is a means to B, which in turn is a means to C, which in turn is a means to D, and so on without ever reaching anything that is valued for its own sake, would we not very quickly develop an indifference about such an endless affair? And it may well be that an overemphasis on extrinsic values has contributed to the disillusionment some have found in modern societies. Consider the man who works very hard, not because he enjoys his work, but because his work provides a large income that enables him to buy a home in the suburbs, join a country club, become a sponsor of the art association, and obtain many other marks of success which, though not the sort of things that the man truly enjoys are, nevertheless, desired because of their usefulness in impressing his business associates, who when thus impressed can be very useful agents in helping him achieve a still greater income. Surely a mark of the liberally educated man is that he knows how to get off such a treadmill. Although unlimited intelligence may be exercised in weighing extrinsic values, surely wisdom includes knowing how to enjoy the intrinsically desirable.

It appears then that the designations *extrinsic* and *intrinsic* are functional or contextual classifications. They do not necessarily point to different kinds of properties that inhere in objects, properties that may be directly differentiated in experience. They designate, rather, different functions that are involved in valuing. Such a distinction has been developed by man in order to facilitate communication and inquiry.

When man inquires, he never "inquires in general"—he never asks all questions at once nor does he question incessantly. Similarly, when man values, he does so in a particular context or situation that is, at least temporarily, bounded. This is to say that in any given situation there will always be some facts and some values that are taken for granted. Otherwise, both intellectual conclusions and value consummations would be impossible.

It follows that if, in a given situation, something is valued extrinsically, there must be something in that situation that is valued intrinsically. For, if one thing is valued because it leads to something else, then some other thing must be that something else. In this sense, then, extrinsic-intrinsic is just another way of saying means-end.

It would be a mistake, however, to conceive experience as made up simply of a series of situations or particular experiences. *Experience* is always more than a summation of "experiences" somewhat in the same way perhaps that a line is more than a series of points. When a line is divided into segments, no matter how small a segment is taken it still remains part of a line; that is, it still has the property of extension, something not possessed by a point, for a point has only position. Any particular experience, event, or situation that can be recognized as such always has a thread of meaning involved in it that transcends the boundaries that mark off the particular experience. In other words, particular experiences are meaningful only as they remain a part of the continuing line of experience.

Thus it is that, when it is said that an intrinsic value is "valued for its own sake," reference is intended to the consummative function it may perform in a given situation or a particular experience. Intrinsic value should not be construed to be an *end in itself* that stands, as a point, isolated from the continuing line of meaningfulness. When a person enjoys something intrinsically, that is, for its own sake, it does not mean that he is *deliberately disregarding* its relations and consequences.[3] Quite the other way around. A person comes to enjoy something intrinsically only as it becomes an integral part of a pattern of meaning or of a way

---

[3] Contrast with C. L. Stevenson, *Ethics and Language*, Yale University Press, New Haven, p. 177.

of structuring experience, with respect to value, that transcends the particular situation. In a complex web of values the intrinsic function is performed by those focuses where attention and interest more or less temporarily fixate, permitting a consummating experience.

Since value, like knowledge, is typically dealt with largely on the level of recognition, it is true that normally one is not consciously aware of the ramifications or consequences of his intrinsic values—they are treated "as if" they were ends in themselves. But this is merely the correlate of treating knowledge of *recognizable* objects and events as if it were immediate knowledge. On the other hand, when some value problem arises, then it frequently becomes appropriate to question what has been taken for granted and to make explicit at least portions of the web or structure of meaning that has been functioning implicitly. This permits examination and judgment, that is, *evaluation*, in contrast to the valuing that goes forward at the level of recognition.

If it turns out that a person finds there are some intrinsic values that he believes everyone ought to value in every situation, he then designates these as *absolute values*. For example, it is sometimes said that human personality is an absolute value—it ought to be valued by everyone under every conceivable circumstance.

This way of viewing such value designations as extrinsic, intrinsic, and absolute suggests the possibility that they could be treated as the axiological correlates of the epistemological terms factual and formal, systemic, and analytic. We have seen that a statement performs the factual function in inquiry when it asserts something about existential affairs. Factual assertions are assessed as true or false in terms of empirical evidence. In contrast, statements performing only a formal function, that is, the asserting of a relation of meaning, are determined to be true (i.e., valid or consistent) by logical analysis, since they contain no implicit predictions about the content of experience. Formal statements that are held to be true under every system of thought (that is, held to be true come what may in experience) are said to be analytic. Finally, through our examination of the nature of science it was suggested that some statements (notably those that assert conceptual typologies and certain theoretical laws) appear to be *systemically* true. Their truth rests on neither clear-cut factual nor clear-cut formal considerations, but on the more complex matter of assessment of systemic economy and explanatory power.

Now, since to value extrinsically means to value because one believes that what is valued will, in fact, lead to or facilitate the attainment of something else, the ascribing of extrinsic value amounts to a factual assertion which should, in principle, stand or fall on the basis of empirical evidence. On the other hand, to value intrinsically means to value because one has adopted some system or web of values for structuring experience. An assertion that ascribes intrinsic value should, in principle, be determined to be valid or invalid by logical analysis, once the system has been made explicit. And to the extent that a web of values has been systematically organized, then of course one could raise and investigate questions about systemic economy and power. For example, one could, in principle, raise such questions about the Golden Rule. Finally, if one holds that certain values are absolute, that they ought to be valued at all times "come what may in experience," it is clear that the assertion of such a value performs an analytic function.

## THE IS-OUGHT DICHOTOMY

At the beginning of this chapter it was noted that the distinction between fact and value is largely taken for granted. There is no doubt that this distinction is a very useful one. Without such a distinction it is doubtful that human thought could have progressed beyond the first stage, noted by Comte, in which "the is" is viewed as simply the embodiment of the more or less whimsical desires or preferences of the gods. Moreover, without the distinction between what actually is the case in contrast to what one might wish were the case, it is difficult to see how science as we now know it, or even common sense, could have developed at all.

Unfortunately, man-made distinctions—especially the ones that are most obviously useful—tend to harden into dichotomies. These, in turn, become discontinuities that rend asunder human experience in a way that makes the philosophic attempt to see life steadily and to see it as a whole a logical impossibility. Let us, therefore, analyze the is-ought dichotomy to see whether there are some limits to its usefulness.

Consider the following two statements:

1. This is a knife.
2. You ought not to murder your neighbor.

The first is said to be an *is* statement; the second an *ought*. Now if there is a true dichotomy of the is-ought, then every such declarative statement should be one or the other, that is, there should be no middle ground between the is and the ought. But consider the statement, "You ought to sharpen this knife." It contains the word ought and, therefore, appears to be like number 2 above. On the other hand, the sense of the statement does not seem to convey any heavily value-laden imperative, as does number 2. It therefore seems to occupy some middle ground between 1 and 2, and there is, in fact, widespread agreement that such a statement should be given a third designation, such as "a prudential ought statement." Hence, we have before us the following:

1. This is a knife.—An *is* statement.
2. You ought to sharpen this knife.—A *prudential ought* statement.
3. You ought not to murder your neighbor.— A *categorical ought* statement.

Three-way divisions, or trichotomies, are, however, notoriously unstable. Let us, therefore, examine the matter further to see whether some middle ground now exists between 1 and 2, and between 2 and 3. Consider the statement, "This knife is dull." At first glance it appears to be just another type-1 statement. But, if we examine the meaning it conveys (especially when it is punctuated by an exclamation point), we see that it performs at least a mild ought function. In intent, it is elliptical for "you ought to recognize that this knife is dull" or "this knife ought to be characterized as dull." Let us name this use of ought the *characterizing ought.*

Consider now the statement, "You ought to let the police deal with your criminal neighbor." The sense of such a statement suggests that something more than simple prudence is involved. On the other hand, it does not seem to convey the same categorical quality as the admonition against murder. Let us therefore place it between the prudential ought and the categorical ought and call it a *judicial ought.*

We now have the following array:

1. This is a knife.—An *is* statement.
2. This knife is dull.—A *characterizing ought* statement.
3. You ought to sharpen this knife.—A *prudential ought* statement.
4. You ought to let the police deal with your neighbor.—A *judicial ought* statement.
5. You ought not to murder your neighbor.— A *categorical ought* statement.

We could explore further for middle ground. For example, since the word "dull" is frequently a pejorative, perhaps "This knife is dull" should be called an *appraising ought* statement and the label *characterizing ought* should be reserved for the ground between 1 and 2 occupied by such statements as "This is a steak knife." But with the spread already obtained it should prove more interesting (for our purposes) to examine the end cases of what now appears to be some sort of continuum. Before doing so, however, it may be useful to note that even number 1 performs a mild ought function. For the sense conveyed when such a statement is actually spoken is, "You ought to recognize this as a knife." This could be called a *typological ought* statement.

Moreover, though one would not normally do so, one could

accomplish the intent or purpose behind each of the statements in the above array by using "is language." For example:

1. This is a knife.
2. This knife is dull.
3. A prudent man keeps his knife sharp.
4. The police are authorized to deal with one's criminal neighbors.
5. To willfully kill one's neighbor is murder.

We are now ready to examine the end cases.

Logically prior to the inclusion of an existent object under a type (such as "knife") is the assertion of the existence of the object. Hence, prior to statement 1 is the statement "This is." And, of course, prior to the assertion of any particular existent is the assertion of existents in general, that is, the denial of solipsism. This seems to be the sense conveyed by the primitive statement "Isness is."

At the other end of the array, the injunction against murder in general is logically prior to the injunction against a particular instance of murder. But prior to "You ought not murder" is the still more general imperative "You ought to obey at least one ought," or perhaps, "You ought to do what you ought to do." And this is the sense of the primitive assertion that denies moral solipsism, "Oughtness ought to be." Since the intent of the entire array may be expressed in either *is* language or *ought* language, we could just as well have said "Isness ought to be" and "Oughtness is."

It turns out then that is and ought are designations used to call attention to what is at issue in a given context or situation. For example, if I believe that my friend, perhaps a recent immigrant to this country, is unaware of the way the police behave, I may say to him, "The police are authorized to deal with your neighbor—you ought to report to them what he has done." On the other hand, if I believe he is already fully aware on this score but is on the verge of impulsively taking the law into his own hands, then I might say "To willfully kill your neighbor would be murder." The point is, we choose various combinations of is and ought language according to the way we interpret the communication needs of the situation.

Furthermore, since our array suggests that there are various kinds or degrees of oughtness, to dichotomize appears to be a highly artificial procedure, undertaken for logical or methodological reasons rather than because of some natural or ontological significance of the distinction.

Now a logical dichotomy is a division of a class into two subclasses. We should inquire, therefore, what class it is that has been subdivided into is-ought, descriptive-normative, fact-value. At first glance it would appear to be the class statements or assertions that has been subdivided. (Perhaps declarative statements or propositions—actually, it is difficult to name the parent class without prejudicing the question of whether the ought side of the dichotomy is essentially noncognitive.) Further thought suggests, however, that it is, rather, the function or intent of statements that may properly be designated descriptive or normative. And it is right here that we find our limit of usefulness.

Any linguistic expression of a belief (indeed, any manner of expressing a belief other than a complete acting out of the belief) is never more than a partial or elliptical expression. This is to say that what is asserted is not the full-blown belief, with all its interrelated nondiscursive meanings, formal relations, and implicit predictions, but merely the contextually significant and appropriate aspects of the belief. These elliptical expressions are intended to further communication or inquiry and their intent or function may be usefully differentiated by the normative-descriptive distinction. But the underlying belief—the full pattern of meaning, the willingness to act—remains undifferentiated with respect to fact and value. Man acts neither in terms of valueless facts nor factless values.[4] Each man acts in terms of the value-

---

[4] This is why the so-called neutral facts of science never impel man to act. He may look at the conclusions of a science and say, "Just so, but so what?" On the other hand, the more sublimely abstract versions of heaven have not typically been a great motivating force in human affairs. Religions have generally found it necessary either to promise a more corporeal paradise or to threaten with an exquisitely concrete hell.

laden reality that he accepts. It is his *actions* that, over a period of time, reveal both what he believes *is* and what he believes *ought to be.*

## ATTITUDES, PREFERENCES, DESIRES

When the is-ought dichotomy is extended beyond its limit of usefulness and is employed in examining a man's patterns of meaning, it is customary to refer to his beliefs about what *is* as his *beliefs* in contrast to his beliefs about what *ought to be* as his *attitudes, preferences, and desires.* So long as one remains clear about how language is being used such designations are not objectionable. Other expressions such as "a willingness to act" or "a psychophysical state" can be used to name the underlying undifferentiated parent class that supports the logical dichotomy. Unfortunately, however, once belief is placed in contrast to attitude, there is a tendency to set affective or emotional meanings in contrast to other kinds of meanings—presumably factual or descriptive meanings. Such usage, in addition to pushing the is-ought dichotomy beyond its limit of usefulness, generally opens the door to another differentiation having an even more restricted range of usefulness, namely, the emotional or "the passions" versus the rational or intellectual. Such careless use of language may lead one to assume that descriptive or factual judgments (especially scientific judgments) are entirely intellectual or rational (not necessarily rationalistic) whereas all valuations are basically emotional, nonrational, even irrational.

Now, even when such a cognitive-noncognitive division is resisted, it is still commonly alleged that there is something peculiarly personal, subjective and/or conventional (perhaps nominal) about values, whereas facts are impersonal, objective, and real. A large range of extrinsic or instrumental values may be brought into the cognitive fold but at some point, in order to avoid the absurdity of an *absolute* instrumentalism, some terminating value judgment is declared to be "a matter of heart rather than head." So the cognitive-noncognitive dichotomy triumphs in the end.

Now oddly enough, the adoption of this dichotomous view signifies the presence of an attitude rather than an intellectual judgment. In other words, to set intellectual judgments in such a sharp contrast to valuations is to display one's *feelings* or attitude about these matters. Such behavior reveals some of the emotive dimension of meaning attached to such words as *intellectual* and *valuation*. Furthermore, since under this view one does not expect attitudes or the values of the heart to be rational or based on "good reasons" there is no feeling of obligation to examine this attitude about attitudes to see whether it is based on any good reasons.

All of this suggests the need for careful empirical-theoretical study of the formation and function of the emotive meanings revealed in attitudes, preferences, and desires. Although such scientific study never automatically answers philosophic questions, it should provide a base against which both epistemology and axiology may be checked for parsimonious compatibility. Such a procedure would at least open the possibility of an intellectual defense for whatever attitudes are adopted concerning the nature of knowledge and valuations.

For our purpose, which at this point is simply to explore some of the problems involved in the emotive dimension of valuations, the following definitions may be helpful: An attitude is a psychophysical posture or disposition toward a person, object, or situation. It is thus the affective or emotive aspect of a pattern of meaning or willingness to act. Preference is the name given an attitude of favor toward something, especially when what is preferred is placed in contrast with something toward which a less favorable attitude is held. A preference is called a desire when one becomes aware that attention has focused upon the preferred object. When one desires something, the underlying pattern of meaning—the willingness to act—becomes incipiently overt.

## The Formation of Attitudes

If we view attitudes as the affective dimension of patterns of meanings, the question of attitude formation becomes a part of the larger question of the formation of meaning patterns. As we noted in Chapter 4, in the absence of more exact information, a parsimonious assumption would seem to be that a human infant is born with the minimum of built-in responses or meanings necessary to insure his survival in a beneficent environment in which he quickly builds his fund of meanings through processes that, at least in the early stages, resemble classicial conditioning. As patterns of meaning are formed and reformed, they involve, right from the beginning, an affective or attitudinal dimension. In fact, since an infant, or even a young child, is intellectually unsophisticated, his actions frequently reveal that he has not yet grasped the appropriateness of placing the is-ought screen between his reality and the partial expressions of his reality that he presents to others.

When one examines the formation and function of patterns of meaning from the standpoint of theory of valuation, however, certain problems come to the fore that remained unobtrusively in the background during discussions of the nature of knowledge. Consider, for example, the effect of biological drives and narcotics upon patterns of meaning. It is now widely recognized that even such basic drives as those connected with sex or hunger are heavily overlaid with cultural mediations. Nevertheless, it is generally assumed that biological factors, essentially beyond rational control, constitute a base for preferences and desires whereas knowledge is built upon some other base—presumably a more rational one. Under such an assumption, it is no wonder that many have concluded that all valuations are essentially noncognitive.

When we consider the possibility, however, that both beliefs and attitudes are expressions of the same basic pattern of meaning (that is, an individual's reality), we recognize that whatever role, great or small, is played by biological factors, it applies with equal force to both the *is* and the *ought* of a person's reality. And this remains the case even though scientific knowledge, as we have seen, is depersonalized. For what science has struggled to exclude is not the biological base of knowledge but the person-to-person variations. Objectivity is not the opposite of subjectivity. Objectivity means control of judgment by evidence that is publicly verifiable.

Many thoughtful persons will point out, however, that in valuing (in contrast to knowing) it is precisely the personal that is at issue. Actually, however, both knowing and valuing are equally personal. The crux of the matter is whether publicly verifiable evidence may be used by an individual to control his valuing in a way that is at all comparable to his use of such evidence in knowing. In other words, is a science of valuation possible? But first, let us consider further the nature of attitudes.

The fact of habits—especially "bad habits"—tends to confuse the matter. An individual may habitually prefer, even habitually desire. And, of course, habits are not necessarily passive mechanisms, lying dormant until aroused by a specific stimulus. Habits are frequently quite dynamic patterns of meaning that may be triggered by a wide range of mediators or generalized stimuli. Good and useful habits are no less habits than are bad habits. A good habit is a pattern of meaning that enables us to act smoothly and efficiently in a way that is just the way we would prefer to act if we stopped to think about it. A bad habit expresses behavior that runs counter to deliberate judgment. Consequently, our bad habits cause us problems; our good habits keep us out of problems.

Now habitual ways of behaving are no less frequent in knowing than in valuing and one can certainly develop bad habits with respect to what *is* as well as to what *ought to be*. Indeed, since behavior—especially nonverbal behavior—is an expression of a pattern of meaning that lies beneath the is-ought dichotomy, it is frequently difficult for an impartial observer to tell whether the victim of a bad habit is confused in his knowing or his valuing. Consider the following rather trivial case: Suppose you lived for many years in a house in which the light switch for the bathroom is just to the right of the doorway. Then you move to a house where the light switch is to the left of the doorway. It may take quite a while to extinguish completely the habit of reaching to the right of the doorway for the light switch, even though when you stop and think about it "you know better."

In the case of more complicated knowing situations involving elaborate conceptual schemes, theories, models, or systemic patterns, do not certain approaches to experience become habitual? And are not such "intellectual habits" really *attitudes,* that is, postures or dispositions that we adopt toward the *is* of reality? If two scientists agree on "the facts" but disagree on what is the most appropriate way of incorporating these facts into a pattern of meaning, what is the nature of the problem? Is it a problem of the *is* or of the *ought*? Is it an attitude or a belief that is at issue? And what will characterize the arguments? Will they be intellectual or emotional, objectively evidential or personally persuasive?

Once it is recognized that there is no sharp break between the intellectual and the emotional and that man is capable of being intellectual about his emotions just as he may be emotional about intellectual questions, then it should be clear that attitudes, preferences, and desires, even habitual ones, may be subjected to orderly evaluation and reorganization. Deeply ingrained habits are not broken by a single act of will, and this is true whether it is the factual or the value dimension that is at issue. But there appears to be no good reason to assume that objective evidence and rigorous argument is more effective in changing a person's reality with respect to fact than changing it with respect to value. What is or is not effective with various persons under various circumstances is an empirical question.

It is certainly possible to condition or train a person to believe that certain factual propositions are true and later recondition or retrain him to believe that contrary propositions are true. The same may be done with respect to attitudes. Educators generally recognize, however, that simple training is not enough to produce an educated man—at least with respect to the factual dimension of reality. Teachers encourage students to reconstruct thoughtfully their patterns of meaning in the light of objective evidence and careful reasoning. Moreover, students are encouraged to develop the habit of thoughtful reconstruction and to develop habitual preference for such an approach—again, at least with respect to factual matters.

Unfortunately, teachers, parents, and others concerned with the education of the young seem generally to have been willing to settle for careful training rather than thoughtful reconstruction when it comes to attitudes, preferences, and desires. In fact, a popular image of the virtuous man is that he seldom is bewildered or even perplexed by moral problems. He simply knows and does what is right. It is frequently thought to be a sign of moral weakness or lack of fiber if a man has to stop and think before he can decide what is right. No doubt one reason why adequate empirical evidence is lacking concerning the possibilities of the educative construction and reconstruction of attitudes (in contrast to training and retraining) is that education for attitudes has so generally been assumed to be impossible that it has seldom been tried. People have learned that, simply by taking thought, they do not change their habitual desires for food or tobacco, and they have concluded that such desires are typical of all valuing.

## A SCIENCE OF VALUATION

There are three things that a science of valuation should not be expected to provide: (1) a logical demonstration of why a person should accept obligation in general—that is, why he ought to do what he ought to do, (2) a perfect or absolute justification for any value judgment, (3) a system or hierarchy of values that would eliminate all personal valuation-problems.

To require these of a science of valuation would be like requiring factual science to (1) refute solipsism, (2) give up the principle of permanent control, (3) eliminate a scientist's everyday, common-sense problems. What a science of valuation may, hopefully, be expected to do is to develop methodologies for control of those valuation judgments that men would like to see made in an objective fashion, and to develop a systematically organized body of knowledge about what is worthy of being valued upon which individuals may draw as they attempt to be more intelligent about their personal valuation-problems.

Unfortunately, there is a long history of the quest for unattainable goals, and little systematic effort toward attainable ones. John Dewey has pointed out the following:

> Ethical theory began among the Greeks as an attempt to find a regulation for the conduct of life which should have a rational basis and purpose instead of being derived from custom. But reason as a substitute for custom was under the obligation of supplying objects and laws as fixed as those of custom had been. Ethical theory ever since has been singularly hypnotized by the notion that its business is to discover some final end or good or some ultimate and supreme law.[5]

As unfortunate as the quest for ethical certainty has been, equally unfortunate have been two other ideas concerning the relation of a science of valuation to other sciences. First, there has been considerable hope that a science of valuation could somehow reduce all value judgments to factual judgments. In effect, this would limit a science of valuation to the investigation of extrinsic or instrumental values. The second idea has been that, as more extensive knowledge is developed about man and society, especially about what men actually value and how these values stand in relation to basic needs, somehow a science of valuation will emerge. In effect, it is hoped that a fuller knowledge of what *is* will generate a knowledge of what *ought to be*. We have already noted that the kind of knowledge gained from the hominological sciences may help us become more intelligent about our value choices, but this is not the same as saying that the *ought* will spring from the *is*. Description and explanation of human behavior, no matter how extensive, is not the same thing as an evaluation of human conduct.

[5] John Dewey, *Reconstruction in Philosophy*, enlarged ed., Beacon Press, Boston, 1948, p. 161.

It is true of course that a science of valuation, if it is to be "a science," should display the basic characteristics of science in general. It is certainly not the case, however, that science can deal only with factual assertions. We have already noted the important role in science of formal and systemic assertions. Again, what is at issue is whether public verifiability is attainable with respect to *intrinsic* values. Rather than adopting a negative assumption in advance of inquiry we need a sustained effort to explore this question.

As for the role of the empirical study of valuing (that may be developed systematically in the hominological sciences), we should note that although descriptive science does not answer categorical ought-questions it does develop characterizing and typological oughts, or norms that are supportable on systemic grounds. In principle, there appears to be no reason why the hominological sciences should not thus develop typological distinctions that would mark the line of departure for a science of valuation.

Once the domain of a science of valuation were suggested, the first task of the science would be to explore ways of controlling judgments made within this domain. Presumably, such judgments could be cast in the form "X is good" (or "X is worthy of being valued," "you ought to do X," or the like). Can such assertions be subjected to orderly inquiry that brings to bear in a decisive manner evidence that is publicly verifiable? In short, can such value-assertions be warranted?

Now, before an assertion can be judged warranted or not warranted, it must first be understood. This is to say that all concerned need to understand what it means—or, more precisely, what meaning is intended by the person making the assertion. It appears that "X is good" may mean one or more of the following:

1. X leads to or facilitates the attainment of some other value, say, Y.
2. The goodness of X is entailed by some other value or value scheme, say, S.
3. I like X.

To what extent may each of these types be treated as scientifically decidable?

In the case of a type-one statement asserting specific extrinsic value to X, it is clear that it is a factual assertion and there is general agreement that, at least in principle, such assertions are open to scientific investigation. For example, if I assert "Smoking is bad" and mean by this that "Smoking leads to lung cancer," we should all agree that scientific inquiry may be expected to develop evidence that would either support or refute the assertion.

There has been less exploration of the nature of the type-two statement. Consider, for example, that "Smoking is bad" may mean "Smoking is a violation of the Christian religion." What is involved here is a relation of meanings. Most value schemes, such as Christian ethics or the core values honored by a given society, consist of a collection of more or less ambiguous rules, maxims, or exhortations, rather than a systematic set of axioms, postulates, and definitions. Nevertheless, important disagreements do arise over what are thus, essentially, *formal* questions, and it appears that, in principle, value schemes could be systematized to the point that such disagreements could be subjected to the kind of logical analysis that commands public agreement.

It is the type-three statement that has led many persons to assume that there is something essentially arbitrary or non-cognitive about valuing, hence, that in last analysis a true science of valuation is impossible. Can the assertion "I like X" be opened to controlled inquiry and judgment? Can such an assertion be either true or false?

There is an obvious sense in which "I like X" may be true or false. It may be a truthful report or a bald falsehood. In its more obvious sense, this is not of crucial concern to a science of valuation. What is of concern is the more subtle and complex matter of whether the speaker is deceiving himself when he says "I like X." Involved here is the ancient admonition "Know thyself," and the problem of deciding whether one's surface or impulsive inclinations are in harmony with one's basic self is certainly a matter that may be opened to investigation. Such an inquiry may typically include not only both the factual and formal considerations involved in types 1 and 2, but also considerable introspective, perhaps psychiatric, investigation. For to assert "I like X" is to report that desire has focused upon X as an intrinsic value. If, for any reason, the question arises as to whether X is worthy of being valued, then the decision called for is of a systemic nature. What is at issue is the way one is structuring experience with respect to value—in short, what is at issue is one's *character*. The question of the possibility of a science of valuation, therefore, reduces to the question of whether controlled judgments can be formed concerning the comparative worth of alternative ways of structuring character.

## Disagreements about Value

It should be remembered (as in the case with knowing) that as long as valuing goes forward at the level of recognition there is no problem and no occasion for deliberate judgment or inquiry. It is especially important to remember this in connection with type-three assertions. As long as an individual has no doubts about what he likes and dislikes, he will see no point to inquiring into the matter, because *for him* there is no problem. This is true whether we are considering questions of value or of common sense or of, say, physics. In other words, the first condition or step in problem-solving is recognizing that a problem exists.

It follows that the kind of disagreements a man has with himself, so to speak, is more fundamental than disagreements that arise *between persons*.[6] When two persons disagree about what they like or dislike, unless one or both also disagrees with himself the problem they face is not, strictly speaking, a valuation problem at all. They are confronted by a problem in human relations treated typically as calling for some stratagem either to avoid the conflict or to make the most of it in terms of self-aggrandizement

[6] Contrast with Stevenson, *Ethics and Language*, esp. pp. 130-134.

or self-effacement, according to the characters of the individuals involved.

There are occasions, however, when for one reason or another an individual does honestly ask himself whether his intrinsic values are worthy of being valued—whether his own character is satisfactorily structured. Moreover, there are occasions when men sincerely inquire of one another on such matters and long for cooperative, orderly investigation of the problem. Consider our Founding Fathers declaring independence or formulating a Bill of Rights. To be sure there was much maneuvering of human relations, but there was also, evidently, considerable honest inquiry as to what is worthy of being valued, what should constitute the focuses of interest and attention—the main knots in the web or value-structure for the new society. The Founding Fathers were faced, in principle, with a systemic question calling for creation of the most powerful and parsimonious set of value-assertions that could be formulated.

It may be instructive to ponder the significance of the language used in the Declaration of Independence, a language that eschewed the is-ought dichotomy and offered no warrant for the assertions made save self-evidence. It seems clear that the intent of this language was to claim for the propositions of the Declaration the same sort of validity accorded to, say, the axioms of Euclid in geometry. Today, of course, we would not hold that the axioms of geometry are self-evident truths in a synthetic or factual sense. Yet we do not conclude that they are merely a matter of personal feeling, attitude, or preference. When viewed as the bases for a system of interpreted or applied geometry, they enjoy a systemic justification that falls within the domain of public verifiability. In much the same way, such conceptions as the equality of man and his right to life, liberty, and the pursuit of happiness are publicly verifiable. As foundations for character, they are powerful and parsimonious ideas and, when incorporated in an applied social system, they surely enjoy a warrant that transcends private preference.

It turns out then that disagreements in attitudes or values are sometimes rooted in disagreements about factual affairs, sometimes in disagreements about the correct way of interpreting or relating meaning within some system of values, and sometimes in disagreements about how experience is to be structured with respect to value. In each case, what is at issue is diverse or disparate patterns of reality. Where the disparity is relatively slight or superficial, the disagreement can usually be settled by inquiry that is relatively simple and straightforward. Where the disparity is more fundamental, the process of reorganizing or reconstructing reality-patterns is more complex. When a person remains obdurate in the face of what is generally agreed to be overwhelming evidence, then it is recognized that knowing and valuing have a common base and we say that a person is "out of touch with reality" or "refuses to face reality."

Another way of understanding the nature of disagreements about value is to take a further step in unpacking the meaning of the assertion "X is good." This may be done by considering the following schema:

$$X \text{ is good}$$

because
$\left\{\begin{array}{l} \text{1. X leads to Y} \\ \text{2. the goodness of X is entailed by S} \\ \text{3. I like X} \end{array}\right\}$
$\left.\begin{array}{l} \text{and that} \\ \text{is sufficient} \\ \text{reason for} \\ \text{valuing X.} \end{array}\right.$

We have shown that, in principle, the three statements within the brackets may be subjected to controlled inquiry. It is always possible, however, that men may agree concerning the outcome of such inquiry and still disagree concerning the value of X. For example, men may agree that X does, in fact, lead to Y, but still not agree as to whether this fact constitutes good reasons or justification for valuing X. In the face of such disagreements, orderly inquiry may be continued by agreeing, so to speak, to move the brackets one place to the right. That is, if the disagreement is over the value of Y the the assertion "Y is good" must be unpacked. If, for example, it can be shown that Y leads to Z or that the goodness of Y is entailed by S, then perhaps it may be agreed that this is a good reason for valuing Y and, hence, for valuing X.

A crucial case is, of course, one in which someone asserts that "I like X" is sufficient reason or justification for valuing X. Now, either the matter at issue is trivial or is important. If trivial, then "I like X" may be construed in trivial fashion and still be deemed sufficient justification. If important, then "I like X" must be construed to mean "Valuing X is in harmony with my basic character." Once again, then, we face the question of whether character can be subjected to orderly investigation and reconstruction.

Now, there is a sense in which the fact that "X is in harmony with my basic character" is always sufficient reason or justification for valuing X—indeed, the only sufficient reason possible. For a person who understands himself fully and is fully in control of himself will value X if and only if X is in harmony with his basic character. It follows that for such a perfect being justification of a value judgment must remain a personal rather than a publicly verifiable affair and all values would be reducible to personal relativism. Since, however, we are less than perfect, we sometimes can and do call our own character into question and seek better ways of structuring experience with respect to value. When, however, an individual is entirely satisfied with his present way of valuing, that is, when a person behaves as if he were perfect, he simply pays no attention to what others advance as good reasons for viewing matters otherwise. And, of course, the same remark may be made with respect to knowing. All this, once again, shows that in both knowing and valuing some dissatisfaction with one's present patterns of meanings is a necessary condition for inquiry and judgment. In the absence of a recognized problem, both knowing and valuing go forward on the level of recognition and there is no occasion for inquiry and judgment.

It follows that, from the standpoint of teaching, a student's environment should be arranged so that a problematic situation is created in which, with the help of the teacher, the student can create and test reconstructed patterns of meaning. How best to accomplish this with various students in a variety of situations is an empirical question that may properly be studied by a developing science of teaching.

## EDUCATING FOR IMPROVED VALUING

No attempt has herein been made to discuss in detail all of the many varieties of disagreement about value that do, in fact, arise, nor to analyze all of the complexities involved in the valuations that man is daily called upon to make. The intent has been simply to suggest that in our present state of understanding there appear to be no compelling reasons for concluding that valuations must always remain beyond scientific control. In any event, since both philosophy and education profess to be concerned with the integration of human experience—with "seeing life steadily and seeing it as a whole"—both should work at the challenge of trying to put together again the worlds of fact and value that have been rent asunder by the development of science.

As far as the schools are concerned, they should no more be expected to give students the "right answers" to their personal valuation-problems than to *give them* the answers to other personal problems: What's wrong with the car when it won't start on a cold morning? Which is the better radio kit for the money? What should I do for acne? On the other hand, most educators would agree that something is wrong with a curriculum that remains totally unrelated to such personal problems. A well-rounded program of school experiences should help students increasingly to gain control over all their experience. More specifically, it should (1) increase their knowledge and understanding of the forces and mechanisms that operate in their natural and social environment, (2) develop and strengthen habits of orderly inquiry and controlled judgment, and (3) perhaps most important of all it should lead students into an increasingly comprehensive and integrative reconstruction of their patterns of meaning—their structuring of reality, including their own character.

Unfortunately, even where it is recognized that such objectives involve value as well as fact—involve the emotional dimension of meaning as well as the rational, there is frequently still a tendency to assume that radically different kinds of teaching procedures or approaches are necessary in order to relate the curriculum to a student's personal value problems in contrast to his personal factual problems. For example, in order to increase knowledge and understanding of the environment, the schools provide a program of science—studies beginning in the early elementary grades, building toward the formal study of mathematics, biology, physics, and chemistry in the high school years. When viewed as a whole, this program of studies is intended not merely to provide students with certain facts or truths of natural science, but to help them grasp how man has struggled to gain understanding and control over his natural environment and how he has constructed, tested, and reconstructed his patterns of meaning with this end in view.

By contrast, where is a program of studies to build a grasp of the way man has struggled to understand and regulate the moral dimensions of his life? In the science program, we learn not only that the sun is the center of our solar system but also that wise men formerly thought otherwise, what some of the difficulties were, how the view came to be changed, and what are some of the advantages of the present view. We learn something about the value of such scientific progress and something about the methods by which it is accomplished. Should not the school also teach about how man has tried to structure his moral experience by developing various principles or codes for the regulation of behavior, how wise men have disagreed about the validity and adequacy, what reasons have been advanced, and something of the value and methods of developing moral judgments? In short, isn't it time the schools recognize that a program of training (in contrast to education) is no more adequate in morals and aesthetics than in science and literature?

It would be easy to conclude that the schools should introduce a program of studies in social, moral, and aesthetic values paralleling present programs in science and history. Such an innovation would probably mark a step forward, but it would not come to grips with the fundamental educational problem. Moreover, introduction of a new program of studies would simply aggravate the pressing educational problem noted in the last chapter —the problem of how to cope with the fact of rapidly expanding knowledge. What is needed, therefore, is once again an emphasis upon fundamental structures and principles, building an intuitive grasp in the early grades as a foundation for an increasingly systematic and comprehensive understanding in succeeding years of schooling.

Even if we were competent to write it, adequate discussion of this suggestion would obviously run far beyond the limits of an introductory study in philosophy of education. There is, however, one aspect of the problem that is so closely related to the main concerns of this chapter that a brief discussion may be in order. It is the matter of so-called intrinsic versus extrinsic motivation.

It is frequently said that teachers should encourage students to develop an interest in the school's various subject matters just for their own sake, rather than because it is necessary to do well in school in order later to attain vocational and social success as an adult citizen. It is said, and correctly so, that, in the first place, an emphasis on schooling as a means to remote adult goals is a weak motivator and, second, that if, nevertheless, the student should adopt such a view of schooling he would be missing the point of the liberal dimension of education. In less comprehensive terms, emphasis on intrinsic rather than extrinsic motivation is taken to mean that grades, rewards, and punishments of various sorts in connection with academic competition should be deemphasized, whereas teachers should strive to make lessons interesting, either in their own right or by tying them to the immediate problems and interests of students. Although many teachers would agree to all this in principle, most find it difficult to translate it into practice, especially at a time when the public has become afraid that we may lose the educational sector of our many-sided competition with Russia.

When it is recognized, however, that intrinsic and extrinsic are simply the names we use to designate and differentiate, in a contextually significant manner, functions or aspects of our valuing, then it can be seen that the problem of developing motivation (that is, developing, enlarging, and refining, attitudes, preferences, values) is never a matter of intrinsic *versus* extrinsic but the more fundamental matter of restructuring patterns of meaning and, hence, of habitual modes of behavior. The trouble with so-called extrinsic motivators is not that they are not in fact extrinsically important. It is rather that, when attention is focused too exclusively upon them, they tend to be viewed as intrinsically valuable and, worse still, that educationally inappropriate or even immoral means may be adopted in order to attain them. Thus it is that where great emphasis is placed upon academic prizes of one kind or another students may resort to cramming, even cheating, in order to attain the prize or the more subtle rewards that accrue to the prizewinner.

What is needed, of course, is an educational-social climate in which the whole process of formal schooling may develop as part of a progressively enlarged and refined pattern of meaning. It has often been remarked that our really great teachers seldom seem to be directly concerned with either motivation or discipline. Problems in this area are somehow taken care of by the very act of teaching. No doubt such teachers, either consciously or intuitively, recognize that interest, effort, and meaning are all parts of the same package. The very attitude they adopt toward the subject matter and toward the teaching of it enables students to gain the kind of meaningful perspective that elicits interest when the subject is viewed intrinsically, and effort when viewed extrinsically. Under such a perspective, subject matter does not remain in a compartment by itself where it may be viewed as more or less interesting in its own right and more or less valuable as a means to something else. On the contrary, it may become for the student, as it already has for the teacher, an integrated part of the complex web of meanings by which reality is structured. It thus enriches both fact and value and increases control over the course of subsequent experience, while personality and character emerge in the process.

### Suggestions for Additional Reading

Chapter 22 through 26 in Titus, *Living Issues in Philosophy*, and chapter XII in Randall and Buchler, *Philosophy, an Introduction,* provide a good introduction to the basic problems involved in theory of value. Chapter 7, in Beck, *Philosophic Inquiry,* covers about the same ground and in addition presents Beck's own point of view known as "Objective Relativism."

Students interested in a more extensive analysis of the major contemporary points of view with respect to value should read such books as Rice, *On the Knowledge of Good and Evil,* and Pepper, *The Sources of Value.* One of the most influential analyses of valuation at the present time is Stevenson, *Ethics and Language.* Two other recent works that students usually find insightful are Brandt, *Ethical Theory,* and Baier, *The Moral Point of View.*

Students interested in studying Dewey's point of view in connection with problems of valuation should, probably, first of all consult Dewey's *Logic: The Theory of Inquiry,* since his theory of valuation is part of his theory of inquiry. Chapters IX and XXIV are especially concerned with judgments of value. There is a paperback edition of a collection of Dewey's essays called, *Philosophy of Education,* part III of which is devoted to "Value and Thought." In *Reconstruction in Philosophy* (also in paperback) chapter VII is devoted to value considerations. More extended discussion of value questions will be found in Dewey, *The Quest for Certainty,* and Dewey and Tufts, *Ethics.*

A number of books in philosophy of education give attention to the nature of value judgments and their relation to the work of the schools. Students may wish to read chapter 5 in Brubacher, *Modern Philosophies of Education,* and chapters 8, 9, and 10 in Morris, *Philosophy and the American School.*

# CHAPTER 8

# *What Is Man?*

FROM A biological standpoint man is *Homo sapiens.* Along with the apes (i.e., gorillas, chimpanzees, orangutans, and gibbons), man is an anthropoid and together they constitute a portion of the order Primate. Primates, in turn, are a portion of the larger order Mammalia. It is sometimes said that man is thus a distant cousin of the apes since it appears that somewhere in the long course of evolution man and apes came from a common ancester. Their lines of descent (or ascent?) diverged, however, some seven million years ago.

All men and women now living are members of the same species, and there appears to be no reason for assuming that any group or race of modern man is inherently superior to any other group as a whole. It is customary, nevertheless, to classify modern man into so-called *races,* based chiefly on the simple matter of skin color. We thus speak of the white or Caucasian race, the yellow or Mongolian, the black or Negroid, the brown or Malaysian, and the red or Amerind. The arbitrariness involved in such classification can be noted when it is realized that some "white men" actually have darker skin than some "brown men" or "black men." Actually, in addition to skin color, other factors such as type of hair, eyes, lips, and nose are usually considered, but of course the deciding factor is usually a matter of what is merely assumed concerning the ancestors of the individual in question.

## MAN AND NATURE

There is an obvious sense in which man is part of nature. The same substances and chemicals that are found in man are found in other parts of nature, and without natural nourishment man dies. Moreover, it is difficult to be sure that any of man's alleged distinctive characteristics, such as rationality, self-consciousness, and the ability to make and use tools and language, mark a sharp break or discontinuity. It may be that as far as these characteristics are concerned, it is in degree rather than in kind that man differs from the other animals. On the other hand, in addition to being an integral part of nature there is the perennial question as to whether man is also something more. Does man, either innately or by development, transcend the rest of nature?

During the course of some twenty-five hundred years of Western culture, an almost endless variety of views concerning the nature of man have been developed. Even today when we are in a position to survey these views, there is no general agreement among scholars concerning a simple but adequate classification. There are, of course, certain major themes that run through many of the interpretations—for example, the notion that the distinctive aspect of man is his rationality. This theme was highly developed in classical times and was revived and modified during the Rennaissance. Largely, but not entirely, in contrast to this theme is the Hebrew-Christian view that the essential nature of man can be understood only in relation to his divine origin and destiny. In the Middle Ages, particularly through the work of Aquinas, a synthesis of these two themes was developed. Partially contrasting with both of these themes is the emphasis of naturalism which, in its long development from pre-Socratic times to the present, has produced such numerous interpretations as materialism, mechanism, atheism, humanism, evolutionism, and vitalism.

From the standpoint of their direct bearing on educational procedures, perhaps one of the more useful ways of looking at various interpretations of man is to group them according to whether they view man as essentially in conflict with nature, essentially delimited by nature and hence incapable of truly opposing nature, or essentially a "nature maker," that is, a creature who is a significant factor in making nature what it is and what it will become. Each of these views has some obvious and some not so obvious bearings on education, ranging from attitudes about aesthetics to views about the proper conservation of natural resources.[1]

## Man Against Nature

It is sometimes difficult for middle-class Americans, living in our midcentury affluent society, to recognize how arduous life has been and continues to be for most members of the human race. Nature has appeared to be man's enemy. Only by unceasing efforts has man been able to protect himself against the rigors of nature's hostile winds and rains, the scorching heat of summer, and the bitter cold of winter, to say nothing of nature's earthquakes, tornadoes, floods, forest fires, landslides, and volcanic eruptions. In addition to these inanimate forces arrayed against him, the flora and fauna of nature have not willingly supplied man with food and clothing. Let man stumble and the jungle overruns his garden, the smaller animals escape his traps, and the larger animals pounce upon him, while night and day pestilence and infirmity are never far away.

Moreover, it is not only the natural environment that is man's enemy but also the nature within. The same energies within man that enable him to be violent and rapacious enough to overcome his natural enemies tend to drive him into violent struggle with his fellow men and even with himself. Indeed, when conditions are such that man has time and energy left over from the struggle against nature, he tends to get into trouble. Idle hands are the instrument of the Devil and holidays from work are times for increase in violence and debauchery. At the present time when

[1] For a brief discussion of some of the bearings on education see chap. 10 and 11 in Phenix, *Philosophy of Education*.

there is serious talk of a four-day work week, a number of thoughtful people are pointing out that without increased emphasis on education for leisure time it could be very dangerous to so shorten the time that man must labor. It is no simple matter for man to learn how to utilize his leisure hours in ways that are, at best, socially beneficial and, at least, not injurious to others and to himself.

When nature is viewed as man's enemy, civilization is said to represent man's more-or-less-successful subjugation of nature. And in some ways the record of man's achievements is rather impressive, although the imbalance between his conquest of the natural environment and his frustrating cold war with the nature within is rather obvious. Even the most optimistic reading of the record may, however, lead to eventual pessimism, for just as the most successful individual is finally overtaken by death the human race itself is evidently doomed by an entropic universe. The philosopher Schopenhauer (1788-1860) after a careful look at history had this to say:

The will to be, the will to live, is the cause of all struggle, sorrow, and evil in the world. A world of ceaseless striving and battle, in which the different forms of the blind will to exist struggle with one another, a world in which the little fishes are devoured by the larger ones is not a good world, but an evil one, indeed, the worst of all possible worlds. The life of man is not worth living because it is full of misery: It follows from the very nature of the human will that it would be full of pain and misery. Life consists of blind craving, which is painful so long as it is not satisfied, and which, when satisfied, is followed by new painful desires, and so on, *ad nauseam*. We are never permanently satisfied, there is a worm in every flower. We are like shipwrecked mariners who struggle and struggle to save their wearied bodies from the terrible waves, only to be engulfed at last. Every breath we draw is a protest against the death that is constantly threatening us, and against which we are battling every second. But Death must conquer after all, for we are his by birth, and he simply plays with his prey a little longer before devouring it.

. . . After one life has run down, the will repeats the same old process in new individuals. The life of most men is weary yearning and torture, a dreamy tottering through the four ages toward death, accompanied by a succession of trivial thoughts. It is like a clockwork that is wound up and goes without knowing why; and everytime a man is conceived and born, the clock of human life is wound up anew, in order to grind out the same old hackneyed tune which it has played so many countless times before, measure for measure, beat for beat, with insignificant variations.

. . . man is a heartless and cowardly egoist, whom fear makes honest and vanity sociable, the only way to succeed in the world is to be as grasping and dishonest as the rest. The progress of knowledge and civilization does not mend matters; it simply brings with it new needs and, with them, new sufferings and new forms of immorality. The so-called virtues, love of labor, perseverance, temperance, frugality, are merely a refined egoism. In much wisdom is much grief, and he that increaseth knowledge increaseth sorrow. History is an interminable series of murders, robberies, intrigues, and lies; if you know one page of it, you know them all.[2]

In order to avoid the eventual pessimism inherent in the view that nature is man's enemy, many elaborate theological and religious ideas have been developed. These have taken many forms, involving so many subtleties that generalizations are bound to be overly simple. Many such forms have centered around a belief that man may transcend his natural death and enter into another life in a realm in which he is less alien. Life in our world is thus viewed as essentially a preparation, or perhaps a test, for life after natural death. Sometimes it has been thought that those who do well in this life will be specially rewarded in the next, and other times it has been said that the reverse is true, that is, that in the next life rewards will be in inverse proportion, so that the last shall be first. And, of course, there has been much disagreement concerning the proper concrete or behavioral meanings to attach to "do well" and "reward." One interesting version that has been believed by millions of people is that the spirit or soul of man is born again and again in various bodies, even in the bodies of animals, until the spirit is purified to the point where it is released from all further struggle, thus attaining nirvana.

A belief in life after death may produce a wide range of moti-

[2] As presented by Frank Thilly, *A History of Philosophy*, Holt, New York, 1914, pp. 488-489.

vations with respect to natural life. On the one hand, where life is unusually difficult, it may provide through its promise of eventual reward the consolation and resignation that enables man to endure his hardships, although it has frequently been necessary, in order to prevent attempts to gain the reward prematurely, to teach that suicide is sinful. On the other hand, the desire to live in a way best calculated to attain rewards in the next life has motivated some to undertake most remarkable deeds. Depending upon their understanding of what kinds of behavior would be most highly rewarded, some individuals have devoted their lives to missionary work or to social service; others have concentrated upon stamping out sin, even burning sinners at the stake in order to save the sinners' souls and hence to collect the special rewards reserved for those who have not only saved themselves but have also saved others. And, of course, throughout history, individuals and organizations have capitalized on beliefs of this kind, using them to make men tractable slaves or zealous crusaders.

Fortunately, one of the more profoundly influential versions of "man against nature" is the belief that God has created man and placed him in a world specially designed as a maturing ground or school in which he may learn of the Fatherhood of God and the brotherhood of man. Although it appears that life in this specially planned environment presents rather more than an optimally educational challenge, God's grace makes it possible in the life after death for man to attain reward and perhaps further challenge. It follows that if man is to learn the lessons of this world he must find a kind of equilibrium between succumbing to nature and withdrawing from nature. In other words, man must live in the world but not become too much a part of it. Herbart (1776-1841) spoke to this point as follows:

It would be disastrous if ethics set its aim so high that it appeared to debase the things of this world. . . . An active and mature man will not be subject to a tempestuous fate that urges him on to an unknown goal, unaware whether he is driving or being driven. On each level of life he will attempt to attain serenity and reason. He will aim to attune his soul to accord with his environment, and from his vision of the Absolute he will derive his faith of the ultimate victory of the good. He will strive to acquire a harmony of mind that will allow him to move freely, but prudently, between the finite and the infinite, between the transient and the permanent. By noble participation in the joys and griefs of human life he will be led to a fuller appreciation of the pure light of the spirit, and his deeds will reflect the elation of his soul.[3]

Where nature is viewed as man's enemy, a prime objective of education is preparing the young for combat. Logically, this could mean that school should be the place where each new generation learns to develop, through study and experimentation, new and more effective ways of advancing civilization. Actually, however, societies have generally assigned an essentially conservative role to their schools. Why? In very early societies it is understandable that people may have been so afraid of losing the arts of civilization that they insisted upon the conservative function of teaching. No doubt in every age there have been some thoughtful persons who considered it desirable if young people were taught to be critical and inventive, hence more capable of improving the status quo, but it is only when a society is predominantly secure and self-confident—only when it feels it can afford a number of misfits and generally nonproductive members—that it will support a program of education designed to encourage serious experimentation and novelty. This is so because thinking is dangerous to all established institutions and customs and common sense says that it is better for young people to be right than original.

The United States emerged from World War II as, perhaps, the most overwhelmingly powerful and successful society the world had ever seen. At first glance it appeared that civilization was finally secure and a base had been established from which it would be possible to explore man's hidden potentials. The possibilities staggered the imagination. In a world at peace, the methods of combating nature developed by Western culture and

---

[3] *Samtliche Werke* vol. 11, pp. 456 and 458 as translated and presented by Robert Ulich, *History of Educational Thought*, American Book, 1950, p. 283.

applied so successfully in this country could be applied around the world, forcing nature to yield the food and fiber that would supply a material base upon which man could stand secure as he confidently reached for the stars. There would, of course, be mistakes and failures as blind alleys were explored, but man's adventurous spirit would triumph eventually.

But immediately something went wrong. In the first place, the complex world weighed a bit more on our shoulders than was anticipated and, second, since other nations were not willing to allow the atom bomb to remain our private property, we suddently recognized that rather than having secured civilization we had, in fact, simply made it possible for man (in a more individualized sense than ever before) to destroy civilization. Under these circumstances it is no wonder that a cautious conservativism gained in popularity and a society that had in the past romantically exaggerated the effectiveness of its schools then switched to an almost vicious criticism. In this period of confusion and lack of self-confidence, it is again not surprising that many professional educators have pessimistically concentrated upon finding ways of making the schools technologically right rather than optimistically searching for right ways of being original.

## Man Delimited by Nature

Aristotle once noted that whatever is according to nature cannot be changed by training. For example, it is a stone's nature to fall when left unsupported and, consequently, a stone cannot be trained to go upward even though it is tossed into the air 10,000 times. In the same way man cannot be taught to fly as a bird nor to breathe under water as a fish. In this sense man cannot fight against nature; he may kick and scream as he is pulled along or he may follow nature willingly. Freedom is thus, a subjective category and consists of recognizing necessity.

Under this view one may assume, either that the nature that engulfs man is a blind, purposeless force, or that it is a grand design for bringing to fruition a divine purpose. Perhaps the two most elaborate systems based on these alternative assumptions are the absolute idealism of Hegel and the dialectical materialism of Marx. Under either view, individual man viewed apart from the sweep of history has little meaning. Man attains significance only as he voluntarily identifies himself with the way things are going to go anyway. Of course, operationally, this usually means accepting a set of directives supplied by some leader supposedly endowed with superior discernment. It follows that the purpose of education is to set men free by preparing them, individually and collectively, to play the roles proper "in the nature of things."

More typically, the view that man is essentially bounded by nature has been coupled with the belief that man, nevertheless, has a considerable range of choice left open to him. Aristotle, for example, pointed out that nature supplies man with neither intellectual nor moral virtues—nature gives man merely the capacity for acquiring them. And, as we noted in Chapter 2, it was in this connection that Aristotle developed the pedagogical advice, "we learn by doing."

At first glance it might appear that there is little practical difference between the view that nature is man's enemy and the view that man, though having a considerable range of choice, is delimited by nature. The basic difference is in the way the area of freedom is regarded. Shall man use his freedom to study nature and learn how to fight against her, or to understand nature and cooperate with her? We have seen that, when nature (within and without) is regarded as his enemy, man has found it necessary to turn to God in order to avoid an overwhelming pessimism. In contrast, when nature is acknowledged as master, man may assume that evil arises only because men are still relatively ignorant. Even "natural evils," such as earthquakes and floods, cause misery only because men have not yet learned enough of nature's laws to control or to get out of the road of such lawful happenings.

Perhaps the most common theological view held in conjunction with this view of man is deism. One might say that a deist believes that God created and set in operation an orderly, lawful universe. Since God is perfect (all knowing, all powerful, all good), he created the universe without mistakes or omissions of any kind. Consequently, he never finds it necessary to interfere with its orderly operation. Miracles should be expected only from a less-than-perfect Creator—a Creator who either changes his mind in midstream or else had failed to plan adequately in the first place. Moreover, if the plan provides for man having a certain amount of freedom and enough intelligence to learn from the consequences of his acts, then, in the long run, miracles that shield man from the consequences of his own mistakes are not really benevolent from an educational standpoint.

Carried to its conclusion, this approach to the nature of man results in what has sometimes been called "The Theory of Natural Goodness," which stands in sharp contrast to the traditional doctrine of the Church known as "original sin." The Biblical account of Adam and Eve tells of their banishment from the Garden of Eden. Whether viewed as history or as metaphor, the Church taught that their sin was perpetually shared by all their descendants. In other words, because of this original sin each human child is born evil and can be saved only by the sacraments and ministrations of the Church. But, in spite of this tradition, men such as Rousseau reasoned that an all-good and all-powerful God would not create something evil. There was no doubt that men do evil things, but it surely is in spite of their divine creation, not because of it.

Rousseau taught, therefore, that man should return to nature and seek to learn again the simple, unsophisticated life that God must have intended. Midst the corruption of Europe's absolute monarchies of the eighteenth century, such reasoning had a strong appeal to many intellectuals and others sensitive to the injustice of the prevailing social system. There is little doubt that such teaching was influential in producing both the American and the French revolutions. And, as we noted in Chapter 2, the philosophy of education developed by Rousseau exerted considerable, although delayed, effect upon American educators. Indeed, the more extreme forms of permissiveness and "child centeredness" of progressive education was, no doubt, due much more to the influence of Rousseau than of John Dewey, even though in the popular mind all of "progressivism" has become linked with Dewey's name.

From the standpoint of the nature of man, however, the point to be noted, in reference to the views of man discussed thus far, is that whether man is thought to be born evil or good—whether man is thought to be in essential conflict with nature or essentially a part of (and thus delimited by) nature—man is viewed as endowed with a definite *nature,* that is, a universally common set of (natural and/or supernatural) instincts, faculties, or enfolded potentials or forms that constitute the distinctive *essence* of man. It follows that education should take its cues (for both objectives and methodology) from this alleged "nature of man." For, even if one desired to establish a system of schools designed deliberately to miseducate, one would still need to understand the nature of his prey, just as big-game hunters find it advantageous to become thoroughly familiar with the instincts, the abilities, and the limitations of the object of their quest.

## Man as Nature Maker

There is an obvious sense in which man is changing the face of the world and is thus making or remaking nature. Increasingly, it is the artificial or man-made parts of his environment that captures the focus of man's attention. He has not only rearranged to suit himself such molar parts of nature as hills, streams, stones, and metals, but has literally created new combinations of elements to further purposes that he has developed for himself. When this view of man is emphasized, civilization is neither the record of man's fight against nature nor the unfolding history of nature's grand design; civilization is, rather, that part of nature (both within and without) that man himself has wrought. It all began when, after countless years of using natural objects as implements, man had the temerity to look at a natural object and say "I can make one better than that!"

All of this can be recognized without conceding that man has in any fundamental way vaulted out of nature's bounds or basically altered the design of the universe. But, repeatedly over the centuries, some men have asked why it is necessary to assume that either the universe or the design of the universe is already completed. Once it was noted that the universe appeared to be dynamic rather than static—in a state of becoming rather than of simple being—it became natural to ask why we should assume that the answer to "Becoming what?" is already fixed. Perhaps the universe is truly open-ended. Perhaps the sense of choice that man experiences subjectively is an objectively significant aspect of the universe. Rather than being fixed in advance, perhaps the essence of a thing is contingent upon what happens to that thing—contingent upon the context into which it is placed and the use to which it is put. And, in the case of a self-conscious, living thing such as man, perhaps his essence or nature is at least in part determined by what he decides. Perhaps we *are* what we *do*. And, to the extent that we could have done otherwise, we could now *be* otherwise.

In any event, when the universe is viewed as open, thus providing (as William James once suggested) some "elbow room" for man, education cannot take its cue from a fixed, universal "human nature." When viewed as a process of personal development, education is a process in which significant selves are created. Education is thus essentially character development, and all forms of both scientific and humanistic knowledge are auxiliary to the building of rich and disciplined character. By evaluating the past, man can create ideals for guiding his decisions that affect the future, but if the universe (including his own character) is truly open, then all such guidelines should be held as tentative—subject to reconstruction from the vantage point of additional experience.

Over the years, this view of man as nature maker has tended to take two main forms which we shall call the *personalist* and the *impersonalist* views. Either of these forms may or may not be combined with appropriate theological assumptions. What is at issue is whether man discovers the openness of the universe primarily from looking inward or from looking outward.

When man looks inward and sees openness, it is likely to take the form of the discovery that *to be* carries with it the obligation *to be something*. This presents the individual with more of a quandary than a problem. A problem has been described as a "forked-road" situation but, when one suddenly grasps the truth that he must decide for himself his own essence, it is not a matter of choosing this road or that; it is more like finding oneself in the middle of an endless desert with no roads of any kind in sight. This kind of quandary tends to produce despair or, at the very least, anxiety. And, since introspection is often confused with a view of the world, it is easy to conclude that everyone else is in the same predicament.

. . . you must take the position that you are the most important being in the world. There is no other possible platform from which to view life. You are the center of everything, the focal headquarters for all that you experience. And you always place a higher valuation on your continuing existence than on any other being in the world. Heroic suicides to the contrary notwithstanding, every individual's conscious selfhood exerts a continuing existential judgment in its own favor. That is to say, we assign to our own selves—without any help from Christian doctrine or democratic preachments about the worth of the individual—we assign to our own selves, I say, an *absolute* value and an ultimate worth.[4]

In contrast, when one discovers openness by looking outward and noting the unsettled or problematic character of experience viewed objectively, one is likely to adopt a more sanguine attitude. The inescapability of choice that a personalist views as an "awful responsibility" may appear, when viewed in a more impersonal manner, to be an exhilarating opportunity. After all, before a person can think about himself, he must already be a thinking person. A person must already be something before he can ask "What am I?" The question should really be "What am I thus far?" When generalized, the question becomes "What is man *thus far*?" and although available evidence is not such to warrant unbridled optimism concerning what man may become, still it hardly seems to point to unqualified pessimism. Conse-

[4] Van Cleve Morris, "Existentialism and the Education of Twentieth Century Man," *Educational Theory*, vol. XI, No. 1, p. 53, January, 1961.

quently, the openness of the universe, when interpreted by an impersonalist, tends toward meliorism—that is, the belief that man has at least a fighting chance to correct some of the evils of this world and to make still better some of the goods.

In spite of the fact that the personalist view does frequently lead, as noted above, to the assignment of absolute worth to one's own existence, it is generally coupled with a plea for recognition that cosmic fairness somehow demands realization that every other person, at least from *his* point of view, is also of absolute worth. Consequently, it is urged that one should deal with others, not as objects but as subjects.

In contrast, an impersonalist urges that one should deal with oneself as objectively as possible, and thus avoid the conclusion that one's own existence is always of supreme value. It is an interesting question as to which is the more difficult, to relate empathically to others in terms of their subjectivity, or to objectify one's own character and thus evaluate one's own desires and aspirations in terms of impersonal criteria. Indeed, an interesting question is whether the two views do not amount substantially to the same thing.

When these views are coupled with religious doctrines about the nature of man and of the universe, there is a tendency for a personalist mystically to reaffirm the Fatherhood of God whereas an impersonalist tends toward rational judgment in favor of the brotherhood of man. Since the two are mutually implicative, the question again arises as to whether there is any essential difference between the two points of view. Some have concluded, therefore, that, once the openness of the universe is grasped and man's role as "nature maker" is recognized, the question of personalist versus impersonalist approach is largely a matter of differing individual temperament rather than of fundamental philosophic disagreement. It may be that from an ontological or metaphysical point of view there is little difference. But in epistemology the difference becomes noticeable and in axiology there is a parting of the ways, with the personalist adopting a noncognitive personal relativism and the impersonalist insisting

upon the cognitivist principle of the continuity of inquiry.[5]
Finally, with respect to religion, since it may be possible that
these two views represent the present growing edge of religious
thought, it would be premature to attempt a definitive
assessment.

## MAN AND SOCIETY

Since education may be viewed as a sociopolitical institution
as well as a process of personal growth, the educational bearings
of the various views concerning the nature of man may be more
clearly seen when these views are extended to include comment
upon the relation of the individual to society. Again, the countless
variations in the way that this relation is conceived may be
grouped under three main themes that correspond roughly to the
positions already discussed. The individual may be viewed as in
essential conflict with society. This view holds that any form of
social organization and regulation is a more or less necessary
evil. A second view is that the individual is essentially a creature
of society having little or no meaning or significance apart from
the social organization that molds his personality and character.
The third alternative presents man as a socially creative force in
the universe. The indivudual is thus viewed as a nexus of social
activity.

### The Individual Versus Society

We have noted that the passions and energies that enable man
to fight against nature tend to get men into conflict with each
other. It has been argued, therefore, that man, in his natural
state, is at war both with nature and with all other men. Thomas
Hobbes (1588-1679) noted that this natural state of man is a
miserable condition and reasoned that early men, recognizing
this, must have been willing to subjugate themselves to the will

---

[5] The "Empirical Personalism" of Harold O. Soderquist may be an exception. See his *The Person and Education*, Merrill, Columbus, Ohio, 1964.

of some king or ruler in order to defend themselves against invasion and the injuries to one another. In other words, men formed a *commonwealth*.

Hobbes believed that human nature is such that it leads men toward "partiality, pride, revenge, and the like," and against "justice, equity, modesty, mercy, and, in sum, doing to others as we would be done to." Consequently, men need some "visible power to keep them in awe, and tie them by fear of punishment to the performance of their covenants." He said:

The only way to erect such a common power, as may be able to defend them from the invasion of foreigners and the injuries of one another, and thereby to secure them in such sort as that, by their own industry, and by the fruits of the earth, they may nourish themselves and live contentedly; is, to confer all their power and strength upon one man, or upon one assembly of men, that may reduce all their wills, by plurality of voices, unto one will: which is as much as to say, to appoint one man, or assembly of men, to bear their person; and everyone to own and acknowledge himself to be the author of whatsoever he that so beareth their person, shall act or cause to be acted in those things which concern the common peace and safety; and therein to submit their wills, everyone to his will, and their judgments, to his judgment. This is more than consent or concord; it is a real unity of them all, in one and the same person, made by covenant of every man with every man, in such a manner as if every man should say to every man, "I authorize and give up my right of governing myself to this man, or to this assembly of men, on this condition, that thou give up thy right to him, and authorize all his actions in like manner." This done, the multitude so united in one person, is called a *commonwealth*, in Latin, *civitas*. This is the generation of that great LEVIATHAN, or rather, to speak more reverently, of that *mortal god*, to which we owe under the *immortal God*, our peace and defense. For by this authority, given him by every particular man in the commonwealth, he hath the use of so much power and strength conferred on him, that by terror thereof he is enabled to perform the wills of them all, to peace at home and mutual aid against their enemies abroad. And in him consisteth the essence of the commonwealth; which, to define it, is, one person, of whose acts a great multitude, by mutual covenants one with another, have made themselves everyone the author, to the end he may use the strength and means of them all, as he shall think expedient, for their peace and common defense.

And he that carrieth this person is called *sovereign*, and said to have sovereign power; and everyone besides, his *subjects*.[6]

Two points should be noted: first, that individual man is the locus of all strength, will, and "natural rights," and second, that in order to promote "the common peace and safety" he enters into a covenant (including realistic means for its enforcement) that diminishes his individual rights and power. The individual buys an orderly society, so to speak, and the price is his own "natural sovereignty."

John Locke (1632-1704), reasoning from these same general premises concerning individual man's natural rights, nevertheless questioned whether human nature is such that men must so largely relinquish their rights in order to obtain peace and security. Perhaps man's natural state, although a state of liberty, is not a state of license. Since it is widely acknowledged that the views of John Locke exerted a profound influence upon our Founding Fathers, let us quote at length from his essay on civil government.

. . . though man in that state have an uncontrollable liberty to dispose of his person or possessions . . . yet he has not liberty to destroy himself, or so much as any creature in his possession, but where some nobler use than its bare preservation calls for it. The state of nature has a law of nature to govern it, which obliges everyone; and reason, which is that law, teaches all mankind who will but consult it, that, being all equal and independent, no one ought to harm another in his life, health, liberty, or possessions. For men being all the workmanship of one omnipotent and infinitely wise Maker—all the servants of one sovereign Master, sent into the world by His order, and about His business—they are His property. Whose workmanship they are, made to last during His, not one another's pleasure; and being furnished with like faculties, sharing all in one community of nature, there cannot be supposed any such subordination among us, that may authorize us to destroy one another, as if we were made for one another's uses, as the inferior ranks of creatures are for ours. Everyone, as he is bound to preserve himself, and not to quit his station willfully, so, by the like reason, when his own preservation comes not in competition, ought he, as much as he can, to preserve the rest of mankind, and not, unless it be to do justice on an offender, take away or impair the life,

[6] Thomas Hobbes, *Of Commonwealth* (Part Two of *Leviathan*). Portions quoted are from the early pages of chap. XXVII.

or what tends to the preservation of the life, the liberty, health, limb, or goods of another.[7]

Furthermore, Locke reasoned, perhaps man's natural rights include the right of enforcing natural law. This is to say that, if any man should transgress natural law, every other man has the right to punish the offender. Moreover, Locke concluded that anyone injured by such a transgression has also the right of enacting reparation.

From all this, Locke reasoned, first, that it is not inevitable that men must give up their natural rights to some sovereign in order to attain peace and safety and, second, that when men do enter into social compacts of one kind or another it does not mean that they have given up all their natural rights.

To this strange doctrine—viz. that in the state of nature everyone has the executive power of the law of nature—I doubt not but it will be objected that it is unreasonable for men to be judges in their own cases, that self-love will make men partial to themselves and their friends. And on the other side, that ill nature, passion, and revenge will carry them too far in punishing others; and hence nothing but confusion and disorder will follow; and that therefore God hath certainly appointed government to restrain the partiality and violence of men. I easily grant that civil government is the proper remedy for the inconvenience of the state of nature, which must certainly be great where men may be judges in their own case, since 'tis easy to be imagined that he who was so unjust as to do his brother an injury, will scarce be so just as to condemn himself for it. But I shall desire those who make this objection, to remember that absolute monarchs are but men, and if government is to be the remedy of those evils which necessarily follow from men being judges in their own cases, and the state of nature is therefore not to be endured, I desire to know what kind of government that is, and how much better it is than the state of nature, where one man commanding a multitude, has the liberty to be judge in his own case, and may do to all his subjects whatever he pleases, without the least question or control of those who execute his pleasure; and in whatsoever he doth, whether led by reason, mistake, or passion, must be submitted to, which men in the state of nature are not bound to do one to another? And if he that

[7] John Locke, *An Essay Concerning the True Original Extent and End of Civil Government,* par. 6.

judges, judges amiss in his own or any other case, he is answerable for it to the rest of mankind.[8]

x   Whosoever therefore out of a state of nature unite into a community must be understood to give up all the power necessary to the ends for which they unite into society, to the majority of the community, unless they expressly agreed in any number greater than the majority. And this is done by barely agreeing to unite into one political society, which is all the compact that is, or needs be, between the individuals that enter into or make up a commonwealth. And thus what begins or actually constitutes any political society is nothing but the consent of any number of freemen capable of a majority to unite and incorporate into such a society. And this is that, and that only, which did or could give beginning to any lawful government in the world.[9]

But though men when they enter into society give up the equality, liberty and executive power they had in the state of nature into the hands of the society, to be so far disposed of by the legislative as the good of the society shall require; yet it being only with an intention in everyone the better to preserve himself, his liberty and property (for no rational creature can be supposed to change his condition with an intention to be worse), the power of the society, or legislative constituted by them, can never be supported to extend farther than the common good, but is obliged to secure everyone's property by providing against those three defects above-mentioned that made the state of nature so unsafe and uneasy. And so whoever has the legislative or supreme power of any commonwealth is bound to govern by established standing laws, promulgated and known to the people, and judges, who are to decide controversies by those laws; and to employ the force of the community at home only in the execution of such laws, or abroad, to prevent or redress foreign injuries, and secure the community from inroads and invasion. And all this to be directed to no other end but the peace, safety, and public good of the people.[10]

All of this, rather obviously, leads to the conclusion that the proper form of commonwealth is some type of constitutional and representative government, a government in which sovereignty is retained by the people and officers of the government are held accountable to the people. In the next chapter we shall want to examine this in greater detail, but in the context of our present concerns—that of the nature of the relation of man to society—we

---

[8] *Ibid.*, par. 13.
[9] *Ibid.*, par. 99.
[10] *Ibid.*, par. 131.

see that these views suggest that *human nature* exists prior to and is independent of society and that in order to form a society men must enter into social agreements that restrict or curb their "natural" inclinations or natures. Social arrangements are therefore extraneous and artificial and, in this sense, opposed to human nature.

With this in mind, we see that education gets involved in an inescapable conflict. On the one hand, when education is viewed as a process of personal development it appears that it should take its lead from the nature of human nature. Even though men disagree concerning this "human nature," they may still agree that some theory or view of human nature is an essential starting point for any theory of education.[11] Furthermore, since human nature is what it is, independent of particular and changing social relationships, it follows that education (as a process of personal development) should at all times and at all places be essentially the same: education should be a process by which man's distinctively human capabilities are developed.

Suppose, for example, that one believes the following five characteristics are the distinctive human qualities:

1. Self-consciousness.
2. Rationality—the power of abstract thought and the power to generalize.
3. The power of ethical discrimination and the power to choose.
4. Aesthetic appreciation.
5. The power to transcend the particular physical and cultural conditions in the midst of which life is lived.[12]

It is, then, the business of education, both formal and informal, to provide the kind of experiences that promote expansion and refinement of these five powers or qualities. In addition, a par-

[11] See, e.g., Charles D. Hardie, *Truth and Fallacy in Educational Theory.* It should be noted that in discussions of human nature and education the expression "human nature" is systematically ambiguous. Sometimes it refers to what is fixed in man by virtue of his being a man rather than a horse or tree or angel. Aristotle noted that what is by nature cannot be altered by training. But more often "human nature" refers to those distinctively human capacities that may be developed by proper education.

[12] This follows closely a list of characteristics discussed by Titus, *Living Issues in Philosophy*, 2nd ed., p. 129.

ticular school may, of course, offer some vocational training just as it may, for example, open a cafeteria or even a barber shop. But these additional services should never be confused with true education since they cater to the "needs" of a particular time and place rather than to the development of essential and unchanging human nature.

On the other hand, since, as Aristotle noted, education should be compatible with the constitution and should be of first importance as a matter of public concern and legislation, it is not sufficient to view education solely as a process of personal development; it must also be viewed as a sociopolitical institution. And it is here that the problem arises. For, if man's human nature is in essential conflict with his social arrangements, then education (as a series of experiences sponsored by a sociopolitical institution) will surely not be fully compatible with maximum development of each individual's natural capabilities.

This fundamental conflict is frequently glossed over in one way or another. Typically, in democratic societies, it is argued that the nature of democracy (and consequently, the legitimate demands of a democratic sociopolitical organization) is not in true conflict with man's basic nature. After all, democracy may be said to be based on respect for man's "natural rights" and concern for individual freedom. But, as we shall see in the next chapter, an actual nation, existing at a particular time and location, can never simply choose democracy in the abstract nor freedom in general; it must adopt specific forms of social and political organization involving specific freedoms and specific constraints. Reduced to overly simple terms, the problem that an educator thus faces is how to implement the ideal of the optimal development of each individual's natural endowment while at the same time promoting the kind of adjustment (or even conformity) necessary for harmonious continuation of sociopolitical arrangements that make possible such complex undertakings as formal education.

One way to solve this problem (at least intellectually) is to push the conception of "man versus society" to its radical conclusion. Few men have had the courage to do this, but Rousseau (1712-1778) suggested that man's original state of nature (as discussed by Locke, for example) had been long lost before men entered into the kind of social arrangements known in historical times. So-called social contracts were made not by men living in a state of nature but by men already corrupted by notions of property and inequality. Moreover, all social arrangements, even those of a democratic character, tended eventually to pervert man's original nature and to evolve toward depotism. Indeed, any form of government that could actually succeed in maintaining justice and the general welfare would be a government that really wasn't necessary. "For a country, in which no one either evaded the laws or made a bad use of magisterial power, could require neither laws nor magistrates." Rousseau's arguments seem to point to the conclusion that all sociopolitical arrangements are essentially evil and would be unnecessary if man could recapture the virtues of his original state, but that a government in which the people retain the right and feasibility of revolution is probably not so bad as other forms. Ideally, mankind should, through proper education, work back toward man's original nature and concomitantly disinvolve all sociopolitical entanglements. Rousseau wrote:

The first man who, having enclosed a piece of ground, bethought himself of saying *This is mine,* and found people simple enough to believe him, was the real founder of civil society. From how many crimes, wars, and murders, from how many horrors and misfortunes might not any one have saved mankind, by pulling up the stakes, or filling up the ditch, and crying to his fellows, "Beware of listening to this impostor; you are undone if you once forget that the fruits of the earth belong to us all, and the earth itself to nobody." But there is great probability that things had then already come to such a pitch, that they could no longer continue as they were; for the idea of property depends on many prior ideas, which could only be acquired successively, and cannot have been formed all at once on the human mind. Mankind must have made very considerable progress, and acquired considerable knowledge and industry which they must also have transmitted and increased from age to age, before they arrived at this last point of the state of nature.[13]

The first expansions of the human heart were the effects of a novel situation, which united husbands and wifes, father and children, under one roof. The habit of living together soon gave rise to the finest feelings known to humanity, conjugal love and paternal affection. Every family became a little society, the more united because liberty and reciprocal attachment were the only bonds of its union. . . . From living a softer life, both sexes also began to loose something of their strength and ferocity: but, if individuals became to some extent less able to encounter wild beasts separately, they found it, on the other hand, easier to assemble and resist in common.

The simplicity and solitude of man's life in this new condition, the paucity of his wants, and the implements he had invented to satisfy them, left him a great deal of leisure, which he employed to furnish himself with many conveniences unknown to his fathers: and this was the first yoke he inadvertently imposed on himself, and the first source of the evils he prepared for his descendants. For, besides continuing thus to enervate both body and mind, these conveniences lost with use almost all their power to please, and even degenerated into real needs, till the want of them became far more disagreeable than the possession of them had been pleasant. Men would have been unhappy at the loss of them, though the possession did not make them happy.[14]

From this radical view of the nature of man there follows an equally radical educational proposal: education should be taken out of the hands of the state and made largely an individual or small-group affair. At the very least, children should be removed from the corrupting influence of city life and allowed to develop close to nature under the protection of a teacher who would largely shield them from adults. Since a child's original nature is implanted by a beneficent God, the teacher should encourage full and free development of the child's natural impulses. Thus shielded from the corrupting influence of adult society, the child will develop a strength of character that will make it possible safely to introduce him gradually to experiences designed to teach him the realities of adult society while enabling him to

[13] From the opening paragraph of *The Social Contract*.
[14] *Ibid.*, par. 13 and 14.

recognize and immunize himself against such evil. As adults, the products of this education might then be expected to move toward dissolution of complex sociopolitical regulations, which would be an unnecessary evil were man to return to a state of natural goodness.[15]

### ✕ The Individual as a Creature of Society

Another way in which the conflict between individual and society may be resolved is by going to the other extreme and asserting that society or "the state" is the true locus of value, of human rights and significance. Hegel (1770-1831), working within the general philosophic traditions of idealism and rationalism, objected to the more or less sentimental romanticizing of man's so-called state of nature. Hegel reasoned that God created the universe to operate in a rational manner. Yet, rather obviously, the world is not now, nor has it ever been, in a perfect state. It is therefore, in a state of *becoming*. This is to say that it is moving toward actualization of its own perfect Ideal or Reason. Hegel believed that study of human history reveals the operation of a dialectic or evolutionary process toward such actualization of Divine Reason. Man, in his primitive or "natural" state is *merely* primitive, hence further removed from the actualization of Reason and Freedom than in later societies developed according to Natural dialectic.

Hegel believed that the course of history displays how, through operation of their natural impulses and desires, men have not only furthered evolution of the world toward the Ideal and at the same time accomplished their own desires, but have also accomplished a transformation of human desires, making possible a still higher form of dialectic progress. For example, it is now possible for man, through study of science and history, to recognize at least some of the rational processes that operate in the world. Such recognition was not possible for primitive man. Man may now, therefore, *consciously* cooperate in furthering the movement toward actualizing the Ideal. It follows, therefore,

[15] Rousseau made similar educational suggestions in his *Emile*.

that society, rather than being viewed as the source of restraint and limitation, should be viewed as the means by which actualization of the Ideal is promoted and Freedom is realized.

Concerning the then-current conceptions of man's "natural state," Hegel had this to say:

The error which first meets us is the direct contradictory of our principle that the state presents the realization of Freedom; the opinion, viz., that man is free by *nature*, but that in *society*, in the State—to which nevertheless he is irresistibly impelled—he must limit this natural freedom. That man is free by Nature is quite correct in one sense, viz., that he is so according to the Idea of Humanity; but we imply thereby that he is such only in virtue of his destiny—that he has an undeveloped power to become such; for the "Nature" of an object is exactly synonymous with its "Idea." But the view in question imports more than this. When man is spoken of as "free by Nature" the mode of his existence as well as his destiny is implied. His merely natural and primary condition is intended. In this sense a "state of Nature" is assumed in which mankind at large are in the possession of their natural rights with the unconstrained exercise and enjoyment of their freedom. . . . That assumption is one of those nebulous images which theory produces; an idea which it cannot avoid originating, but which it fathers upon real existence without sufficient historical justification.

What we find such a state of Nature to be in actual experience, answers exactly to the Idea of a *merely* natural condition. Freedom as the *ideal* of that which is original and natural, does not exist *as original and natural*. Rather must it be first sought out and won; and that by an incalculable medial discipline of the intellectual and moral powers. The state of Nature is, therefore, predominantly that of injustice and violence, of untamed natural impulses, of inhuman deeds and feelings. Limitation is certainly produced by society and the state, but it is a limitation of the mere brute emotions and rude instincts; as also, in a more advanced stage of culture, of the premeditated self-will of caprice and passion. This kind of constraint is part of the instrumentality by which only, the consciousness of Freedom and the desire for its attainment, in its true—that is Rational and Ideal form—can be obtained.[16]

Like Rousseau, Hegel had the courage to push his ideas to radical conclusions. The individual, his will and personality,

---

[16] G. W. F. Hegel, *Philosophical History*, from par. 34 and 35.

is relatively short lived and unimportant in and of himself in contrast to the State which is more permanent and more objectively Real. Individual desires are *subjective* while the "will of the state" can be said to have objective existence. Hegel thus spoke of:

> . . . the moral Whole, the *State*, which is that form of reality in which the individual has and enjoys his freedom; but on the condition of his recognizing, believing in and willing that which is common to the Whole. And this must not be understood as if the subjective will of the social unit attained its gratification and enjoyment through that common Will; as if this were a means provided for its benefit, as if the individual, in his relation to other individuals, thus limited his freedom, in order that this universal limitation—the mutual constraint of all—might secure a small space of liberty for each. Rather, we affirm, are Law, Morality, Government, and they alone, the positive reality and completion of Freedom. Freedom of a low and limited order, is merely caprice; which finds its exercise in the sphere of particular and limited desires.[17]

Under this view it is clear that wherever there appears to be some degree of conflict between individual and society, the will of the state should be given the right of way. Man may choose to swim against the current but, where the current is overwhelming, such a decision gives only an illusion of freedom. True freedom consists of recognizing necessity. It follows that education consists of enabling the individual to identify with the will of the state and thus to attain a significant place in the stream of Reality.

Hegel hesitated, however, to predict in any detailed way precisely what the will of the state should be in any given instance. In other words, Hegel's confidence was in the over-all, long-range outcome of the Process. At any given time, individual men can attain freedom only by identifying with the will of the state as it then and there exists. But there is no guarantee that any given state can be identified as the particular bud out of which the main branch of further dialectic evolution will continue.

[17] *Ibid.*, from par. 31.

Although men can now grasp the nature of the Process, it is not yet possible to forecast the Perfect Actualization.

Karl Marx (1818-1883) was less hesitant. Interpreting history in materialistic terms, he saw the dialectic process at work as a series of class struggles eventuating in one all-embracing, world-wide, Communistic state in which all of the usual notions of social class, private property, and individual rights will dissolve. Only in such a universal and classless society can man live in perfect freedom. In such a society, government as now known, will gradually wither away. For, as Rousseau noted, in a society where there is no conflict there is no need for law-enforcement agencies.

Furthermore, Karl Marx, in collaboration with Friedrich Engles, issued in 1847 *The Communist Manifesto* in which they declared it is the duty of the proletarians or working class to become the conscious agents of destiny and, through violent revolution, to establish one or more national states which can then work more effectively toward world-wide Communism.

> The Communists disdain to conceal their views and aims. They openly declare that their ends can be attained only by the forcible overthrow of all existing social conditions. Let the ruling classes tremble at the Communist revolution. The proletarians have nothing to lose but their chains. They have a world to win.
>
> Working men of all countries, unite![18]

Depending upon where emphasis is placed, the views thus far discussed suggest a wide variety of educational arrangements. For example, if the Hobbes "Leviathan" is viewed as more objectively *real* than its individual members, then, as in the case of the Hegelian state, any educational conflict between individual and society will always be resolved in favor of society. On the other hand, under the Lockean approach, if one differentiates between society and government (as Locke actually did), then the basic conflict may be thought of as between the individual and the state rather than between individual and society. In this

---

[18] The closing lines of *The Communist Manifesto*.

country, there has been a strong tendency to identify the national government as the state, hence as the villain, while state and local governments are cast in the role of defenders of individual freedoms. It is understandable that in the early days of the Republic men feared central government because it was more remote and represented a wider range of social and economic interests than were found in any of the provincial communities of that time. Moreover, it was "a remote government" that the colonies had found so distasteful.

Today, however, after a long history of the federal courts protecting individuals against violations of their rights by state and local governments, one cannot help but suspect that many who insist that it is only the federal government that is the "Lockean state" do so simply because they have found it much easier to extract special privileges from state and local governments than from federal. In any event, this kind of argument can be used for ignoring the inherent educational conflict between individual and society, as long as education as a sociopolitical institution is thoroughly dominated by provincial social traditions and by state and local politics.

In contrast to all this and, no doubt, in reaction to it, there are *Neo-Liberals* some persons who insist that we now know enough (conceptually and technologically) to build a new social order in which evils such as slums, illiteracy, malnutrition, and many forms of physical and mental ill-health can be largely eliminated, if we will use the schools to promote realistic social and political education and commitment. The way in which this sort of educational proposal is related to a conception of the nature of man is seldom stated as fully as one could wish. It may be that its advocates have managed to combine the idea that the universe is open and man (as mankind) is a nature-maker, with the notion that man (as an individual) is (or should be) delimited by society. In fact, there is talk to the effect that the very meaning of truth, beauty, goodness (hence all knowledge, wisdom, and morality) is delimited by various forms of social consensus. In any event, it is argued that the idea that education (as a sociopolitical institution and as the technology and profession of teaching) should be devoted to *education* (as a process of personal development) is an outmoded and ineffective idea. It is claimed that, when schools concentrate upon *individual* growth or reconstruction, their graduates are simply gobbled up by society's unreconstructed institutions, which remain essentially unaffected. After all, a cannibal doesn't become Christian by eating Christians. The schools should, therefore, embark upon building a new social order by a direct attack of double envelopment: on the one hand, students should be taught the realities of social, economic, and political power-structures, coupled with experiences designed to elicit commitment to certain democratic ideals and programs (based on an uncoerced social consensus); on the other hand, educators, as an organized socioeconomic power group, should undertake political action to insure that conditions will be favorable to the school playing such a role. The result would be a democratic "planning society" in contrast to a "planned society" of totalitarian form, although there still remains the question of the schools' function with reference to the plans that are progressively developed by such a "planning society."

### Man as a Nexus of Social Activity

Over the years, many have struggled to construct a way of understanding man that avoids both the paradoxes and the extremes involved in the views so far discussed.[19] Perhaps "man and society" can best be understood as a special case of "organism and environment." It has frequently been observed that man does not merely live in an environment, but *by means of* an environment. Even this observation, however, is only transitional to grasping the insight that life is an affair of organism *and* environment. In other words, the environment is in the organism just as much as the organism is in the environment. Either organ-

[19] The particular version presented here draws heavily upon the work of Arthur F. Bentley. See especially his *Inquiry into Inquiry*, and his *Process of Government*, Sect. II.

ism or environment may be discussed separately *as an abstraction,* but what is directly given for observation is the behavior of organism-environment.

At the level of physiological studies, it is becoming increasingly clear that to regard the human skin as the boundary between organism and environment is rather arbitrary. An embalmed corpse could, perhaps, be said to have existence *in* an environment, but wherever there is life there is constant transaction between and among elements that one moment may be viewed as part of the organism and the next as part of the environment. An organism cannot exist *as organism* apart from an environment, and, indeed, an environment has no existence *as environment* except as it is in transaction with an organism.

As for individual and society, to conceive, either of man existing apart from society in some so-called state of nature, or of a society or state as having existence and "will" apart from actual individuals is to create abstractions. Such abstractions may be useful tools for certain types of studies, but to imagine that these abstractions represent actual entities or a locus of values is to block further progress in understanding man as a nexus of social activity, which is, again, what is directly observable. In other words, man's behavior is social behavior just as his life is "environment life." By the same token, all of a society's desires and institutions are the desires and institutions of men—actual, particular men—just as any given environment is always the environment of particular organisms.

Under this view, the abstract conflict between individual and society resolves into particular conflicts—at particular times and places—between specific social individuals acting singly or in organized groups. Frequently, these conflicts center around differences of opinion concerning the proper dividing line between public and private affairs. In the next chapter, we shall need to look at this matter in considerable detail, but for now the point to be noted is that, since all human behavior is social (just as all living involves environment), the fact that a given instance of behavior can be shown to have social consequences does not mean that it should necessarily be a matter for public regulation. For, as John Dewey once noted, "the public has no hands." No matter how complex the machinery, "public or social control," the "will of the state," etc., is always a matter of actual human behavior undertaken for the purpose of controlling other actual human behavior. In every instance, what is at issue is not an abstract conflict between abstract entities, but the real problems of real men. And there can be no legitimate importing, a priori fashion, of principles, based on these abstractions, that authoratively settle problems in terms of either a privatism or a publicism (i.e., individualism or totalitarianism).

It follows that education (even in the case of an individual privately undertaking his own instruction) is always a social affair, for it is a human affair. Nevertheless, education as an abstract process of human development can be said to have no aims outside itself—that is, there is nothing in the process itself that dictates what particular direction it must take except as certain directions may be found *in fact* to close off or terminate the process while other directions are found to open up or promote the process. In this sense it may be said that education should be subordinate to nothing save more education. On the other hand, wherever education is actually taking place there are always involved specific persons with more or less clear aims on purposes. The view of man as a nexus of social activity does not, therefore, provide *the* answer to man's educational problems any more than it does to any other of the problems of men. It merely sweeps off the table the traditional doctrinaire solutions and, especially with respect to education, it denies that the starting point for educational theory must be some doctrine concerning the nature of man (or of society) *conceived abstractly*.

## SUGGESTIONS FOR ADDITIONAL READING

There was a time when a man could, perhaps, afford ignorance with respect to much that is now studied systematically by physical and cultural anthropology. That time, if it ever existed, is now long past. If one is to live, in any adequate fashion, in today's world, it is necessary to reconstruct narrow racist views concerning the nature of man. Students who have not had the advantage of formal course-work in general anthropology should study some of the standard texts available in this field. In this connection, Jacobs and Stern, *General Anthropology* (Number 20 in the College Outline Series) should prove helpful.

Another, more popular paperback on the nature of man is Ashley Montagu's, *The Biosocial Nature of Man*. Students frequently report that they find this little book very enlightening.

Some of the standard introductory texts in philosophy have chapters or sections devoted to views concerning the nature of man, as, for example, Titus, *Living Issues in Philosophy*, chapters VIII-XI. Other texts discuss the nature of man indirectly under topics such as "The Quest for Final Answers" and "Theological Dualism" (see Beck, *Philosophic Inquiry*) or "The Speculative Function of Philosophy" (see Randall and Buchler, *Philosophy: An Introduction*).

Most of the standard texts in philosophy of education do not present, as a separate topic, comparative views (or even a single view) of the nature of man. Noteworthy exceptions are Brubacher, *Modern Philosophies of Education*, chapter 3, pp. 44-72; Butler, *Four Philosophies*, which provides short statements of five different views of man, see pp. 119-20, 391-92, 403-7, 506-7; and Phenix, *Philosophy of Education*, pp. 117-209, 461-505. More frequently it is necessary to search for discussions of the nature of man under more or less indirect headings. In some cases this is worth doing, for example, chapter 3, "The Structure and Dynamics of Personality" in Broudy, *Building a Philosophy of Education*.

Many of the more helpful discussions of the nature of man, in the general literature of philosophy of education, focus upon the relation of the individual to society. For example, in Sayers and Madden, *Education and the Democratic Faith*, chapter 2 discusses the meaning of "individualism" and its relation to equality, freedom, and authority. In Kilpatrick, *Philosophy of Education*, there are chapters on "The Social Nature of Man," "The Culture," "The Individual and Society," etc., in which various views about man, his abilities and capabilities, are discussed in close relation to a consideration of alternatives for classroom organization and management, curriculum, school plant construction, and the like.

# CHAPTER 9

# *What Is Democracy?*

THE NATURE of language is such that certain words may mean different things to different people. Chameleonlike, words take on differing shades of meaning from context to context and, in the case of the word *democracy,* meaning has grown over the years until today it generally conveys considerably more than "rule by the people." This is true even when it is used to name a form of government and, in many contexts, democracy calls up a range of ideals and behaviors that run considerably beyond questions of political arrangements.

## DEMOCRACY AS A FORM OF GOVERNMENT

### Greek Democracy

Some five hundred years before the birth of Christ there evolved, primarily in the city-state of Athens, political arrangements that placed final authority in the hands of the people rather than in the hands of a few or of a single person. In attempting to assess the meaning of early Greek democracy two extremes should be avoided. On the one hand, some persons (especially those wishing to emphasize the influence of Christianity upon modern democracy) point out that in reality the "rule of the people" in Athens meant the rule by "the citizens"— an elite group of slave owners who, because of an economy built on human slavery, had the leisure to devote themselves to the arts, including the art of government. It is said that under these conditions the ideas of equality and justice were so restricted that it is very misleading to claim that our modern conceptions of democracy had their roots in pre-Christian or pagan Greece.

On the other hand, some persons (especially those who emphasize only the political meaning of democracy, in isolation from all economic, social, and moral considerations) maintain that democracy means specifically the political arrangements developed in ancient Athens. Since what was feasible in a small city-state could hardly be expected to work in a modern complex industrial nation, such persons usually point out that the United States of America is a *Republic*, and not a democracy at all.

One way of avoiding these extremes is to note that words such as democracy, justice, and equality have two dimensions of meaning: an intensive dimension of ideal, and an extensive dimension of actual human behavior, with neither dimension being static or fixed. For example, there is some evidence to suggest that, from a moral standpoint, slavery in democratic Athens was, at worst, no worse than slavery in ante-bellum Christian America. And, for that matter, if the meaning of democracy is to be explicated entirely in terms of its extensive dimension, why was the United States called a democratic nation before women were permitted to vote? Evidently more than the extensive dimension was involved.

It follows that a more satisfactory way of exploring the meaning attached to democracy by the early Greeks is to consider what they had to say about it. A number of such studies have been made,[1] but for our purposes some of the words of Pericles (*circa* 500-429 B.C.) will suffice.

We are happy in a form of government which cannot envy the laws of our neighbors—for it has served as a model to others, while being original at Athens. And this our form, as committed not to the few, but to the whole body of the people, is called a democracy. How different soever in a private capacity, we all enjoy the same general equality our laws are fitted to preserve; and superior honors in propor-

[1] See e.g., Walter R. Agard, *What Democracy Meant to the Greeks*, University of Wisconsin Press, 1960.

tion as we excel. The public administration is not confined to a particular family, but is attainable only by merit. Poverty is not a hindrance since whoever is able to serve his country meets with no obstacle to preferment from his first obscurity. The offices of the state we go through without obstructions from one another; and live together in the mutual endearments of private life without suspicions; not angry with a neighbor for following the bent of his own humor, nor putting on that countenance of discontent, which pains though it cannot punish—so that in private life we converse without diffidence or damage, while we dare not presume on any account to offend against the public, because of the reverence we bear to the magistrates and the laws, chiefly to those enacted for the redress of the injured, and to those unwritten laws, a breach of which is thought a disgrace. . . . The Grandeur of this our Athens causeth the product of the whole earth to be imported here, by which we reap a familiar enjoyment, not more of the delicacies of our own growth than of those of other nations.

In our manner of living we show an elegance tempered with frugality, and we cultivate philosophy without enervating the mind. We display our wealth in the season of beneficence, and not in the vanity of discourse. A confession of poverty is disgrace to no man; no effort to avoid it is disgrace indeed. There is visible in the same persons an attention both to their own private concerns and those of the public; and in those engaged in the labors of life there is competent skill in affairs of government. For we are the only people who think that one who does not participate in state affairs—not indolent, but good for nothing. And yet we pass the soundest judgments, and are quick at catching the right apprehensions of things, believing not that words are prejudicial to actions, but rather what is prejudicial is the not being duly prepared by previous debate before we are obliged to proceed to execution. Herein consists our distinguishing excellence, that in the hour of action we show the greatest courage, and yet debate beforehand the expediency of our measures. The courage of others is the result of ignorance; deliberations make them cowards. And those must undoubtedly be owed to have the greatest souls, who, most acutely sensible of the miseries of war and the sweets of peace, are not hence in the least deterred from facing danger.

In acts of beneficence, further, we differ from the many. We preserve friends not by receiving, but by conferring, obligations. For he who does a kindness hath the advantage over him who, by the law of gratitude, becomes a debtor to his benefactor. The person obliged is compelled to act the more insipid part, conscious that a return of kindness is merely a payment and not an obligation. And we alone are splendidly beneficent to others, not so much from interested motives as for the credit of pure liberality. I shall sum up what yet remains by only adding that our Athens in general is the school of Greece; and that every single Athenian amongst us is excellently formed, by his personal qualification, for all the various scenes of active life, acting with a most graceful demeanor and a most ready habit of despatch.[2]

These words are probably a subtle blend of the two dimensions of the meaning of democracy. Pericles, no doubt, painted an idealized picture. Nevertheless, it was a picture of behavior, not merely of ideals.

Three points seem to stand out: the right and responsibility of every citizen for participation in lawful government, a separation between public and private affairs (this amounts to a denial of totalitarianism), recognition that even private affairs should be regulated by a social-moral code that is in harmony with the principles that guide governmental affairs (this amounts to a denial that democracy can be viewed as merely a form of government in isolation from and independent of economic, social, and moral considerations).

## Laissez-faire Democracy

The desire for some form of democratic government frequently arises because of the evils of dictatorship, monarchy, or aristocracy. People long for freedom and, under such conditions, freedom means mainly removal of the restraints imposed by arbitrary rulers. Thus it is that the focus of democratic aspirations sometimes fixes upon only the first of the three points, noted above, concerning Greek democracy. Since rule by the people is thus placed in sharp contrast to rule by tyrants, and since the most noticeably objectionable feature of the tyrant's rule is the restraints imposed on individual freedom, democracy becomes equated with individualism, or a minimum restriction

[2] From a funeral oration delivered in 431 B.C., as a memorial to the first Athenian soldiers who fell in the Peloponnesian War.

on individual behavior. It may then be said that "that government is best which governs least."

Even in Greek thought there was a minority point of view to the effect that a proper democracy should permit every man to live as he pleases, that is, according to his own fancy. This idea was given powerful reinforcement in later times by the view of the nature of man as being in essential conflict with both nature and society and by the Lockean notion of the social contract. Government is necessary to protect a commonwealth against invasion and to establish a minimum of laws for regulation of private enterprise. Beyond that, any attempt by government to exercise control or even leadership is the beginning of tyranny. Adam Smith (1723-1790) was a very influential spokesman for this point of view, especially in respect to economic matters. His *An Inquiry into the Nature and Causes of the Wealth of Nations* was an eloquent plea for the defense of free trade and free enterprise.

From the standpoint of those who believe in protective tariffs and other political measures designed to insulate industrial capitalists and the landed aristocracy from the rigors of free competition, the ideas of Adam Smith seemed excessively liberal. On the other hand, from the standpoint of the laborer or of what the Communists call the proletariat, this "classical liberalism" did not appear so liberal, for, under this view, labor was treated as a commodity to be manipulated, as all commodities were, in order to maximize profits. Ricardo (1772-1823), a British economist, spoke very frankly about this matter.

> Labour, like other things which are purchased and sold, and which may be increased or diminished in quantity, has its natural and its market price. The natural price of labour is that price which is necessary to enable the labourers, one with another, to subsist and to perpetuate their race, without either increase or diminution.
>
> The power of the labourer to support himself, and the family which may be necessary to keep up the number of labourers, does not depend on the quantity of money which he may receive for wages but on the quantity of food, necessaries, and conveniences becomes essential to him from habit which the money will purchase. The natural

price of labour, therefore, depends on the price of the food, necessaries, and conveniences required for the support of the labourer and his family. . . .

The necessity which the labourer would be under of paying an increased price for such necessaries would oblige him to demand more wages; and whatever increases wages, necessarily reduces profits. . . .

It is when the market price of labour exceeds its natural price that the condition of the labourer is flourishing and happy, that he has it in his power to command a greater proportion of the necessaries and enjoyments of life, and therefore to rear a healthy and numerous family. When, however, by the encouragement which high wages give to the increase of population, the number of labourers is increased, wages again fall to their natural price, and indeed from the reaction sometimes fall below it. . . .

Under a system of perfectly free commerce, each country naturally devotes its capital and labour to such employments as are most beneficial to each. This pursuit of individual advantage is admirably connected with the universal good of the whole. By stimulating industry, by rewarding ingenuity, and by using efficaciously the peculiar powers bestowed by nature, it distributes labour most effectively and most economically: while, by increasing the general mass of productions, it diffuses general benefits, and binds together, by one common tie of interest and intercourse, the universal society of nations throughout the civilized world. It is this principle which determines that wine shall be made in France and Portugal, that corn shall be grown in America and Poland, and that hardware and other goods shall be manufactured in England. . . .[3]

When it is thought that man is by his very nature a competitive animal destined to spend his life struggling against a hostile environment and against his fellow man and when it is thought that government should do no more than referee the fighting and provide protection against outside interference, the result is *rugged individualism.* To the victor belong the spoils, and concern for the vanquished is labeled as unnatural sentimentalism (or squeamishness). Moreover, any voice raised to protest—any suggestion that this may not be the best of all possible systems—is squelched with the retort, "If you're so smart, why ain't you rich?"

[3] David Ricardo, *The Principles of Political Economy and Taxation,* Dutton, New York, 1926, pp. 52, 70, 53, 81.

Drawing on the survival-of-the-fittest model provided by Darwin, Herbert Spencer (1820-1903) attempted to justify a laissez-faire version of government. He argued that:

In common with its other assumptions of secondary offices, the assumption by a government of the office of Reliever-general to the poor, is necessarily forbidden by the principle that a government cannot rightly do anything more than protect. In demanding from a citizen contributions for the mitigation of distress—contributions not needed for the due administration of men's rights—the state is, as we have seen reversing its function, and diminishing that liberty to exercise the faculties which it was instituted to maintain. Possibly . . . some will assert that by satisfying the wants of the pauper, a government is in reality extending his liberty to exercise his faculties. . . . But this statement of the case implies a confounding of two widely-different things. To enforce the fundamental law—to take care that every man has freedom to do all that he wills, provided he infringes not the equal freedom of any other man—this is the special purpose for which the civil power exists. Now insuring to each the right to pursue within the specified limits the objects of his desires without let or hindrance, is quite a separate thing from insuring him satisfaction. . . .

Pervading all nature we may see at work a stern discipline, which is a little cruel that it may be very kind. That state of universal warfare maintained throughout the lower creation, to the great perplexity of many worthy people, is at bottom the most merciful provision which the circumstances admit of. . . . The poverty of the incapable, the distresses that come upon the imprudent, the starvation of the idle, and those shoulderings aside of the weak by the strong, which leave so many 'in shallows and in miseries,' are the decrees of a large, far-seeing benevolence. It seems hard that an unskilfulness which with all its efforts he cannot overcome, should entail hunger upon the artizan. It seems hard that a labourer incapacitated by sickness from competing with his stronger fellows, should have to bear the resulting privations. It seems hard that widows and orphans should be left to struggle for life or death. Nevertheless, when regarded not separately, but in connection with the interests of universal humanity, these harsh fatalities are seen to be full of the highest beneficence—the same beneficence which brings to early graves the children of diseased parents, and singles out the low-spirited, the intemperate, and the debilitated as the victims of an epidemic. . . .[4]

[4] Herbert Spencer, *Social Statistics*, London, 1851, pp. 311, 322-323.

## American Democracy

There is little doubt that the basic tenets of classical liberalism, as developed by British and French writers, exerted a profound influence upon the thinking of the leaders of the American Revolution. Consider, for example, whether in the Declaration of Independence there is involved the notion of "natural rights" and "social contract" conception of government with its justificaiton of the "right of revolution" and "government by consent of the governed."

When in the Course of human events, it becomes necessary for one people to dissolve the political bands which have connected them with another, and to assume among the powers of the earth, the separate and equal station to which the Laws of Nature and of Nature's God entitle them, a decent respect to the opinions of mankind requires that they should declare the causes which impel them to the separation.

We hold these truths to be self-evident, that all men are created equal, that they are endowed by their Creator with certain unalienable Rights, that among these are Life, Liberty and the pursuit of Happiness.—That to secure these rights, Governments are instituted among Men, deriving their just powers from the consent of the governed,—That whenever any Form of Government becomes destructive of these ends, it is the Right of the People to alter or abolish it, and to institute new Government, laying its foundation on such principles and organizing its powers in such form, as to them shall seem most likely to effect their Safety and Happiness. Prudence, indeed, will dictate that Governments long established should not be changed for light and transient causes; and accordingly all experience hath shewn, that mankind are more disposed to suffer, while evils are sufferable, than to right themselves by abolishing the forms to which they are accustomed. But when a long train of abuses and usurpations, pursuing invariably the same Object evinces a design to reduce them under absolute Despotism, it is their right, it is their duty, to throw off such Government, and to provide new Guards for their future security.—Such has been the patient sufferance of these Colonies; and such is now the necessity which constrains them to alter their former Systems of Government. The history of the present King of Great Britain is a history of repeated injuries and usurpations, all having in direct object the establishment of an absolute Tyranny over these States. To prove this, let Facts be submitted to a candid world.

On the other hand, many of the Founding Fathers were also familiar with the older Greek conceptions of democracy and, perhaps still more important, they believed that political forms in the new nation need not be dominated by any European doctrines. They felt free, for example, to argue about what equality should mean in the new nation—Was it to mean merely "equality before the law" (the laissez-faire emphasis) or was it also to include equality of right and responsibility to participate in government (a Greek emphasis), and should it include "equality of personal dignity" (a Greek conception reinforced by Christian doctrine)? And, indeed, perhaps it should be construed to mean "equality of opportunity" (a notion that seemed much more feasible in America than in crowded Europe).

What actually happened, of course, was that viewpoints and doctrines had to be compromised. In a few cases, the ideas of a European writer could be accepted intact. For example, consider the following, written by Charles Louis de Secondat, Baron of Montesquieu (1689-1775):

> The political liberty of the subject is a tranquility of mind arising from the opinion each person has of his safety. In order to have this liberty, it is requisite the government be so constituted as one man need not be afraid of another.
>
> When the legislative and executive powers are united in the same person, or in the same body of magistrates, there can be no liberty, because apprehensions may arise lest the same monarch or senate should enact tyrannical laws, to execute them in a tyrannical manner.
>
> Again, there is no liberty, if the judiciary power be not separated from the legislative and executive. Were it joined with legislative, the life and liberty of the subject would be exposed to arbitrary control; for the judge would be then the legislator. Were it joined to the executive power, the judge might behave with violence and oppression.
>
> There would be an end of everything, were the same man or the same body, whether of nobles or of the people, to exercise those three powers: that of enacting laws, that of executing the public resolutions, and of trying the causes of individuals . . .[5]

But, in many more cases, laissez-faire doctrine was modified by American common sense and the more optimistic conceptions of

[5] Montesquieu, *The Spirit of Laws*, Hafner, New York, 1959, I, p. 183.

the nature of man nurtured by the frontier spirit. For example, the to-promote-the-general-welfare statement in the preamble of the Constitution appears to be more than laissez-faire doctrine.

Perhaps the two most difficult problems, calling for compromise, that faced the framers of the Constitution were the following: first, even though the task before them was to create a constitution for a new nation, they were not, in fact, preparing a contract to be signed by a people living in a state of nature. The hard, political reality was thirteen loosely confederated but more-or-less independent and sovereign former colonies. They exhibited considerable variation in economic, social, and religious customs and traditions, as well as considerable difference in size, wealth, and sources of wealth. On the one hand, there was the desire to create a true nation, unified and strong enough to take its place in the world along side other nations. On the other hand, each state (former colony) wanted assurance that its interests and welfare would not be submerged in the union. And, of course, the smaller the state the more apprehensive were its representatives.

The second problem was to find some feasible political meaning for the principles set forth in the Declaration of Independence. Again, the social reality was far removed from a state of nature. The people who were to make up the new nation, rather then being free and equal, exhibited a nearly maximum possible range of difference with respect to ownership of property and other forms of wealth, education (including political experience), and personal-social privilege, ranging from landed aristocrats to slaves. On the one hand there was the desire to create a government in which all final authority rested in the hands of "the people," on the other hand there were deep rooted fears of the consequences of unstable, irresponsible "popular opinions."

Separately, these two problems appeared impossible to resolve. Viewed in relation to one another, however, they yielded to a series of compromises. For example, the states were stripped of sovereignty[6] and the Constitution was declared to be

---

[6] See Art. I, sect. 10, of the Constitution.

an instrument, not of the states, but of "We the people . . ." On the other hand, each state was retained as a political entity, not merely a subdivision of the national government, but a separate political organization of the people of that state. Moreover, by dividing the national legislature into two branches, both of the basic problems could be compromised at one stroke. Since each state government was to select two senators, the smaller states were assured of influence in national affairs at the same time that this highly indirect election of senators assured those who were fearful of popular government that national policies would not be subjected to "mob rule."

Finally, before the Constitution was ratified there were included ten amendments designed to protect fundamental individual rights. It is interesting that while these amendments were obviously written to protect citizens against possible encroachments by the federal government, over the years it has in fact increasingly been the case that citizens have turned to the federal courts to protect them against infringement of such basic rights by state and local political powers.

But perhaps the crowning stroke of genius was the inclusion in the Constitution of the provisions for amendments and for an Independent Supreme Court. This court has developed, over the years, the power to pass on the constitutionality of legislation and has, in effect, developed the power to interpret the meaning of both Constitution and legislation. These two provisions prevent American political arrangements from becoming static or fixed. In the words of Carl Wittke, American Democracy is something "Forever Unfinished." He has said:

Lincoln defined the American experiment in democracy as "government of the people, by the people, and for the people." That definition implies that democracy is a process forever unfinished, not a society frozen into a rigid political, economic and social order. The prime objective in this country is not to build up the authority of the state, but to secure the maximum of fulfillment for every individual.

Democracy will live only as long as it survives in the hearts of our people, for it depends upon an attitude toward life, rather than upon laws. Democratic government does not drop like manna from the heavens upon a chosen people. It must be defended and won by each succeeding generation. It will be lost when we abandon our faith in the sanctity of the individual.

Democracy functions through the peaceful give and take of legislative compromise. It is radical enough to believe that competing and conflicting groups must be given the opportunity to be heard, and to exert their powers of argument and persuasion in the open, and to the maximum of their ability. In no other way can people form an intelligent, reasoned judgment.

No form of government is ideal, but a democracy is more stable, peaceful and palatable in the long run than any other form yet devised by the ingenuity of man. . . .

We have faith in orderly change, predicated upon free discussion and free choices. We believe in the right of still unpopular minorities to be heard, within the framework of the law, the constitution, and the full protection of the courts, provided only that they operate in the open; do not resort to conspiracy; observe the laws against libel, obscenity, and treason, and stop their arguments short of advocating the use of force and violence.

It is a wholesome historical exercise to see how far we have come since 1776. When Jefferson wrote the immortal Declaration, thousands of men and women were held in slavery in a free America where all men were supposed to be created equal. Women, both by law and custom, were considered low-grade inferiors of the human race. Only from 8% to 16% of the male adults could vote, and still fewer could hold office. Many honestly believed universal manhood suffrage was evil, and imposed a responsibility too great for the average man to bear.

It took a Civil War to start the Negro along the slow, hard road toward equal rights. Universal manhood suffrange was won only after many political encounters, and not until 1920 were women finally enfranchised by the federal constitution.

Not theories nor ready-made ideologies, but pure American common horse sense produced our anti-monopoly legislation, the Interstate Commerce Commission, the Federal Reserve System, the Securities and Exchange Commission, federal bank deposit insurance, workmen's compensation, mother's pensions and social security, the public health nurse, the food inspector, the forest ranger and the playground supervisor. Railroads were built with large government subsidies, and agriculture long ago ceased being an unprotected, private industry. Subsidies were granted to shipping and air lines; conservation and irrigation projects, and public highways were developed at the public expense.

The people wanted it so. Probably none of us like all of these measures, and we change our laws from decade to decade, but the most conservative today would approve most of them as essential to a healthy and progressive America. Several generations ago, all of them were the radicalism of wild crusaders. By frank and persistent experimentation, we have kept our stability, and by the flexibility of the democratic process, we were able to substitute peaceful evolution for destructive revolution.[7]

## DEMOCRACY AS AN INDIVIDUAL-SOCIAL ETHIC

Perhaps the most striking feature of modern democracy, whether in the United States or elsewhere, is the increasing tendency of its advocates to include in its meaning considerably more than the literal transcription *rule by the people*. Of course, not all advocates of democracy have agreed to the wisdom of extending the meaning of the term. Some have argued, for example, that *democracy* should be used only as the name for the *process* and any attempt to include in its meaning some statement of direction or purpose introduces a limitation upon the sovereignty of the people and hence an inconsistency in the meaning of the term.[8] A little analysis suggests, however, that rule by the people implies "ruling." Or, said differently, for "a sovereign" to be *sovereign* he must exercise his sovereign authority. Said still more generally, a process is never random action, it is systematic action or a series of actions directed by some purpose or some end-in-view. It does not follow that the purpose or end must be forever fixed or absolute but it does follow that, in general, any action that may properly be designated "a process" or, in particular, any action that is an incident of "ruling" must, at that time, be directed by some purpose or intent. Furthermore, over a period of time encompassing a number of such

[7] Condensed from an address "Forever Unifinished" by Carl Wittke, Dean of the Graduate School, Western Reserve University, Cleveland, Ohio. By permission.

[8] See, e.g., Ernest E. Bayles, *Democratic Educational Theory*, Harper & Row, New York, 1960, chap. 10.

actions, if there is no consistency or if there are no discernible trends of any kind, then we realize that what we have called "ruling" should more properly be called anarchy or the absence of *rule*.

In any event, the fact remains that people are these days using the term democracy as a name for a set of principles as well as for a process or way of governing. As soon as the word is given this larger meaning, it becomes clear that it is related to the various conceptions of the nature of man—man and nature, the individual and society, and indeed, to a whole cluster of other meanings: freedom, equality, authority, justice, and many others. Moreover, it turns out that, rather than democracy implying a particular conception of man, each of the various views of man suggests a form or meaning for democracy, first as an ethic, and secondarily as a form of government. It follows that two societies, having substantially different views of the nature of man, will employ the term democracy to refer to substantially different ideals and practices. Even within a single society, to the extent that differences exist in conceptions of the nature of man, similar differences in the meaning of democracy will be noticeable.

Now an ethic is made up of a set of guiding principles. For example, the golden rule is a key principle in the Christian ethic. It is instructive to note that, although the golden rule is customarily identified with the Christian religion, a number of other religions suggest a similar ethical principle. In much the same way, each of the various conceptions of man suggests ethical principles, some of which are similar to principles suggested by other conceptions. In other words, just as several persons of differing religions may all agree that each should deal with others in the way he would like to have others deal with him, so persons holding various views concerning the nature of man and society may still be able to approximate consensus concerning some guiding principles for the regulation of individual-social affairs, including political affairs.

*Logically*, all this appears as follows: A person accepts or constructs a systematic philosophy including a systematic view of the nature of man and society. In the light of this, he constructs principles for the guidance of individual-social affairs. In the light of these principles, he erects political structures that seem best calculated to embody or give operational meaning to the principles. In contrast, *what actually happens,* of course, is that every person is born into some sort of society, in which he becomes more or less committed to a range of individual-social (including political) practices. Concurrently, he is taught or manages to formulate for himself certain guiding principles. Eventually, some persons are either taught or manage to construct a more-or-less systematic view of the nature of man, along with other parts of a more or less systematic philosophy. Consequently, it is not at all surprising that we find people agreeing, for example, to a certain principle but disagreeing concerning both its philosophic justification and its meaning in practice. Or we find people agreeing on, say, a certain course of political action, but disagreeing as to what is the guiding principle.

The question then arises as to whether, in a given society or nation, enough agreement can be found *at the level of principles* to constitute a guide for the continuing development and reconstruction of individual-social and political arranagements. Since, as indicated above, the task is not one of direct logical construction de novo, but rather of taking stock of where we are thus far, a sensible course would appear to be the examining of those documents and statements most prized by the society in question in the hope of determining what principles seem to be embodied in the arrangements to which the society is thus far actually committed. In the case of the United States of America, we would certainly want to look at the Declaration of Independence and Constitution, especially the Bill of Rights, the more important Supreme Court Decisions, and certain highly regarded statements, such as Lincoln's Gettysburg Address, Washington's Inaugurals, etc.

A number of such studies have actually been made[9] and,

[9] See, e.g., the work of Harold Hand, reported in Smith, Stanley, and Shores, *Fundamentals of Curriculum Development*, pp. 76-78.

although there is not complete agreement as to the principles embodied, the following would probably command majority assent. These statements, along with their explication, may, therefore, be viewed as a hypothesis concerning the meaning of democracy, as an individual-social ethic, in midcentury America.

Democracy involves:

1. Respect for individuality and for the conditions that promote the growth of human personality
2. Confidence in human intelligence, formed and informed through the processes of free, autonomous inquiry
3. The right and responsibility for appropriate participation in investigation and resolution of problems of shared concern

### Respect for Individuality

It should again be remembered that various views of the nature of man will suggest various meanings for democratic principles. A person who believes that the individual attains significance only as he identifies completely with his society will obviously give a different meaning to "individuality" than a person committed to rugged individualism. It follows that they will hold radically different opinions concerning what conditions will best promote growth of human personality.

Evidently, the majority of midcentury Americans reject both of these extreme views and consequently the range of disagreements that arise as we attempt to institute arrangements in the light of this principle is significantly less than the range that is theoretically possible. There seems to be widespread agreement, for example, that every individual, regardless of economic, social, racial, or religious considerations, or even if he be a criminal or insane, is *at least ideally* entitled to a certain amount of privacy in those matters that are not of public concern and to equality before the law and "due process" in those matters that are of public concern. We do not always live up to this ideal but when cases of failure are brought to our attention we concede that a wrong has been done. And this is of no small importance, because, although acknowledgement of an ideal does not of itself improve conditions, they are far less likely to be improved without the guidance that an acknowledge ideal can give.

As we have just noted, a respect for individuality involves a distinction between public and private affairs. How is this distinction to be drawn? Some 100 years ago, John Stuart Mill (1806-1873) had this to say:

. . . The notion that the people have no need to limit their power over themselves, might seem axiomatic when popular government was a thing only dreamed about, or read of as having existed at some distant period of the past. . . . In time, however, a democratic republic came to occupy a large portion of the earth's surface, and made itself felt as one of the most powerful members of the community of nations; and elective and responsible government became subject to the observations and criticisms which wait upon a great existing fact: It was now perceived that such phrases as "self-government" and "the power of the people over themselves" did not express the true state of the case. The "people" who exercise the power are not always the same people with those over whom it is exercised; and the self-government spoken of is not the government of each by himself, but of each by all the rest. The will of the people, moreover, practically means the will of the most numerous or the most active *part* of the people, the majority, or those who succeed in making themselves accepted as the majority: the people, consequently, *may* desire to oppress a part of their number, and precautions are as much needed against this as against any other abuse of power. The limitation, therefore, of the power of government over individuals loses none of its importance when the holders of power are regularly accountable to the community, that is, to the strongest party therein. . . .

Like other tyrannies, the tyranny of the majority was at first, and still vulgarly, held in dread chiefly as operating through the acts of the public authorities. But reflecting persons perceive that when society is itself the tyrant—society collectively over the separate individuals who compose it—its means of tyrannizing are not restricted to the acts which it may do by the hands of its political functionaries. Society can and does execute its own mandates; and if it issues wrong mandates instead of right, or any mandates at all in things with which it ought not to meddle, it practices a social tyranny more formidable than many kinds of political oppression, since, though not unusually upheld by such extreme penalties, it leaves fewer means of escape, penetrating much more deeply into the details of life, and enslaving the soul itself.

Protection, therefore, against the tyranny of the magistrate is not enough: there needs protection also against the tyranny of prevailing opinion and feeling; against the tendency of society to impose, by other means than civil penalities, its own ideas and practices as rules of conduct on those who dissent from them; to fetter the development, and, if possible, prevent the formation of any individuality not in harmony with its ways, and compels all characters to fashion themselves upon the model of its own. There is a limit to the legitimate interference of collective opinion with individual independence; and to find that limit, and maintain it against encroachment, is as indispensable to a good condition of human affairs, as protection against political despotism.

But though this proposition is not likely to be contested in general terms, the practical question, where to place the limit—how to make the fitting adjustment between individual independence and social control—is a subject on which nearly everything remains to be done. All that makes existence valuable to anyone, depends on the enforcement of restraints upon the actions of other people. Some rules of conduct, therefore, must be imposed, by law in the first place, and by opinion on many things which are not fit subjects for the operation of law. What these rules should be is the principal question in human affairs; but if we except a few of the most obvious cases, it is one of those which least progress has been made in resolving. . . .[10]

After noting that, for the most part, people do not have or do not even recognize the need for "good reasons" in attempting to justify the values that are embodied in social customs and that are imposed upon individual dissenters, and after remarking that "The only case in which the higher ground has been taken on principle and maintained with consistency, . . . is that of religious belief . . .," Mill offers the following guide:

. . . the sole end for which mankind are warranted, individually or collectively, in interfering with the liberty of action of any of their number, is self-protection. That the only purpose for which power can be rightfully exercised over any member of a civilized community, against his will, is to prevent harm to others. His own good, either physical or moral, is not a sufficient warrant. He cannot rightfully be compelled to do or forbear because it will be better for him to do so, because it will make him happier, because, in the opinion of others, to do so would be wise, or even right. These are good reasons for remon-

[10] John Stuart Mill, *On Liberty*, Regnery, Chicago, 1955.

strating with him, or reasoning with him, or persuading him, or entreating him, but not for compelling him, or visiting him with any evil in case he do otherwise. To justify that, the conduct from which it is desired to deter him must be calculated to produce evil to someone else. . . .[11]

It should be clear, of course, as it was to Mill, that borderline cases are bound to arise in which it is hard to tell whether a proposed line of individual behavior will eventuate in serious enough harm or inconvenience to others to warrant interference. Dewey once pointed out[12] that what actually happens is that individuals are let alone to behave as they please until the hurtful effects of their actions are noticed by other people. The people who thus become concerned constitute "a public." According to the size and composition of this "public," it will employ various kinds of social or political actions to regulate the type of behavior it has become concerned about. Such regulating action may range from neighborhood or community social sanctions to national legislation such as the Pure Food and Drug Acts.

Furthermore, as Mill also recognized, his principle applies to acts of omission as well as commission. Individuals may thus be required to install automatic garbage-disposers in every house built in certain residential areas, automobile manufacturers may be required to equip all new automobiles with turn signals, and, presumably, every state could be required to maintain a system of public schools, to say nothing of requiring individuals to pay taxes and to serve in the armed forces. But, in any event and regardless of how much disagreement there may be about borderline cases, the point to be noted is that respect for individuality entails a recognition of some area of privacy and independence, otherwise democracy may not be differentiated from totalitarianism.[13]

Intimately related to all these considerations is the matter of respect for the conditions that promote the growth of human

[11] *Ibid.*
[12] See *The Public and Its Problems,* Gateway Books, Chicago, 1946.
[13] See The Rockefeller Panel Report, *The Power of the Democratic Idea,* esp. pp. 6-7 and pp. 53-56.

personality. We shall need to look at this in more detail when we consider the meaning of democracy for education but, for the present, two points should be noted: First, "growth," as we found in the case of "process," is the name of a conception that is not totally directionless. (Such words are similar to the word "velocity" in contrast to "change" or "alteration.") Second, the effects of various conditions upon growth of personality is an empirical matter. It turns out, therefore, that the question of what particular conditions are to be respected at any given time involves both conceptual and factual material. On the one hand, there is the image that people hold of the chief characteristic of a mature, harmoniously developed, and growing personality, and, on the other hand, the state of development of the hominological sciences of the time. Since neither conceptions nor scientific knowledge need ever become static, this principle does not impose closure upon democracy—it can remain "forever unfinished" and presumably, new potentials of human personality will be recognized as further gains are made under the guidance of present conceptions.

### Confidence in Human Intelligence

We are so accustomed to living in an age of science and technology that it is easy to overlook the remarkable confidence that we have in human intelligence when it is formed and informed through the processes of free, autonomous inquiry. Whether one is considering what is true and right in general, or with respect to sociopolitical arrangements in particular, a review of history reveals that generally men have not displayed this confidence in their own collective intelligence. A more penetrating look at our own age reveals that the temptation to abdicate—to shift allegiance to some authority other than human intelligence—is still very real and pervasive in all areas of life except science. Yet, if democracy or rule by the people implies ruling, that is, that the people must actually exercise authority rather than abdicating it, then a democratic community, as is the case with the scientific community, must be autonomous: it must develop for itself its own methods and criteria and designs—in short, its own intelligence. So far as we know there is nothing built into the universe that requires men to be either scientific or democratic, but without confidence in human intelligence neither science nor democracy can exist.

More specifically, what does this principle mean? Does it mean, for example, that one must believe that intelligence is spread evenly throughout the population, that truth and right can be determined by majority vote, that popular opinion is always right or just or wise? Does it mean that expertness is undemocratic? Does it mean, finally, that faith in God is out of place in a democracy?

Not at all! Confidence in human intelligence means substantially the same from a democratic standpoint as it does in science. In the words of Jefferson, it means that we are not afraid to follow truth wherever it may lead nor to tolerate error as long as truth is left free to combat it. In the scientific or democratic community, the expert, the genius, the gifted, the talented can be set free to develop their ideas, without being told what truths their inquiries must confirm. And, equally important, the less gifted can find honorable work to do and can, at least ideally, command a fair hearing for their own ideas or suggestions. At any given time, what is actually accepted as a basis for further action or inquiry depends, of course, upon the general level of perspicacity. Confidence in human intelligence means, therefore, not that we believe that every decision will be the best that conceivably could have been made, but that the collective intelligence (given at least approximate conditions of free inquiry) will be astute enough to keep open the avenues for correction and will, in the long run, be more successful than any available alternative.

Since neither science nor democracy constitutes a philosophy (and certainly not a theology), there is nothing in either that demands any sort of religious or antireligious commitment. The individual scientist may engage in as much or as little metaphysical speculation as he pleases. He may, as many scientists have, find inspiration and guidance for his work in such speculation. As scientist, however, he recognizes that other members of the scientific community are equally free and that such individual speculation is not part of the corpus of science. In similar fashion, an individual member of a democratic community may, as far as democracy is concerned, adopt whatever justification for the democratic principles seems best to him. He may, for example, adopt a Jewish, a Christian, or some other religious justification for "respect for individuality," or he may justify his commitment to this principle on humanistic or naturalistic grounds.

There is a sense, however, in which both science and democracy place limitations upon certain matters that have historically fallen within the jurisdiction of organized religions. Before the rise of either modern science or modern democracy, ecclesiastical authorities, being frequently the best educated or most learned men of their time, often made pronouncements about troublesome human questions that are now recognized as falling within such dispersed fields as astronomy, geology, political science, and dietetics. A number of such pronouncements hardened into dogma and became interwoven with theological considerations. Consider, for example, the doctrine of the divine right of kings. A commitment to either science or democracy logically requires the rejection of such theocratic (in contrast to theological) doctrine.

Finally, we should recognize that the problems involved in attaining, or even approximating, conditions of free inquiry are sometimes quite complex and baffling. We have previously touched upon some of these problems[14] and shall need to look at others in connection with the meaning of democracy for education. But at this point we should note that, although modern methods for rapid and mass communication of ideas carry enormous potential benefit for free inquiry, these same methods may

[14] See, e.g., footnote pp. 91-92.

be used effectively for suppressing inquiry. What is at issue here is not simply the obvious matter of the dissemination of truth versus falsehood, of "good propaganda" versus "bad propaganda," but the more subtle affair of the influence of mass media upon the criteria of credibility accepted by a people.

It has been said that, in the early days of movable type, since people were accustomed to seeing the Bible as the only printed book and since the Bible was regarded as literally true, there was a strong tendency to regard any statement found on a printed page as "the gospel truth." Whether or not there is any truth to this story, it illustrates the point here at issue. Mass media of communication not only either inform or misinform but they also set the standards for what will be regarded as believable. Furthermore, the way in which "information" is treated by such media provides a compelling model. It is difficult enough even in a classroom, to teach the instrumental role of information in furthering inquiry, but when commentators, journalists, and editorial writers repeatedly confuse or interchange information and conclusion, it is no wonder that the public accepts "quiz kids" as *experts* and thinks that dogmatic assertion is the hallmark of authority. The public is poorly served by syndicated columnists who offer advice for twenty cents under the general rubric that all the problems of men, from sexual relations to international relations, can be solved by common sense "as any fool can plainly see."

Society can enact regulations to insure that in any given community not all of the media are owned or controlled by a single interest. Strictly speaking, this assures us only that our information about the elephant is not coming from a single blind man. Nor would it solve the problem to place further control in the hands of the public. For, as noted earlier, "the public has no hands"; only individuals have hands. It is only when democracy is construed as an ethic and becomes a widespread personal commitment that mass media of communication become the ally of free inquiry rather than a seductive substitute.

## Right and Responsibility for Appropriate Participation

Given some sort of working distinction between public and private affairs (and, of course, whatever criteria are adopted are matters for public concern and decision), democracy implies that every member of a given public has the right to participate in the investigation and resolution of the problems of that public. But, once again, since rule by the people implies ruling rather than abdication, the right of participation carries with it the responsibility to exercise that right. It does not follow, however, that direct, personal participation (after the manner of an idealized image of a New England town meeting) is necessary or even appropriate in all of the various kinds of problems that arise.[15] As a matter of fact, the problem of devising appropriate (i.e., equitable, feasible, and effective) means for enabling everyone concerned with a problem to participate in its investigation and solution is itself a perennial problem of democracy, and experimentation with various proposals for its solution is one of the features of democracy that keeps it forever unfinished. With respect to governmental and political arrangements, the people of the United States have, right from the beginning, been much too astute to accept across the board such overly simple suggestions as "all questions should be settled by a simple majority vote." Any autonomous group, whether democratic or scientific, must struggle with the problem of developing designs and criteria for the control of judgment and decision making. And there is no more reason for supposing that some simple rule of thumb will be any more adequate or universally appropriate for decision making in complex public affairs than in complex scientific questions.

When democracy is construed as an ethic and its principles are expected to offer guidance for a wide range of affairs that run beyond normal governmental concern (so that it becomes pos-

[15] See The Rockefeller Panel Report, *The Power of the Democratic Idea*, esp. pp. 38-41.

sible to speak meaningfully of, say, a "democratic family" or a
"democratic education" as well as a democratic government),
then it becomes increasingly clear that the principle of participation, along with all other principles, never automatically supplies the answer to any problem. A principle enables one merely
to recognize that a problem exists. But again, this is no small
matter since a problem that is not recognized cannot be *solved*;
at best it can be removed by chance. Thus it is that where
democracy is taken seriously it is recognized that every person,
regardless of age or intelligence or any other consideration that
does not by definition rule him out of the class "human persons,"
actually does have a right to participate in decisions that affect
any public of which he is a part. Children are affected by family
decisions, students are affected by educational decisions, all of
us are affected by political decisions. The problem that this principle calls to our attention is indeed staggering.

In the face of such an overwhelming problem, it is no wonder
that large chunks of it have been sliced away by more or less
arbitrary decisions. In most states a person may not vote until he
is twenty-one. In most families "children are to be seen not
heard" when the time comes for decision making. In most schools
students are not consulted when curriculum decisions are made.
Remembering that democracy does not require direct, personal
participation, still the principle reminds us that in any area of
life even benevolent dictatorship falls short of the democratic
ideal. Once the radical and far-reaching import of this principle
is grasped, we must realize that all the intellectual resources of
man are not at present too great to bring to bear upon this piece
of democracy's unfinished business.

## DEMOCRACY AND EDUCATION

Early in our study of "What is Education?" we recognized that
more than one way of viewing this question is appropriate and
necessary if we are to understand the wide range of meaning
involved. Remembering that the three approaches developed in

Chapter 2 are intended to be suggestive rather than exhaustive, let us now explore briefly the meaning for education of democratic principles under this triune conception.

## Democracy and Education (as a process of personal development)

One of the most common of the many misunderstandings of Dewey's educational writings is the notion that his conception of educational growth is somehow neutral or empty, as far as offering direction for the content and methods of education. Only a little analysis of Dewey's thought is sufficient to make it clear that "growth" is intended as a metaphor. Dewey certainly did not believe that mind, character, intelligence, personality are physical entities (as, say, muscles) that may literally grow. By use of this metaphor, Dewey calls our attention to *actual physical growth* as an instructive model for understanding education as a process of personal development.

Specialists in the field of physical growth or development have long recognized the following points. First, growth is not to be identified with every change or alteration in physical make-up. Muscular dystrophy is not confused with growth nor is it thought that obesity or even a muscle-bound condition is the limit toward which growth moves. Second, empirical study reveals that the idea or image of "superb physical development" has varied from age to age and culture to culture. Nevertheless, these conceptions are not arbitrary or whimsical; they are related both to the practical realities of economic and social success as defined by a culture and to the level of development of the relevant sciences (i.e., physiology, dietetics, etc.). Third, although specialists make use of such guides as "tables of average height and weight," "normal blood pressure," and the like, it is fully recognized that each individual requires a certain amount of more-or-less special consideration. Fourth, the question of what will best promote sound physical development and under what circumstances is an empirical question not to be answered by doctrinaire or a priori conceptions.

Consequently, at any given time, in connection with promoting the physical growth of students or clients, a specialist will project ideals of development as ends-in-view for direction of effort. But only the ill-informed will imagine that a specialist employs an inflexible or fixed standard either in regard to individual differences or with respect to human potential. Actually, the more that is learned about physical development and its complex relation to many factors previously unsuspected, the more the horizon of potential opens up, so that today we can envision possibilities of physical development and fitness undreamed of by earlier generations. The conception of physical growth is only as empty and directionless as is one's understanding of this process as an actual or existential occurrence. So let it be with "educational growth." To a perceptive student of the educative process, the ideal of *growth* is a most suggestive guide when facing problems of content-selection or problems of instructional techniques, or when attempting to isolate valuable research-areas.

It turns out then that the meaning of democracy for education (as a process of personal development) is substantially caught up in this conception of growth. Confidence in human intelligence formed and informed through the processes of free autonomous inquiry is, again, the necessary condition for taking seriously Dewey's admonition that growth should be subordinate to nothing save more growth. And respect for individuality and for the conditions that promote the growth of human personality provides the motivation (running deeper than the political necessity of an educated electorate) for undertaking a program of universal education. What remains is the question of the meaning in an educational setting of the principle of appropriate participation.

When education is viewed as a process of growth—growth of intelligence, skills and understanding, character, personality, then we have a key for unlocking the problem of what kind of participation is appropriate. Often, when it has been recognized that students do have the right and responsibility for participation in decisions involved in their own education, it has been the *forms* of democracy, rather than its substance, that have captured attention. In the name of democracy, we have sometimes asked elementary school children to vote on day-by-day curriculum decisions and we have spread before high school and college students an array of offerings so that they may "elect" courses and programs of study. When it is recognized, however, that, from the standpoint of education as a process of personal development, the reason why students should participate in certain ways is because such participation is necessary for their own educational growth, then it becomes clear that only those modes of participation that actually do promote educational growth constitute appropriate participation. And, because such participation is necessary, it once again carries a responsibility as well as a right.

Can there be too much democracy in the classroom? Experienced teachers know there can be too much voting and too much sentimentalism and romanticism about children's impulses, "felt needs" and "teen-age problems." But there could hardly be too much respect for individuality and for the conditions that promote the growth of human personality, nor too much confidence in human intelligence formed and informed through the processes of free autonomous inquiry. We have discovered that certain forms of student participation are inappropriate for promoting educational growth; development of more appropriate forms constitutes another area of unfinished business.

This is a matter for study within the science and profession of teaching and, though it therefore lies beyond the scope of an introductory course in philosophy of education, a number of relevant suggestions have been made. We might note before leaving the point, however, that, as the older, traditional, authoritarian, and dictatorial teaching-methods and demeanor have been remodeled under the influence of progressive slogans, authority and dictation have tended to become merely benevolent rather than democratic. Most of us greatly prefer the more humane conditions that now generally exist in our schools but we should also realize that benevolent dictatorship tends to build dependence, on the part of students, rather than increasing acceptance of responsibility for self-direction, even with respect to educational growth to say nothing of ethical-social behavior. This dependent attitude of students is very noticeable in our colleges where it appears that a vast majority have never grasped the fact that "educating" is essentially an intransitive activity.

## Democracy and Education (as a sociopolitical institution)

If education is to be compatible with the Constitution, then again attention should focus on substance rather than form. This is the case whether we are concerned with questions of the proper organization and modes of operation for our educational institutions or with the question of the more direct teaching of democracy by these institutions. Let us consider these problem-areas one at a time.

Without repeating what has previously been discussed,[16] we can see that where a society's educational institutions do not embody and illustrate the principles of democracy, in spite of all preachment time spent in school becomes training in and for something other than democracy. The same may be said, of course, for time spent at work, with various clubs, or with religious and political groups, to say nothing of time spent in our penal institutions, hopefully called "correctional institutions."

Many writers have deplored the authoritarian forms that are said to be typical of public school administration and social psychologists have discussed the benefits of "democratic group leadership" in contrast to *laissez-faire* and autocratic structures. But the problem runs deeper than this.[17] The way in which students are seated in a classroom, committee structures within a school and a school system, the way in which the PTA is organized, all exert influence upon communication and morale and, no doubt, upon personality and character development of all

[16] The reader may wish to review what was said in Chap. 2 concerning education as a sociopolitical institution. See pp. 30-38.

[17] See Philip G. Smith, *Philosophic Mindedness in Educational Administration*, Ohio State University Press, 1956.

involved. But the fundamental determining force is the degree to which the substance of democratic principles is there—it is the presence or absence of democratic respect, confidence, rights, and responsibilities that indicate the essential character of an institution.

Recognizing that any institution that is essentially undemocratic will have difficulty in teaching democracy effectively, there remain legitimate pedagogical questions concerning "dealing with controversial issues," the relation of education to indoctrination, propaganda, commitment, and the like. Such questions are, perhaps, more properly a part of "methods courses" than of a course in philosophy of education. Nevertheless, a brief discussion of the meaning of *indoctrination* may be helpful at this point.

Literally, the word *doctrine* means *teachings,* that is, that which is taught or advocated, in contrast to oddments of information or belief that are somehow just picked up and passed around without ever becoming part of the subject of formal or informal instruction. Consequently, *to indoctrinate* means simply to teach, to offer instruction, or to advocate. Over the years, however, the word doctrine has become associated with dogma, a set of principles, beliefs, or "teachings" put forward authoritatively as being either beyond the reach of ordinary inquiry or so settled as to require only acceptance rather than further investigation. Thus it is that to indoctrinate has come to mean, especially in educationist circles, to teach a set of beliefs or a point of view in such manner as to create the impression openly or subtly that what is taught is so true and important to individual or social well-being that, by contrast, all possible alternatives are false and dangerous. Propaganda, emotional persuasion, using films with suitable background music, and the like, in order to shortcut or bypass reflective investigation, or else the use of drill and catechism in order to implant, inculcate, or otherwise build "conditioned meanings"[18] have come to be thought of as deliber-

[18] The reader may wish to review the discussion of education versus training, p. 23 and pp. 78-79.

ate methods of indoctrination. In its most subtle and effective form deliberate indoctrination is disguised as free, reflective inquiry—but with sources of information and criteria of credibility so rigged or manipulated that the process produces only the illusion of yielding warranted assertions. And, of course, educationists recognize that indoctrination can also be non-intentional.

Now, since the content of regular academic school-subjects is not thought of as dogma, questions of indoctrinating, say, arithmetic or geography do not normally arise. It is true, however, that the way in which certain aspects of some subjects are presented (say, a particular theory in psychology, economics, political science) might well bear watching. But just as a quick rule of thumb, it is in connection with viewpoints that are commonly named in English by words ending in "ism," that serious questions about indoctrination arise, notably: Protestantism, Catholicism, Communism, capitalism, socialism, individualism, patriotism, jingoism. Any objective appraisal of our present situation will recognize that there are many individuals and organized groups in this country who would like to see the schools indoctrinate one or more of the above isms, and they frequently bring pressure to bear upon the schools. Probably, most experienced teachers, when they fully recognize such pressures, try to resist them, although many of us believe that, unfortunately, teachers have not brought effective *organized effort* against such pressures.

In relation to the meaning of democracy, however, all this comes to a head when sincere defenders of democracy propose that the school, as a democratic sociopolitical institution, should embark on a deliberate program of "indoctrination for democracy." No doubt some who make this suggestion mean nothing more than that the schools should *teach democracy* with as much systematic effort and perseverance as is now devoted to, say, teaching the history of the Civil War or teaching sentence diagramming. Where this is all that is intended, many of us would agree that the suggestion merits very serious attention, including attention to the matter of enabling patrons to understand that both content and methods for teaching democracy are properly areas for professional rather than for lay decision, just as in the case of teaching sentence diagraming.

More troublesome are those who believe the schools should propagandize for democracy or inculcate democratic principles. Such persons are, perhaps, of three sorts: those who confuse democracy with one or more of the isms mentioned above, those who equate "respect," "confidence," "acceptance of responsibility" with certain more-or-less stereotyped, overt behaviors, and those who (encouraged by the unfortunate tendency to refer to democracy as a way of life)[19] see democracy as a direct *alternative* to traditional views of the nature of man and society. Since, as we have seen, such views are generally interwoven with a series of philosophic, theological, and religious commitments, it is no wonder that democracy, conceived as an alternative ideology, is thought to require similar emotional commitment on the part of the faithful. It is quite beyond the scope of this work to discuss tactics for dealing with these three types, but it would appear that the general strategic principle would be the same as for dealing with a person who, for example, wants the schools to teach astronomy but confuses astronomy with astrology. It is difficult, of course, to adopt such a stance if one inclines toward an emotivist or other subjective view of the nature of value with its personal or cultural relativism and its typical correlate of a sharp break between emotion and reason. It is also difficult, if one believes that the significance of the individual is entirely delimited by society. But, when one recognizes that there are "good reasons" for allegiance to the principles of democracy just as there are good reasons for the principles (characteristics and stipulations) of science, then the school's role in "teaching democracy" falls into place without special ritual or emotionalism.[20]

[19] For some objections to calling democracy "a way of life" see Hullfish and Smith, *Reflective Thinking: The Method of Education*, pp. 258-260.

[20] We should once again note the importance of nondiscursive symbols and meanings. Just as the full cognitive-emotional grasp of the principles of science is aided by experience in laboratory and field project, so it is that

## Democracy and Education (as the science and art of teaching)

Under discussion these days are a host of important problems involved in developing education as a profession. Most of these problems are only indirectly related to the meaning of democracy; they are more directly related to particular social, political, economic, even aesthetic structures of society. Since democratic principles permit a very wide range with respect to such structures, the principles offer only indirect guidance to the teaching profession as it strives to develop more effective organizations and policies. But the central problem of education as a profession *is* directly related to the meaning of democracy, namely, what are the locus and the nature of the educator's authority.[21]

It is customary to differentiate intellectual authority and moral authority in terms of the is-ought or the descriptive-normative dichotomy. Since education, as a practice, cannot escape the normative dimension, the profession certainly needs some theory of moral as well as of intellectual authority. How is this directly related to the meaning of democracy?

As far as intellectual authority is concerned, whatever claims a teacher (textbook writer, administrator, curriculum expert, etc.) makes must be based on evidence available through free inquiry. This is true of every person acting in any sort of public capacity in a democracy. As a private individual, anyone in a democracy may accept whatever source of authority pleases him and he may join with others in private organizations or societies devoted to authority that is not based upon publicly verifiable evidence.

---

in teaching democracy the course of study should not be limited to discursive knowledge about democracy. Moreover, even as a subject of general education, democracy should involve physical mastery—that is, the developing of democratic habits of thought and action. Consequently, it is very likely that the schools should develop aesthetically appropriate ceremony and regimen in this connection. The problem is to differentiate this from the more easily understood proposal that we should teach democracy by propaganda and ritual.

[21] For a fuller discussion of this matter see William O. Stanley, *Education and Social Integration,* and Myron Lieberman, *Education as a Profession,* esp. chap. 3, "Authority in Education."

The behavior of such individuals or groups should be regulated only if and to the extent that it violates Mill's principle.

Since students in a classroom constitute a captive audience, teachers have the responsibility of exercising more than normal caution not to violate each individual's right to such "private conclusions." This does not mean that teachers are obligated to protect provincial viewpoints, prejudice, superstition. Quite the contrary, teachers have a definite responsibility to teach and to insist upon objective inquiry. If in the process students find that what they are learning at school conflicts with or causes rethinking of what has been accepted at home and in the community, then this is a sign that taxpayers are beginning to realize a return on their investment. But in protecting the students' freedom to learn (which is the real point of academic freedom),[22] the teacher should be careful not to confuse his own "private conclusions" with matters that are based entirely upon objective inquiry. In other words, concerning matters that are truly controversial even among well-informed people, it should be obvious that the best evidence, argument, or good reasons that free inquiry has produced are still too sketchy or ambiguous to point to a single conclusion. Nevertheless, life is such that we must frequently adopt, at least tentatively, "a position" with respect to such matters. And students would be poorly served were teachers to give the impression that mature, educated people are too timid or too removed from life's realities to "take a stand" on important issues. The point is that a teacher should make it clear to students (and he cannot very well do this unless it is clear to him) that at certain times he expresses opinions that are at least partially based on his private convictions.

Many of us believe that far worse things can happen to students than to be influenced by the personal convictions of their teachers. But in a democracy there is no excuse for badgering students—for making them feel insecure and out of place—because they do not reflect a teacher's value-structures and per-

[22] See H. G. Hullfish, *Toward a Democratic Education*, chap. V, "Academic Freedom."

sonal views. As a general proposition, this is seldom questioned but, until the teaching profession becomes clearer than it now is on the nature and source of its intellectual authority, it is not likely to develop the self-discipline needed to correct even the more flagrant violations.

Concerning moral authority, once again educators must resist the urge to lay claim to any base outside of democratic principles. And fortunately they need not, for here is ample authority for the moral dimensions of pedagogical behavior. Teachers having deep and insightful respect for individuality, and backed by professional organizations that are disciplined and responsible with respect to their role in a democratic society, should never feel it necessary to try to side-step the moral dimension inevitably involved in any attempt to promote the growth of human personality. There appears to be nothing uncovered in our analysis of philosophy, and of education and of the nature of knowledge, science, value, and man that suggests that sound education will necessarily be hampered by democratic principles. Nor did we find anything that suggests that some other underpinning for education would be more productive. It follows that any philosophy of education (as a philsophy *for* education) that does not come to grips with democratic principles (so far as the normative dimensions of its theory of education is at issue) is, *prima facie*, inappropriate in a democratic society.

## SUGGESTIONS FOR ADDITIONAL READING

One might suppose that every American public school teacher would be thoroughly familiar with the major documents of American democracy and with the history and development of our democratic ideals and institutions. But, unfortunately, this is not the case in spite of a wealth of literature readily available. One especially interesting and informative book about the Constitutional convention is *The Great Rehearsal* by Carl Van Doren. For a competent historical analysis of some of today's complex problems, *Living Ideas in America*, edited by Henry S. Commager, is a useful resource. Interesting insights into the way in which certain problems have been resolved in the U.S. Senate may be gained from reading John F. Kennedy's *Profiles in Courage*.

In a more philosophic vein there are many excellent discussions of the nature of democracy in general and of American democracy in particular. Students generally find Smith and Lindeman, *Democratic Way of Life,* very helpful and it is available in paperback. Ralph Barton Perry has written a challenging book called *Shall Not Perish from the Earth.* And many students find John Dewey's *The Public and Its Problems* very thought provoking. Irwin Edman's *Fountainheads of Freedom* is a very useful presentation of the growth of American ideas with specific reference to the Declaration of Independence, Ralph Waldo Emerson's "Self-Reliance," the observations of Alexis de Tocqueville, and addresses of Abraham Lincoln. John Dewey's *Freedom and Culture* is very helpful for building an understanding of the enormous range of meaning attached to "freedom" in American society.

Concerning the meaning of "freedom" as it relates to the nature of man and democracy, a most helpful book is the brief one by Herbert J. Muller called *Issues of Freedom.* This little book should probably be considered "a must" by all who have a serious interest in understanding democracy.

Anyone who has followed the suggestions for additional reading in the preceding chapters has, no doubt, discovered that "Democracy" is a favorite topic for discussion in many of the standard texts in philosophy of education. There is no need to repeat the titles of these texts. But every serious student of education, regardless of personal philosophic orientation, should become familiar with Dewey's classic, *Democracy and Education.*

For an analysis of educational problems in relation to the complexities of modern social organization one should consult William O. Stanley, *Education and Social Integration.* A recent analysis is presented by Kimball and McClellan in *Education and the New America.*

A very readable discussion of the meaning of democracy in relation to selected problems of education is Hullfish, *Toward a Democratic Education.* This is of special interest because it was written for a Japanese audience and consequently the focus is deliberately simplified and sharpened in order that the main features may stand out even for the reader who is not very familiar with American traditions.

Students interested in a more detailed analysis of modern meanings of democracy should study *Democracy, Ideology, and Objectivity* by Naess, Christophersen, and Kvalo. This book is especially useful in that it presents the topic from a viewpoint outside the usual American approach. For an analysis of the decision-making process in modern democratic states, see Dahl and Lindblom, *Politics, Economics, and Welfare,* and/or *A Preface to Democratic Theory* by Dahl. For a provocative analysis of the meaning of modern individualism see David Riesman, *Individualism Reconsidered.*

Finally, for an examination of the question "Is there a rational justification for democracy and, if so, what is it?" see Thorson, *The Logic of Democracy.*

# Bibliography

AGARD, WALTER R., *What Democracy Meant to the Greeks*, University of Wisconsin Press, Madison, 1960.

ARISTOTLE, *Politics*, B. Jowett (trans.), Oxford, Fairlawn, N.J., vol. I, 1885.

AVEY, ALBERT E., *Handbook in the History of Philosophy*, Barnes and Noble, New York, 1954.

BAIER, HURT, *The Moral Point of View: A Rational Basis of Ethics*, Cornell, Ithaca, N.Y., 1958.

BAYLES, ERNEST EDWARD, *Democratic Educational Theory*, Harper & Row, New York, 1960.

BECK, LEWIS WHITE, *Philosophic Inquiry*, Prentice-Hall, Englewood Cliffs, N.J., 1953.

BECKER, CARL LOTUS, *Everyman His Own Historian*, Appleton-Century-Crofts, New York, 1935.

BENTLEY, ARTHUR F., in Sidney Ratner (ed.), *Inquiry into Inquiry*, Beacon Press, Boston, 1954.

BENTLEY, ARTHUR F., *Process of Government*, University of Chicago Press, 1908.

BERKELEY, GEORGE, "A Treatise Concerning the Principles of Human Knowledge," in Benjamin Rand (ed.), *Modern Classical Philosophies*, Houghton Mifflin, Boston, 1908, pp. 263-306.

BERKSON, ISAAC BAER, *The Ideal and the Community*, Harper & Row, New York, 1958.

BODE, BOYD HENRY, *How We Learn*, Heath, Boston, 1940.

BRACKENBURY, ROBERT LEO, *Getting Down to Cases*, Putnam, New York, 1959.

BRAMELD, THEODORE, *Philosophies of Education in Cultural Perspective*, Holt, Rinehart and Winston, New York, 1955.

BRAMELD, THEODORE, *Toward a Reconstructed Philosophy of Education*, Dryden Press, New York, 1956.

BRANDT, RICHARD B., *Ethical Theory*, Prentice-Hall, Englewood Cliffs, N.J., 1959.

BRIDGMEN, P. W., *The Logic of Modern Physics*, Macmillan, New York, 1960.

BRONOWSKI, JACOB, *The Common Sense of Science*, Harvard University Press, Cambridge, 1953.

BROUDY, HARRY S., *Building a Philosophy of Education*, 2nd ed., Prentice-Hall, Englewood Cliffs, N.J., 1961.

BROUDY, HARRY S., *Paradox and Promise*, Prentice-Hall, Englewood Cliffs, N.J., 1961.

BRUBACHER, JOHN SEILER, *A History of the Problems of Education*, McGraw-Hill, New York, 1947.

BRUBACHER, JOHN SEILER, *Modern Philosophies of Education*, McGraw-Hill, New York, 1939.

—— BRUNER, JEROME S., *The Process of Education*, Harvard University Press, Cambridge, 1960.

BRUNER, JEROME S., JACQUELINE J. GOODNOW, AND GEORGE A. AUSTIN, *A Study of Thinking*, Wiley, New York, 1956.

BURNS, HOBERT W., AND CHARLES J. BRAUNER, (ed.) *Philosophy of Education: Essays and Commentaries*, Ronald Press, New York, 1962.

BURTT, EDWIN ARTHUR, *The Metaphysical Foundations of Modern Science*, rev. ed., Harcourt, Brace, New York, 1932.

BUTLER, J. DONALD, *Four Philosophies and Their Practice in Education and Religion*, Harper, New York, 1957.

CAMPBELL, NORMAN ROBERT, *What is Science?*, Dover Publications, New York, 1952.

CHURCHMAN, C. WEST, *Prediction and Optimal Decision*, Prentice-Hall, Englewood Cliffs, N.J., 1961.

CLARK, BURTON R., *Educating the Expert Society*, Chandler Publishing, San Francosco, 1962.

COHEN, MORRIS R. AND ERNEST NAGEL, *An Introduction to Logic and Scientific Method*, Harcourt, Brace, New York, 1934.

COMMAGER, HENRY S., (ed.) *Living Ideas in America*, Harper, New York, 1951.

COMTE, AUGUSTE, *The Positive Philosophy*, Harriet Martineau (trans.), John Chapman, London, 1853.

CONANT, JAMES BRYANT, *On Understanding Science*, Yale University Press, New Haven, 1947.

DAHL, ROBERT A., *A Preface to Democratic Theory*, University of Chicago Press, 1956.

DAHL, ROBERT A. AND CHARLES E. LINDBLOM, *Politics, Economics, and Welfare*, Harper, New York, 1953.

DANTO, ARTHUR, AND SIDNEY MORGENBESSER (ed.) *Philosophy of Science*, Meridan Books, New York, 1960.

DEWEY, JOHN, *Democracy and Education,* Macmillan, New York, 1916.

DEWEY, JOHN, "Education and Social Change," *The Social Frontier,* May, 1937.

DEWEY, JOHN, AND JAMES H. TUFTS, *Ethics,* Henry Holt, New York, 1919.

DEWEY, JOHN, *Freedom and Culture,* Putnam, New York, 1949.

DEWEY, JOHN, *How We Think,* rev. ed., Heath, Boston, 1933.

DEWEY, JOHN, *Logic: The Theory of Inquiry,* Henry Holt, New York, 1938.

DEWEY, JOHN, *Philosophy of Education,* Littlefield, Adams, Ames, Iowa, 1956.

DEWEY, JOHN, *The Public and Its Problems,* Gateway Books, Chicago, 1946.

DEWEY, JOHN, *Reconstruction in Philosophy,* Henry Holt, New York, 1920.

DEWEY, JOHN, AND ARTHUR F. BENTLEY, *Knowing and the Known,* Beacon Press, Boston, 1949.

DEWEY, JOHN, *The Quest for Certainty: A Study of the Relation of Knowledge and Action,* Minton, Balch, New York, 1929.

DURANT, WILLIAM JAMES, *The Story of Philosophy,* Simon and Schuster, New York, 1926.

EINSTEIN, ALBERT, *On the Method of Theoretical Physics,* Oxford University Press, 1933.

FRANK, PHILIPP, *Philosophy of Science,* Prentice-Hall, Englewood Cliffs, N.J., 1957.

GOODMAN, NELSON, *Fact, Fiction, and Forecast,* Harvard University Press, Cambridge, 1955.

HANSEN, KENNETH HARVEY, *Philosophy for American Education,* Prentice-Hall, Englewood Cliffs, N.J., 1960.

HANSON, NORWOOD, *Patterns of Discovery,* Cambridge University Press, London, 1961.

HARDIE, CHARLES D., *Truth and Fallacy in Educational Theory,* N.Y. Bureau of Publications, Teachers College, Columbia University, 1962.

HARRIS, WILLIAM TORREY, "School Discipline," *The Third Yearbook of the National Herbart Society,* University of Chicago Press, 1897.

HAVIGHURST, ROBERT J., AND BERNICE L. NEUGARTEN, *Society and Education,* Allyn and Bacon, Boston, 1957.

HENRY, NELSON B., (ed.) *Modern Philosophies of Education,* the fifty-fourth yearbook of the National Society for the Study of Education, Part I, University of Chicago Press, 1955.

268                                                   BIBLIOGRAPHY

HEGEL, G.W.F., *Philosophical History*, J. Sibree (trans.), Collier, New York, 1902.

HOBBES, THOMAS, *Leviathan*, B. Blackwell, Oxford, 1960.

HORNE, HERMAN H., *Idealism in Education*, Macmillan, New York, 1923.

HOSPERS, JOHN, *An Introduction to Philosophical Analysis*, Prentice-Hall, Englewood Cliffs, N.J., 1953.

HULLFISH, H. GORDON, *Toward a Democratic Education*, College of Education, Ohio State University, Columbus, 1961.

HULLFISH, H. GORDON, AND PHILIP G. SMITH, *Reflective Thinking: The Method of Education*, Dodd, Mead, New York, 1961.

HUME, DAVID, *Enquiries Concerning the Human Understanding*, Clarendon Press, Oxford, 1961.

HUNT, JOSEPH MCVICKER, *Intelligence and Experience*, Ronald Press, New York, 1961.

HUTCHINS, ROBERT M., *The Higher Learning in America*, Yale University Press, New Haven, 1936.

INHELDER, BARBEL, AND JEAN PIAGET, *The Growth of Logical Thinking*, Anne Parsons and Stanley Milgram (trans.), Basic Books, New York, 1958.

IRWIN, EDMAN, *Fountainheads of Freedom*, Reynal & Hitchcock, New York, 1941.

JACOBS, MELVILLE, AND BERNHART J. STERN, *General Anthropology*, (College Outline Series 20) Barnes and Noble, New York, 1952.

KANT, IMMANUEL, *Critique of Pure Reason*, N. K. Smith (trans.), Macmillan, London, 1929.

KENNEDY, JOHN F., *Profiles in Courage*, Harper, New York, 1956.

KILPATRIC, WILLIAM HEARD, *Philosophy of Education*, Macmillan, New York, 1951.

KIMBALL, SOLON F., AND JAMES E. MCCLELLAN, JR., *Education and the New America*, Random House, New York, 1962.

KNELLER, GEORGE FREDRICK (ed.), *Foundations of Education*, Wiley, New York, 1963.

LANGER, SUSANNE K., *Philosophy in a New Key*, Harvard University Press, Cambridge, 1942.

LEWIS, CLARENCE IRVING, *An Analysis of Knowledge and Valuation*, The Open Court, La Salle, Ill., 1947.

LEWIS, CLARENCE IRVING, *Mind and the World Order*, Scribner, New York, 1929.

LIEBERMAN, MYRON, *Education as a Profession*, Prentice-Hall, Englewood Cliffs, N.J., 1956.

LIEBERMAN, MYRON, *The Future of Public Education*, University of Chicago Press, 1960.

LOCKE, JOHN, *An Essay Concerning Human Understanding*, Dutton, New York, 1961.

LOCKE, JOHN, "An Essay Concerning the True Original Extent and End of Civil Government," in *Social Contract, Essays by Locke, Hume and Rousseau*, Oxford University Press, London, 1958.

MADDEN, EDWARD H., (ed.), *The Structure of Scientific Thought*, Houghton Mifflin, Boston, 1960.

MARTIN, WILLIAM OLIVER, *The Order and Integration of Knowledge*, University of Michigan Press, Ann Arbor, 1957.

MASON, ROBERT E., *Educational Ideals in American Society*, Allyn and Bacon, Boston, 1960.

MAYER, FREDERICK, *Philosophy of Education for Our Time*, Odyssey Press, New York, 1958.

MELTER, BERNARD N., HARRY R. DOBY, AND PHILIP M. SMITH, *Education in Society*, Crowell, New York, 1958.

MILL, JOHN & STUART, *On Liberty*, Gateway Edition, Regnery, Chicago, 1955.

MONTAGU, ASHLEY, *The Biosocial Nature of Man*, Grove Press, New York, 1956.

MONTAGUE, WILLIAM PEPPERELL, *The Ways of Knowing*, Allen & Unwin, London, 1925.

MONTESQUIEU, CHARLES LOUIS DE SECENDAT, *The Spirit of Laws*, Tomas Nugent (trans.), Hafner, New York, 1959.

MORRIS, VAN CLEVE, "Existentialism and the Education of Twentieth Century Man," *Educational Theory*, vol. XI. No. 1, January, 1961.

MORRIS, VAN CLEVE, *Philosophy and the American School*, Houghton Mifflin, Boston, 1961.

MULLER, HERBERT J., *Issues of Freedom*, Harper, New York, 1960.

NAESS, ARNE, JENS A. CHRISTOPHERSEN, AND KJELL KAVALO, *Democracy, Ideology, and Objectivity*, Oslo University Press, 1956.

NAGEL, ERNEST, *The Structure of Science*, Harcourt, Brace and World, New York, 1961.

*The New School Science*, American Association for the Advancement of Science, Washington, D.C. Miscellaneous Publications No. 63-6.

OTTO, MAX C., *Things and Ideals*, Henry Holt, New York, 1924.

PARK, JOE, (ed.) *Selected Readings in the Philosophy of Education*, Macmillan, New York, 1958.

PHENIX, PHILIP HENRY, *Philosophy of Education*, Henry Holt, New York, 1958.

PEPPER, STEPHEN COBURN, *The Sources of Value*, University of California Press, Berkeley, 1958.

PERRY, RALPH BARTON, *Shall Not Perish from the Earth*, Vangard Press, New York, 1940.

PIAGET, JEAN, *The Origins of Intelligence in Children*, Margaret Cook (trans.), International Universities Press, New York, 1952.

RANDELL, JOHN HERMAN, JR., AND JUSTICE BUCHLER, *Philosophy: An Introduction* (College Outline Series 41), Barnes and Noble, New York, 1942.

RICARDO, DAVID, *The Principles of Political Economy and Taxation*, Dutton, New York, 1962.

RICE, PHILIP BLAIR, *On the Knowledge of Good and Evil*, Random House, New York, 1955.

RIESMAN, DAVID, *Individualism Reconsidered*, Doubleday, New York, 1955.

ROCKERFELLER BROTHERS FUND, *The Power of the Democratic Idea*, Doubleday, Garden City, N.Y., 1960.

ROUSSEAU, JEAN-JACQUES, *The Social Contract and Discourses*, G. D. H. Cole (trans.), Dutton, New York, 1950.

RUSSELL, BERTRAND, *Human Knowledge*, Simon and Schuster, New York, 1948.

SAYERS, EPHRAIM VERN, AND WARD MADDEN, *Education and the Democratic Faith*, Appleton-Century-Crofts, New York, 1959.

SCHEFFLER, ISRAEL (ed.), *Philosophy and Education*, Allyn and Bacon, Boston, 1958.

SCHRODINGER, ERWIN C., *Science, Theory and Man*, Dover, New York, 1957.

SMITH, ADAM, *An Inquiry into the Nature and Causes of The Wealth of Nations*, 2 volumes, Methuen, London, 1925.

SMITH, B. OTHANEL, WILLIAM O. STANLEY, AND J. HARLAN SHORES, *Fundamentals of Curriculum Devleopment*, rev. ed., World, Yonkers, 1957.

SMITH, B. OTHANEL, AND STANLEY ELAM (ed.), *Education and the Structure of Knowledge*, Rand McNally, Chicago, 1964.

SMITH, B. OTHANEL, AND ROBERT H. ENNIS (ed.), *Language and Concepts in Education*, Rand McNally, Chicago, 1961.

SMITH, B. OTHANEL, ET. AL., *A Study of the Logic of Teaching*, University of Illinois, Urbana, 1963.

SMITH, PHILIP G., *Philosophic Mindedness in Educational Administration*, Ohio State University Press, Columbus, 1956.

SMITH, T. V., AND EDWARD C. LINDEMAN, *The Democratic Way of Life*, New American Library, New York, 1951.

SNYGG, DONALD, "Another Look at Learning Theory," *Educational Psychologist*, (vol. 1, No. 1, October, 1963)

SODERQUIST, HAROLD O., *The Person and Education*, Merrill, Columbus, Ohio, 1964.

SPENCER, HERBERT, *Social Statistics*, Appleton, New York, 1896.

STANLEY, WILLIAM O., *Education and Social Integration*, N.Y. Bureau of Publications, Teachers College, Columbia University, 1953.

STANLEY, WILLIAM O., B. OTHANEL SMITH, KENNETH D. BENNE, AND ARCHIBALD W. ANDERSON, *Social Foundations of Education*, Dryden Press, New York, 1956.

STEVENSON, C. L., *Ethics and Language*, Yale University Press, New Haven, 1944.

STRICKLAND, RUTH G., "The Contribution of Structural Linguistics to the Teaching of Reading, Writing, and Grammar in the Elementary School." *Bulletin of the School of Education*, School of Education, Indiana University, Bloomington, vol. 40, No. 1, January, 1964.

THAYER, VIVIAN TROW, *The Role of the School in American Society*, Dodd, Mead, New York, 1960.

THILLY, FRANK, *A History of Philosophy*, Henry Holt, New York, 1914.

THORSON, THOMAS LANDON, *The Logic of Democracy*, Holt, Rinehart, and Winston, New York, 1962.

THUT, I. N., *The Story of Education*, McGraw-Hill, New York, 1957.

TITUS, HAROLD H., *Living Issues in Philosophy*, 2nd ed., American Book, New York, 1953.

TITUS, HAROLD, *Living Issues in Philosophy*, 3rd ed., American Book, New York, 1959.

ULICH, ROBERT, *History of Educational Thought*, American Book, New York, 1950.

ULICH, ROBERT, *Philosophy of Education*, American Book, New York, 1961.

VAN DOREN, CARL, *The Great Rehearsal*, Viking Press, New York, 1948.

WHITEHEAD, ALFRED NORTH, *Modes of Thought*, Macmillan, New York, 1938.

WHITEHEAD, ALFRED NORTH, *Science and the Modern World*, Macmillan, New York, 1927.

WIENER, NORBERT, *The Human Use of Human Beings*, rev. ed., Doubleday, Garden City, N.Y., 1956.

WITTGENSTEIN, LUDWIG, *Tractauts Logico-Philosophicus*, Harcourt, Brace, New York, 1922.

WYNNE, JOHN PETER, *Theories of Education*, Harper & Row, New York, 1963.

# Index